A Complete Guide to the

SNAKES

of Southern Africa

A Complete Guide to the
SNAKES
of Southern Africa

Johan Marais

ACKNOWLEDGEMENTS

FIRST EDITION

I am indebted to several amateur and professional herpetologists who have given me advice and information over the years. A great deal of information was obtained from various newsletters and journals of the Herpetological Association of Africa – my thanks to the contributors.

Several people assisted during photographic sessions. My thanks to Brandon Borgelt, Timothy Simpkins, Crawford Coulsen, Dave Morgan, Mike Glynn, John Neeves and especially Theuns Eloff for their help. The late Gody Kunzi, Wulf Haacke, Malcolm Paterson, the late John Lougher, John Vorster, Frans Meyer, Kierie Botha, Gavin Carpenter, Donald Strydom, Barry and Karen Stander and Keith Walters made specimens available to photograph while some of the snakes were photographed at the Transvaal Snake Park and Durban Snake Park. My thanks are also due to Rod Patterson and Fritz Muller.

Atherton de Villiers, Richard Boycott, Marius Burger, Peter Dawson, Wulf Haacke, the late Leonard Hoffman, Niels Jacobsen, Steve Spawls, Colin Tilbury and Bill Branch supplied me with superb photographs. Peter Fuhri assisted with the first-aid photographs.

Angelo Lamibiris kindly supplied the line drawing of *Naja nigricollis nigricincta*, *Naja n. woodi*, and illustrations for the chapter on classification and relationships.

Dr O Bourquin supplied the species account, distribution map and line drawings of *Montaspis gilvomaculata*.

My thanks to the directors of Jonathan Ball and Ad Donker Publishers and Dr Donald Broadley for permission to use line drawings from *FitzSimons' Snakes of Southern Africa*.

The distribution maps were drawn by my wife Molleen with help from Theuns Eloff.

Dr Mark Verseput, Dr Ev Cock and Dr Chris Foggin commented on the drug chart in the reptile husbandry section.

Special thanks are due to Lynn Raw, Angelo Lambiris and Mike Bates who had the laborious task of reading through the manuscript and suggesting improvements. Despite their rather hectic schedules, they managed to find the time to help and I value their contributions. I trust that the end product does justice to their efforts. Lynn Raw also wrote the chapter on classification and relationships. Dr L Schrire, head of the serum and vaccine department of the South African Institute for Medical Research, read and commented on the chapter dealing with snakebite and first-aid treatment.

My sincere thanks to Gordon Setaro for all the good times that we have spent in the veld and for his willingness to share his wealth of information with me. His knowledge and understanding of the reptiles and amphibians of southern Africa is unequalled. I would also like to thank my very good friend, Prof. Gerrie Smith, for all his enthusiasm and encouragement.

My working relationship with my publisher has always been a very pleasant one and I thank Rita van Dyke (formerly of Southern Books) and Louise Grantham for their efforts, patience and assistance.

A final word of thanks goes to my wife Molleen, daughter Melissa and my father. This book is the result of many weekend photographic sessions and hours in my study – times that my family had to do without me or actively avoid me. Without their encouragement, support and understanding this book would not have been possible.

JOHAN MARAIS
1992

SECOND EDITION

It has been more than a decade since the first edition of *A Complete Guide to the Snakes of Southern Africa* appeared and much has happened on the snake front in that time.

I have been very busy building up my business and must thank my colleagues and business associates for their support. Many friends, far too many to list, have given me advice, encouragement and support over the years. My thanks to Donald Strydom, Randy Babb, Paul Moler, the Madhav family, Nush Goncalves, Marius Burger, and Graham and Natasha Alexander for all their support.

Prof. Graham Alexander sacrificed many hours of his valuable time to comment on the manuscript and suggest improvements. Dr Bill Branch has always been a great help and his excellent book *Field Guide to the Snakes and other Reptiles of Southern Africa* has been a most useful reference, especially with regards to behavioural and technical information, as well as distribution maps. I also thank Dr Don Broadley for all his help and advice.

Lynn Raw again kindly wrote the chapter on classification and relationships. Most of the line drawings were done by Randy Babb and it is a privilege to be able to include artwork by such an excellent artist. He drew the head line drawings using various reference works including various technical papers, photographs and the drawings in Broadley's *FitzSimons' Snakes of Southern Africa*. He also referred to preserved specimens that were photographed at the Port Elizabeth Museum and Transvaal Museum.

The sections on first aid and snakebite were read and commented on by Dr Colin Tilbury and Dr Roger Blaylock. I thank them for their time and effort.

Excellent photographs were supplied by Prof. Graham Alexander, Randy Babb, Richard Boycott, Dr Bill Branch, Marius Burger, S Davies, Peter Dawson, Dr Niels Jacobsen, Warren Schmidt, Steve Spawls, Dr Bruce Taubert, Dr Colin Tilbury, Andrew Turner and Atherton de Villiers.

I enjoyed working with Pippa Parker and Emily Bowles of Struik Publishers and look forward to future projects, and I thank Janice Evans and Robin Cox for their hard work and the effort that they put into designing the second edition.

To all of the above, thanks for your input. I take full responsibility for this book and trust that the end product meets with general approval.

Last, but by no means least, my thanks to my family. My father has always been very supportive and I thank him for all his love, wisdom and patience. I thank my wife Molleen and daughter Melissa, to whom this book is dedicated, for all their love, patience, enthusiasm, support and understanding. I spend a great deal of time away from home and, when I am with my family, I selfishly work on manuscripts and spend hours taking photographs. Without their support, so much of what I have attempted in life would never have happened.

JOHAN MARAIS
2004

Green Mamba

AUTHOR'S PREFACE

There are 170-odd species and subspecies of snakes in southern Africa, many of which are insufficiently studied and poorly understood. The aim of this book is not only to assist in identifying southern Africa's diverse range of snakes, but also to give the layperson, including snake enthusiasts, a fresh understanding and appreciation of these fascinating creatures.

The response to *A Complete Guide to the Snakes of Southern Africa*, which was first published in 1992, was overwhelmingly positive and evoked many helpful comments. This new edition has been revised in the light of such comments and the many queries and suggestions I have received. The text has been updated and includes accounts of at least 11 new species and subspecies, while more than 30 species and subspecies have been reassigned. Snakes such as the Red Adder (*Bitis rubida*), the Albany Adder (*Bitis albanica*) and the Southern Adder (*Bitis armata*) were described fairly recently, while others such as the Vine or Twig Snakes of the genus *Thelotornis* have been reallocated. With the rapid advance of herpetology in southern Africa, new distributional data has also come to light. Herpetologists now have greater contact with colleagues worldwide and more research is being conducted than before, both locally and by overseas researchers. In addition, new techniques in DNA analysis are proving to be extremely helpful, especially in the field of taxonomy.

As much additional information as possible has been included in the species accounts that relates to behaviour, natural history, reproduction and snake venoms. Colour photographs now accompany the species descriptions and this, together with the simple icons that make essential information readily available at a glance, will, I hope, enhance the guide and make it even more user-friendly.

In view of the fear and superstition that surrounds snakes, it is worth stating that relatively few snakebite incidents are fatal. Snakebites can range from very dangerous to merely painful or even completely harmless. Several authoritative books have been written on the subject of snakebite and its management. Articles appear in scientific and medical journals, popular magazines and newspapers, while colour brochures on the subject are published from time to time. However, many of these contributions are very technical and focus on the medical treatment of snakebite, the use of antivenom in conjunction with steroids, adrenaline, etc. This book avoids technical terminology where possible and is a more general and practical guide that will appeal to the layperson: the farmer, housewife, gardener, hiker, hunter, fisherman or anyone else who spends time outdoors.

While it is crucial that correct procedures be followed if a snake does bite someone, we humans pose a far greater threat to snakes than they do to us. Urban development, industrialization and mass destruction of natural habitats to make way for agriculture have seriously threatened a number of species. Further study of the impact of these activities on snake populations is urgently required. It is my hope that this book will contribute to a more respectful attitude to these sensitive and skilled predators and to a better understanding of their importance in nature.

The author with a juvenile Burmese Python.

Struik Publishers
(a division of New Holland Publishing
(South Africa) (Pty) Ltd)
Cornelis Struik House
80 McKenzie Street
Cape Town 8001

New Holland Publishing is a member of
Johnnic Communications Ltd.

Visit us at
www.struik.co.za.

www.imagesofafrica.co.za

IMAGES OF AFRICA
P H O T O   L I B R A R Y

First published in 2004

4 5 6 7 8 9 10

Publishing manager: Pippa Parker
Managing editor: Helen de Villiers
Editor: Emily Bowles
Design director: Janice Evans
Design concept: Janice Evans
Designer: Robin Cox
Cartography & illustrations: David du Plessis;
Randy Babb; Dr Angelo Lambiris
Indexer: Jeanne Cope
Proofreader: Thea Grobbelaar

Reproduction by Hirt & Carter Cape (Pty) Ltd
Printed and bound by Times Offset (M) Sdn Bhd

ISBN: 1 8 6872 932 X
Also available in Afrikaans as
'n Volledige Gids tot die Slange van Suider-Afrika
ISBN: 1 86872 933 8

Front cover: Eastern Natal Green Snake
Page 1: East African Egg-eater (Wulf Haacke)
Page 2: Black Spitting Cobra
Page 3: Anchieta's Dwarf Python

Puff Adder

Common Brown Water Snake

Marius Burger

CONTENTS

INTRODUCTION 10

HOW TO USE THIS BOOK 14

Chapter 1: BIOLOGY AND BEHAVIOUR 16

Chapter 2: CLASSIFICATION AND RELATIONSHIPS 24

Chapter 3: SNAKEBITE 34

Chapter 4: SNAKES IN CAPTIVITY 48

Chapter 5: SPECIES ACCOUNTS 60

Adders or vipers 62

Mambas, cobras and their relatives 94

Back-fanged and other venomous snakes 134

Fangless and non-venomous snakes 210

Blind and worm snakes 278

Glossary 301

Bibliography 304

Index 308

INTRODUCTION

Snakes have traditionally been looked upon as slimy, repulsive and aggressive creatures that attack people at every opportunity. If cornered or hurt, a snake may well defend itself but, even then, most snakes prefer to move off quickly and quietly if given the chance. Other snakes will remain motionless, hoping that their excellent camouflage will enable them to remain undetected.

The snake is without doubt one of nature's most efficient and skilful predators. For instance, a rodent, once it disappears down its network of burrows, is safe from most predators – except from snakes. With its elongate, limbless body a snake can easily move through the burrows and not only kill an individual rodent, but in many cases eradicate an entire rodent family in one session.

Some snakes rely on muscle power to kill their prey while others have evolved a venom apparatus. The venom is modified saliva and is produced and stored in salivary glands that are situated more or less behind the eyes on either side of the head. Not only does venom enable the snake to kill its prey, but it also assists with digestion. Saliva is one of the digestive juices secreted by animals and is particularly important to snakes, as they cannot chew their food.

FACTS AND FALLACIES

Few living creatures are as fascinating as snakes, yet although a great deal has been written about them, we still know very little about these interesting and misunderstood animals.

Fallacies are passed on from generation to generation and the same old stories are repeated endlessly. Have you heard about the man on horseback who was chased by a Black Mamba for kilometres on end? Or the snake that was so long it stretched from one side of the road to the other? Another favourite is that Puff Adders eat their babies. The most commonly asked questions about snakes are answered below:

Are snakes wet and slimy?
No, they are neither wet nor slimy, but perfectly dry. A snake that emerges from water will obviously be wet, but not slimy. The shiny, highly reflective skin may give the impression that a dry snake is wet.

*Very little is known about the habits
and behaviour of most snakes.*

Do all snakes spit their venom?

The majority of snakes in the world and in southern Africa, including the cobras, cannot spit their venom. We have two common spitters, the Rinkhals (*Hemachatus haemachatus*) and the Mozambique Spitting Cobra (*Naja mossambica*). The other spitting cobras within our range are the Black-necked Spitting Cobra (*Naja nigricollis nigricollis*), the Black Spitting Cobra (*Naja nigricollis woodi*) and the Zebra Cobra (*Naja nigricollis nigricincta*). These snakes do not actually 'spit' their venom but rather squirt it, although 'spit' is commonly used.

Can the forked tongue of a snake sting?

The forked tongue is used only for smelling and cannot sting or harm in any way.

Does the Puff Adder strike backwards?

Contrary to popular belief, the Puff Adder (*Bitis arietans*) cannot strike backwards. Like most other snakes, it is capable of striking forwards or to the sides or, once it has turned around, striking in the opposite direction, but not backwards. This belief probably originated from the snake's habit of snapping into a coiled or striking position when disturbed, which may give the impression that it strikes backwards.

Do snakes lick their prey before swallowing?

A snake may inspect a dead prey item with flickering tongue, but does not lick it. If disturbed soon after eating, a snake may regurgitate its meal, which will be covered in mucus. People then often erroneously assume that it was licked prior to being swallowed.

Does a python need to anchor its tail before or during a kill?

This is not necessary, as the snake needs to throw only one or two coils around its prey in order to subdue it. The tail does not have to be anchored, although it may be an advantage when constricting large prey. Pythons do, however, always latch onto their prey with numerous sharp, strongly recurved teeth to prevent their prey from escaping.

Do snakes move in pairs?

Snakes usually pair up only to mate; at other times they are loners. If you do find a snake in your garden, it is highly unlikely that you will find a second one close by. If you happen to kill a snake you certainly do not need to fear a mate coming to take revenge.

Do snakes have nests?

Although many eggs may hatch from a clutch laid in a hole or other suitable spot, there is no such thing as a nest of snakes. Several snakes may use the same hiding place or hibernate together, but if you find a snake in a hedge, it does not mean that the hedge conceals a nest full of snakes. One exception, not found in this country, is the King Cobra (*Ophiophagus hannah*) of Asia. The female does actually build a crude nest.

Do snakes only die after sunset?

Obviously, a snake dies the moment it is killed. Owing to the normal irritability of muscle tissue when it has been deprived of blood, there may still be movement long after a snake has died.

The forked tongue of a snake is used for smelling and cannot sting or harm in any way.

Snakes such as the Black Mamba may take refuge in neglected areas.

PEOPLE AND SNAKES

Snakes are attracted to dark and neglected areas and will be encouraged to take refuge beneath sheets of corrugated iron or asbestos, building rubble, firewood, grass heaps, and rubbish tips in gardens. Most snakes prey upon rodents, lizards, frogs and toads and will be drawn to gardens that har-bour such creatures. To deter snakes, always keep your property clean and tidy. Dripping taps and fish ponds will attract frogs and toads as well as snakes, which may come to drink water or seek food. Fowl runs, birdcages and rabbits will also attract snakes.

Dense shrubs and hedges or a combina-tion of wall, hedge and a nearby pond may also encourage some of the arboreal species to move in, and if there are plants growing near or against windows there is a greater likelihood of snakes entering your home. Ensure that hedges and other plants do not grow against windows.

If you do happen to see a snake in your garden and it does not move off of its own accord, get someone to watch it from a safe distance of eight metres or more, and contact a competent snake collector. Keep children and pets well out of the way. If you do not know of a collector, try calling the local conservation department, snake park, museum, zoo, fire department, traffic department, health department or police station and ask them to remove it.

If nobody is available to remove the snake and you cannot let it move off at its leisure, the only alternative may be to kill it. Avoid using a firearm, as bullets ricochet. A snake is not an easy target and if you intend killing one with a firearm, a shotgun would be the best choice. Even then, be very careful and think before you shoot. Blasts from shotguns can often cause extensive damage. Also bear in mind that there are

Deadly snakes like the Black Mamba often venture into suburban gardens. In such an instance, call a competent snake collector.

various laws governing the use of firearms, especially in urban areas.

Alternatively, and only if you feel that it is absolutely necessary, approach the snake very carefully (it might be a spitter) and give it one or two heavy blows on the front third of the body with a solid object such as a golf club or broomstick. The idea is to kill the snake by breaking its back. Do not touch the snake with bare hands, as it may be feigning death. Rather sweep it into a cardboard box or a bucket.

Take the dead snake to your local snake park, museum or university for identification. It will, in all likelihood, be the most abundant species in your area and you will probably come across another one sooner or later. Have a good look at the dead snake so that you will be able to identify that species in future. Remember that there will be only a few dangerous snake species in your area and it is therefore worthwhile to get to know them.

Some people take an active interest in snakes and know how to identify and handle many of them. Track down a local snake enthusiast and keep that person's contact number handy in case you ever have to deal with a snake in your immediate environment.

SOUTHERN AFRICAN HABITATS

A habitat is the particular environment in which an organism lives. Southern Africa has eight distinct habitats or vegetation types in which snakes (and other wildlife) may be found. These are depicted on the map below.

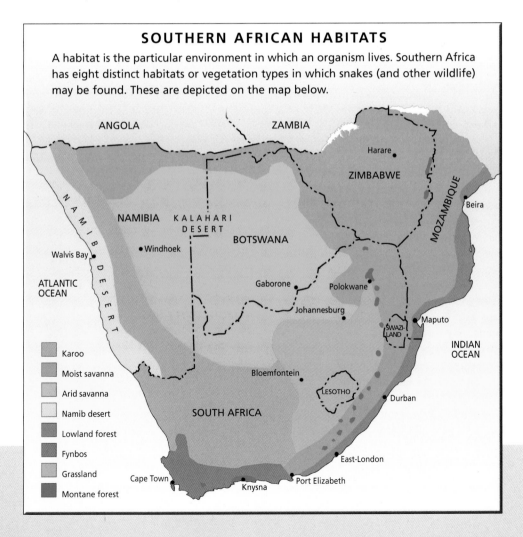

Legend:
- Karoo
- Moist savanna
- Arid savanna
- Namib desert
- Lowland forest
- Fynbos
- Grassland
- Montane forest

HOW TO USE THIS BOOK

The snakes featured in this book have been grouped according to five snake types, namely adders or vipers (pages 62–93), cobras, mambas and their relatives (pages 94–133), back-fanged and other venomous snakes (pages 134–209), fangless and non-venomous snakes (pages 210–277) and blind and worm snakes (pages 278–300).

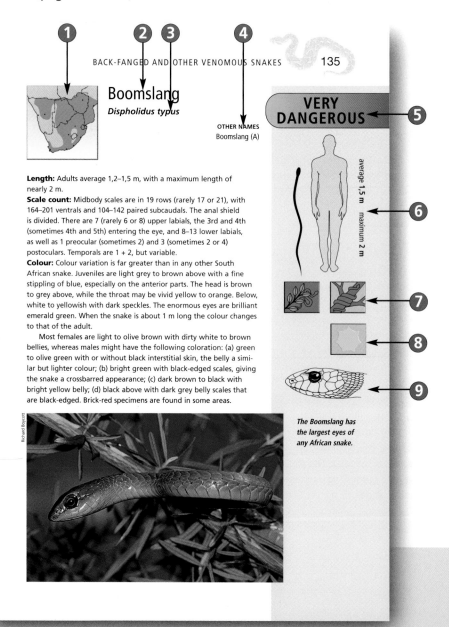

Boomslang
Dispholidus typus

OTHER NAMES
Boomslang (A)

Length: Adults average 1,2–1,5 m, with a maximum length of nearly 2 m.

Scale count: Midbody scales are in 19 rows (rarely 17 or 21), with 164–201 ventrals and 104–142 paired subcaudals. The anal shield is divided. There are 7 (rarely 6 or 8) upper labials, the 3rd and 4th (sometimes 4th and 5th) entering the eye, and 8–13 lower labials, as well as 1 preocular (sometimes 2) and 3 (sometimes 2 or 4) postoculars. Temporals are 1 + 2, but variable.

Colour: Colour variation is far greater than in any other South African snake. Juveniles are light grey to brown above with a fine stippling of blue, especially on the anterior parts. The head is brown to grey above, while the throat may be vivid yellow to orange. Below, white to yellowish with dark speckles. The enormous eyes are brilliant emerald green. When the snake is about 1 m long the colour changes to that of the adult.

Most females are light to olive brown with dirty white to brown bellies, whereas males might have the following coloration: (a) green to olive green with or without black interstitial skin, the belly a similar but lighter colour; (b) bright green with black-edged scales, giving the snake a crossbarred appearance; (c) dark brown to black with bright yellow belly; (d) black above with dark grey belly scales that are black-edged. Brick-red specimens are found in some areas.

VERY DANGEROUS

average 1,5 m　maximum 2 m

The Boomslang has the largest eyes of any African snake.

Richard Boycott

- Photographs accompany most species, including as far as possible any variant colour forms or subspecies. To limit confusion, photographs of similar or easily confused species are also featured along with the snake under discussion.
- To facilitate identification, each species account is split up into several headings and is accompanied by a series of icons (explained below).
- A separate 'Look out for' box highlights each snake's most prominent features for quick identification.
- Essential technical terms are explained in the glossary on page 301.

 1 Locator map: Each species is accompanied by a distribution map. The distributions indicated on these maps reflect the areas in which the snakes may be found, rather than being derived from general museum records, which are not always comprehensive. This is merely a precautionary approach, as in several regions little museum collecting has been done,

although certain species of snakes are known to live there. For more precise distribution information, readers are referred to the various museums that house herpetological collections as well as *Fitzsimons' Snakes of Southern Africa* (see bibliography).

2 Common name: The common name is given at the start of each species account. The same snake may have several common names, and names may also vary from one area to another. Any comments regarding common names will be welcomed and can be e-mailed to **johan@inkbooks.com**.

3 Scientific name: The scientific name is provided for each species. This usually consists of two parts, the first indicating the genus to which the snake belongs, the second giving the actual species name. If there are three names, the third name indicates that the snake under discussion is a subspecies or subgroup of a particular species.

4 Other names: Where available Afrikaans, Zulu and Xhosa names have also been included.

GUIDE TO ICONS

5 Danger bar: Indicates whether the snake is very dangerous, dangerous, mildly venomous, or harmless. Some non-venomous snakes e.g. the Southern African Python, are labelled dangerous because they can inflict a painful wound. Where the venom of species is unknown, the assessment is based on closely related species and anecdotal information.

VERY DANGEROUS

6 Average size: Shows the snake's size relative to an

average human male 1,8 m in height, or to an average human arm of 60 cm.

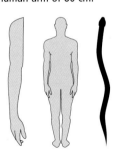

average 90 cm   maximum 1,4 m

7 Habitat: Indicates whether the snake lives mostly in trees,

in shrubs, on the ground or any combination of the three.

8 Nocturnal/Diurnal: Indicates whether the snake is active during the day (diurnal), at night (nocturnal), or both.

9 Head scale diagram: These detailed drawings of the head scales are very useful when trying to identify a snake.

ake eastern congo stiletto snake slender blind snake desert
ng-tailed worm snake forest cobra yellow-bellied house sna
ake berg adder cape cobra anchieta's dwarf python green wat
ake red adder common shield-nose snake. common purple-gloss
ny-horned adder green mamba aurora house snake variegated sl
mba common slug-eater boomslang gaboon adder black-necked

Hatchlings use a fine 'egg-tooth'
on the tip of the nose to cut the
leathery eggshell from the inside

...ain adder swazi rock snake angola file snake olive whip sna
...amibian wolf snake ...southern forest wo
...ake eastern stripe-bellied sand snake schlegel's beaked bli
...ake kunene ...ngwe worm sna
...ter lined olympic snake distant's worm snake puff adder bla
...ing cobra southern african python ornate green snake easte

1 BIOLOGY AND BEHAVIOUR

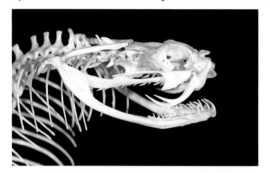

E ven though snakes are related to other reptiles, they are thought to have evolved from lizard ancestors and are most closely related to lizards and amphisbaenids (worm lizards). However, the fossil record is still incomplete and the evolutionary history of snakes is hotly debated. The first snakes appeared about 100 to 150 million years ago, somewhere on the southern continents.

Snakes are most clearly defined by their highly adapted and delicate skulls. The lower jaw bones are not fused in the front, which allows them to operate independently. The upper jaw bones are also loosely articulated and, together with several other adaptions, this allows snakes to consume large prey items, in spite of the fact that they cannot bite off easily manageable pieces. All snakes are, to some degree, long and slender, and their internal anatomy is also elongated. The majority of species have only the right lung, which is greatly elongated in slender species, although some primitive species such as pythons still have a reduced left lung.

Snakes shed the entire skin, from the tip of the snout to the tip of the tail, including the eyecaps.

SNAKE BIOLOGY

Vision

Snakes have good vision, but it is used mainly for detecting movement. However, a snake moving through grass can certainly see and, if it so chooses, carefully avoid even small objects in its path. Hence the old, but true, maxim that if you encounter a snake the best thing to do is to stand perfectly still. Snakes do not strike at stationary objects unless, perhaps, they resemble prey. Two southern African snakes are believed to have superior vision and are capable of seeing stationary prey – the Boomslang (*Dispholidus typus*) and the Twig or Vine Snake (*Thelotornis* spp.). Furthermore, for reasons that are not fully understood, these species have binocular vision, while most other snakes have monocular vision.

Snakes do not have movable eyelids; instead, a fixed transparent shield that is shed with the rest of the skin during sloughing covers the eye.

Hearing

As external ear holes are absent, snakes cannot hear most airborne sounds. They do, however, have an auditory nerve and can hear sounds travelling through a dense medium. Snakes are sensitive to vibrations and can often detect the approach of a person or animal.

Smell

The forked tongue of a snake cannot harm or sting in any way and is used only for smelling. The tongue pushes through a groove in the front of the mouth and is flickered, in order to pick up particles in the air. When it is drawn back into the mouth these particles are deposited onto organs situated in the roof of the mouth, known as the organs of Jacobson. The epithelium of this organ functions in exactly the same way as a human's olfactory epithelium. This means that a snake enjoys a similar sense of smell to our own.

Unlike lizards, snakes do not have movable eyelids and cannot blink. The eye is covered by a fixed transparent shield.

The constantly flickering forked tongue is used for smelling.

The tongue is forked so that the snake can follow scent trails. The tips are kept apart so that it can discern differences in the strength of odours and enable it to locate its prey quickly.

Sloughing or shedding

Shedding of the outer layer of skin occurs as often as 15 times a year in juvenile snakes and about one to four times a year in adults, depending on growth rate. The external layer of skin does not grow and is therefore shed periodically, irrespective of the time of year. The entire skin, from the tip of the snout to the tip of the tail, including the caps that cover the eyes, is shed. Prior to sloughing the eyes become opaque and the snake may go into hiding, as its vision is restricted and it is more vulnerable to predators. The nose is rubbed against a rough surface until a piece of skin comes loose. Then, in most instances, the entire skin is shed in one piece and comes off inside out like an inverted sock. In older and larger snakes, as well as in captive snakes, the skin is often shed in pieces. Prior to shedding, snakes may select higher temperatures (by basking for longer periods) to speed up the development of new skin, effectively shortening the vulnerable period during which they cannot see well.

A Herald Snake with a piece of shed skin on its head. Note the vivid colours immediately after shedding.

SNAKE BEHAVIOUR
Reproduction
In early spring snakes get together to mate, the male usually locating a female by following a scent trail that she leaves behind. Once he locates her, the male will inspect the female with flickering tongue and will eventually twist the base of his tail beneath hers to copulate. Males have two penises, referred to as hemipenes, and one of the penises will protrude for copulation to take place.

Strictly speaking, all snakes hatch from eggs, the majority of them from eggs that are laid and left for external incubation. These snakes are referred to as oviparous or egg-laying and they produce leathery eggs. Some snakes, such as the Southern African Python (*Python natalensis*) and the Rhombic Skaapsteker (*Psammophylax rhombeatus*), coil around their eggs throughout incubation. This serves not only to protect the eggs, but also raises their temperature, which assists with incubation.

Other snakes retain the eggs within their bodies to produce fully developed live young, and are referred to as viviparous or 'live-bearing', although this is not to be confused with mammalian live birth. These eggs do not have the usual leathery shell and the young may be covered in a fine membrane that is easily ruptured.

Between four and eight weeks after mating, a female will select a suitable site to lay her eggs. The eggs are usually deposited in a hollow tree trunk, in rotting vegetation or in some other suitably protected place. The number of eggs, which may depend on the size of the female and, of course, the species, varies from one or two to as many as 60 eggs, or even more. The eggs have soft, leathery shells and require a certain amount of heat and humidity in order to hatch,

usually one to three months later. The young are equipped with an 'egg-tooth' consisting of a sharp ridge on the tip of the snout, which is used to slit the eggshell from the inside. Soon after leaving the egg the 'egg-tooth' is shed. Hatchlings usually resemble the adults and are often perfect replicas of their parents. The young of venomous parents are equipped with fangs and venom glands from birth.

Egg mortality is often high as eggs may be flooded, eaten by scavengers, desiccated or otherwise damaged. This is probably why some snakes retain the eggs within their bodies and give birth to young that are covered in a fine membranous envelope, which is ruptured soon after birth. There are no hard and fast rules as to which snakes are oviparous or viviparous. Mambas, cobras, the Boomslang (*Dispholidus typus*) and house snakes lay eggs, while most adders, the Mole Snake (*Pseudaspis cana*) and the Rinkhals (*Hemachatus haemachatus*) produce live young.

Once the eggs have been laid or the young produced, most snakes show no further interest in their progeny. Recent research indicates that hatchling Southern African pythons (*Python natalensis*), however, may remain with the female for several days after hatching, leaving the burrow during the day to bask, but returning to the protective coils of the female at night.

Bill Branch

The eggs of worm snakes are often stuck to one another, like sausages.

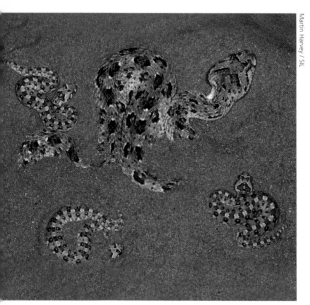

Martin Harvey / SIL

Horned Adders retain their eggs within their bodies to produce fully developed live young.

Hibernation

Snakes are often referred to as being cold-blooded (ectothermic). This does not mean that their blood is cold, but rather that they have no internal mechanism to control body temperature and must depend on the immediate environment to supply their body heat requirements.

In areas where there is a marked difference in temperature between summer and winter, snakes will go into hibernation, or more correctly torpor, for as long as cold conditions prevail. During this period they live off accumulated body fat and show very little, if any, activity. However, on a warm winter's day, a snake may bask near its hideout. Most snakes hibernate in animal holes, beneath rocks, or in deserted termite mounds. Individuals of different species may congregate in the same spot and hibernate together.

Snakes depend on the environment for their heat requirements.

LOCOMOTION AND SPEED

There are four basic modes of progression in snakes:

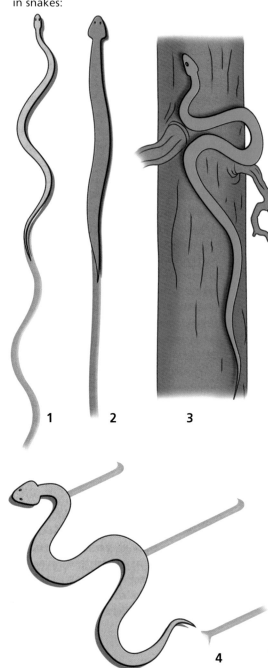

1   2   3

4

1 SERPENTINE MOVEMENT: This is the normal mode that most snakes use, especially when disturbed or when chasing prey. The body undulates from side to side while its hindpart makes contact with irregularities and the body is pushed forward in the direction the snake intends to go. This procedure is also followed when swimming.

2 CATERPILLAR-LIKE MOVEMENT: The snake progresses in a straight line using the ventral scales only. Heavy-bodied snakes, especially the Puff Adder *(Bitis arietans)*, often use this slow method of moving.

3 CONCERTINA-TYPE PROGRESSION: The snake anchors its head and drags the rest of the body along. This can sometimes be seen in trees where snakes may have difficulty negotiating smooth branches. Some burrowing snakes' tails end in sharp spikes, which are dug into the sides of burrows while the snake pushes itself forward.

4 SIDEWINDING: Certain snakes have adopted the sidewinding motion to move about on unstable dune sand. Only one or two sections of the body touch the ground at any one time. A section of the body is thrown sideways and is followed by the next section. One advantage is that most of the body does not make contact with the hot sand while moving.

The speed of snakes has been grossly exaggerated in the past, and still is today. It is highly unlikely that even a snake capable of fast movement, such as a large Black Mamba *(Dendroaspis polylepis)*, would ever exceed 20 km/h. Snakes (and most other reptiles) do not receive as good a supply of oxygenated blood as birds and mammals and therefore tire more easily when compelled to exercise more vigorously than usual for any period of time. Snakes never chase after people and a person could easily outrun any snake if they were both moving rapidly in the same direction.

f adder black mamba common slug-eater boomslang gaboon adde
ake eastern congo stiletto snake slender blind snake desert
g-tailed worm snake forest cobra yellow-bellied house sna
ke berg adder cape cobra anchieta's dwarf python green wate
ke red adder common shield-nose snake. common purple-glosse
y-horned adder green mamba aurora house snake variegated s

The ability to classify is one of the fundamental attributes of human intelligence

2 CLASSIFICATION AND RELATIONSHIPS

BY LYNN RAW

The ability to classify is one of the fundamental attributes of human intelligence. Even before we developed a vocabulary, humankind needed to identify what was good to eat and what was not, what was dangerous and what was benign, what was useful and what was not. Classification systems are limited by the extent of our knowledge. Essentially they attempt to group similar objects or concepts according to a particular purpose or design. They summarize and act as filing or information retrieval systems for our knowledge of the things we classify.

In the case of snakes, early zoologists tended to classify them with other long, slender, limbless animals such as worms and eels. As the knowledge of snake anatomy improved, scientists noticed that snakes have far more in common with lizards than they do with either eels or worms. At a more detailed level, snakes are also further classified into subcategories of snakes. Because certain snakes are venomous, some even dangerously so, their teeth and venom delivery apparatus have been used as a guide to their classification. To a degree, these features are still used, but earlier classifications had to be modified when it was discovered that some similarities did not indicate close relationships but, rather, convergent adaptations.

When VFM FitzSimons published the classic book *Snakes of Southern Africa* in 1962, snake classifications were based on dentition and snakes were grouped as follows: blind snakes (Typhlopidae), thread or worm snakes (Leptotyphlopidae), pythons (Pythonidae), the colubrids (Colubridae), the cobras, rinkhals and mambas (Elapidae), and the adders (Viperidae).

Advances in the knowledge of snake biology have made two things obvious. Firstly, these older classifications group together species that are not closely related, while separating others that are. Secondly, there is still not enough information available to establish a sound classification, and we are still not sure of the relationships of some groups.

For the purposes of this book, we have retained the general guidelines of the old structure, because no new classification is firmly in place.

The binomial system of nomenclature was introduced by Carolus Linnaeus (Carl von Linné) in 1758.

LINNAEAN OR BINOMIAL CLASSIFICATION SYSTEM

The binomial system of nomenclature was introduced by Carolus Linnaeus (Carl von Linné) in 1758 and has formed the basis for zoological scientific names ever since. Most species have just two Latin or Greek names called a *binomen*. The first word always begins with a capital letter and is the genus name given to a group of species, while the second begins with a small letter and is the species name. Both of these names are always printed in italics (or underlined if the situation does not allow for italics), e.g. the Natal Green Snake is named *Philothamnus natalensis* or Philothamnus natalensis. The full citation of the name will also include the name of the person (or persons) who first described and named the species, and the year that this was first published, for example *Philothamnus natalensis* (Smith, 1840). In this example you will notice that the describer's name (Smith) and date (1840) are enclosed in brackets. This parenthesis (bracketing) is used to indicate that Smith originally placed his new species in a different genus (in this case it was *Dendrophis*) that has subsequently been changed to *Philothamnus*.

In some cases three names are used instead of two. If there are three names, the second and third do not start with capital letters and there are no brackets. The third name indicates that this is a subspecies, that is, a subgroup of a particular species differentiated by a particular feature, e.g. colouring. An example of a subspecies name is *Philothamnus natalensis occidentalis* Broadley, 1966, where 'occidentalis' indicates that this is a subspecies of the Natal Green Snake. It is common practice to abbreviate the generic and even the specific name in the case of subspecies, so that the species is referred to as *P. n. occidentalis*. However, the first reference to the species is always written in full.

These definitions will give you an idea of the categories / names used in zoological taxonomy.

● TAXONOMY – the branch of biology concerned with the classification of plants and animals into groups based on their similarities and differences.

● TAXON (plural taxa) – an inclusive group of organisms in a classification. For example, a taxon could be a group at species, genus or family level.

● PHYLUM (plural phyla), CLASS, ORDER AND FAMILY – these are taxonomic groups that are arranged hierarchically (i.e. several classes make up one phylum, several orders make up one class). The members of any one of these units are grouped on the basis that they share unique characters or suites of characters that are not shared by taxa that do not belong (e.g. all and only birds have feathers).

● GENUS (plural genera) – a group of species that share a common suite of characters unique to the members of the genus.

● SPECIES (plural species) – a population of animals that forms a single interbreeding entity. Species may interbreed to produce occasional hybrids and sometimes a hybrid zone at a point of contact with another closely related species. Closely related species that are geographically isolated are more likely to hybridize artificially than those that have overlapping ranges. It is worthwhile noting that there are many definitions of species and that the one given here is based on general considerations that may not agree entirely with all other definitions.

● SUBSPECIES (plural subspecies) – a distinctive subunit of a species, which may be defined by small but consistent differences in traits from other subspecies within the same species. Generally, individuals from different subspecies within the same species can interbreed. Different subspecies within a species are usually geographically separate.

● TRIBE – A taxonomic group between family and genus.

Here is an example of a systematic classification using our previous example:

CLASS
Reptilia
ORDER
Lepidosauria (or Squamata)
SUBORDER
Serpentes (or Ophidia)
SUPERFAMILY
Colubroidea (or Xenophidia
= Caenophidia)
FAMILY
Colubridae
SUBFAMILY
Colubrinae
GENUS
Philothamnus
SPECIES
P. natalensis
SUBSPECIES
P. natalensis occidentalis

In the above classification you will notice some alternative names in brackets. These indicate that some scientists have differing opinions about which names are correct. This is a normal state of affairs in systematics and this disagreement is one of the driving forces of scientific investigation and the search for scientific truth.

IDENTIFICATION AND SCALE COUNTS

Even with little knowledge about the subject, it is possible to identify some snakes (to broader groupings anyway) by virtue of certain characteristics. For example, adders have distinctive coloration; cobras typically spread their hood when alarmed; some species are particularly prevalent in certain areas, etc. However, whereas the group or even the genus might be relatively obvious, it is a greater challenge to identify some snakes to species level. It is at this stage that specific scale counts can help precisely pinpoint a species.

Examination of dead specimens is easiest and safest. Obvious care must be taken when handling a live snake closely. Where the head scales comprise very small, usually keeled scales, the specimen is likely to be an adder; and if a loreal scale is absent (a shield on either side of the head between the nasals and preocular), you may have a cobra or one of its front-fanged relatives.

How to count scales
HEAD SCALES
Count the upper and lower labials (i.e. the scales bordering the lips) on each side, and note which upper labials are in contact with the eye. Check whether the nasal scale is single, semi-divided or fully divided. Check whether a loreal is present. Count the number of preoculars and postoculars. Note the arrangement of the scales on the temples, i.e. the temporal formula. Note any fused scales. Observe the relative sizes of the internasals, prefrontals, frontal and parietals (see the head scale drawings). Note the shape and proportions of the rostral scale at the front of the nose.

Night Adders can be identified without counting scales by the distinct V-markings on the head. However, they may be mistaken for Rhombic Egg-eaters.

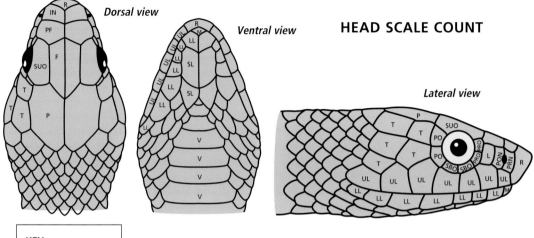

HEAD SCALE COUNT

Dorsal view

Ventral view

Lateral view

KEY
F = frontal
IN = internasal
L = loreal
LL = lower labial
M = mental
P = parietal
PF = prefrontal
PO = postocular
PON = postnasal
PRN = prenasal
PRO = preocular
R = rostral
SBO = subocular
SL = sublingual
SUO = supraocular
T = temporal
UL = upper labial
V = ventral

DORSAL SCALE COUNTS

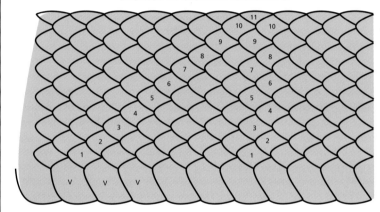

BODY SCALES
Count the number of scales around the body at one head length behind the head, one head length in front of the vent and at mid-body. Do not include the ventral scales. Examine the dorsal scales. Note whether they are keeled or smooth. Some snakes have double keels on the scales over the middle of the back. Often snakes have minute pits on the rearmost tips of the dorsal scales. These can be paired or single.

Scientists have differing opinions about which names are correct. This disagreement is one of the driving forces of scientific investigation and the search for scientific truth.

VENTRAL SCALE COUNT (DOWLING SYSTEM)

To count the ventral scales, begin by locating the first ventral. To do this, look behind the head. The first ventral is the first scale bordered on both sides by the first row of dorsal scales. From that scale, count the ventral scales back to the one immediately before the anal scale. This total is the number of ventrals. Note whether the ventral scales are keeled with a sharp lateral ridge at each side of the body. Check whether these also extend onto the subcaudals.

SUBCAUDAL SCALE COUNT

The first subcaudal is the single scale or pair of scales that meets the lateral scales on each side. Count back along the tail up to and including the scale, or pair of scales, immediately before the conical tip. If the tail appears to have lost the tip or to have been regenerated, indicate this with a '+' after the total. Note whether the anal scale is single or divided.

VENTRAL SCALE COUNT
(Dowling system)

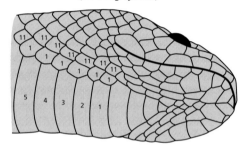

Keeled dorsal scales

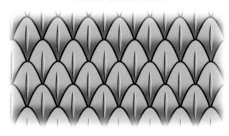

Smooth dorsal scales

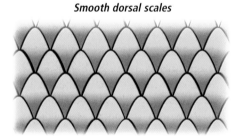

SUBCAUDAL SCALE COUNT

KEY
A = anal
SC = subcaudal
V = ventral

single subcaudals and entire anal

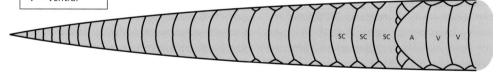

paired subcaudals and divided anal

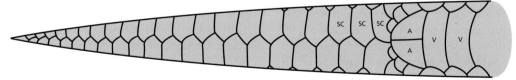

*In practice you may not need to make
all the counts mentioned above.*

USEFUL TIPS FOR COUNTING SCALES

A useful method of obtaining underbody counts in a live snake that is difficult to manage is to place it under a container on a photocopier or scanner and then to make an image of it. It is then relatively simple to count the ventrals and subcaudals from this image.

In practice you may not need to make all the counts mentioned on the previous page. Once you have narrowed down the possible species for your specimen, check the descriptions of these species to find out the differences that will allow you to confirm your identification. Then you will simply need to check the specific counts that will distinguish the species concerned.

If you are still unable to identify the specimen you should send it to a specialist taxonomist at a museum or university for final identification.

PRESERVING AND RECORDING SPECIMENS

The preservation of specimens is a very important aspect of research into snake biology. Virtually all locality and distribution records are based on preserved specimens. These specimens are particularly important if an apparently widespread species is found to consist of two or more nearly indistinguishable species. Unless specimens are available to confirm localities, all previously collected records for the species will be suspect. Preserved specimens are also the source of much of our information on reproduction, food preferences, scale counts and measurements. Scientists working on the ecology or behaviour of snakes also need to preserve representatives of the animals they have been studying, so that their information can

always be related to the correct species. While you should not go out of your way to collect specimens, it is inevitable that you will at some time come across a freshly dead specimen, perhaps killed by a passing car or an ignorant passer-by. It will then be useful to know how to preserve the unfortunate animal so that its death will at least be of some value to science.

Try to record as much information as possible when preserving a specimen. It is essential to note where the specimen was found (a Global Positioning System [GPS] reading is ideal); without a detailed locality, a specimen is of little scientific value. If you do not have a GPS reading, avoid confusion between place names, or obscure localities, by giving the place name, the distance and direction from the nearest major map point, province and country, e.g. 'Farm Rietfontein, 34 km NW of Durban, KwaZulu-Natal, South Africa'. Time and date of collection and the name of the collector are also useful, but the conscientious collector can gather additional valuable information. This includes altitude, temperature, weather conditions, substratum, activity prior to death, measurements, colour photographs and careful notes of the colours before preservation. After taking the details, the specimen can be prepared for preservation. If the snake is fresh, you may be

Preserved specimens in museum collections are relied upon for distribution records. Scientists may do surveys in certain areas to obtain such specimens.

Snakes being prepared for cataloguing.

able to prepare a blood slide that could give some idea of any blood parasites it may have carried. If it is a male, then one or both of the hemipenes can be everted (turned inside out) for preservation. This entails squeezing the base of the tail towards the vent; once the hemipenes begin to evert you can inject preservative into the base of the tail to obtain full eversion. In some cases it may be necessary to make an incision below the tail in order to cut the retractor muscles and so allow full eversion. Some scientists recommend that the mouth should be held open until the specimen is fixed. At this point the specimen should be thoroughly injected with preservative, or a deep longitudinal incision should be made along the belly and preservative poured over it. The specimen should be completely covered with preservative during the fixing stages. Specimens can be frozen if no preservatives are available. Freezing is also sometimes used to kill snakes humanely for scientific research.

The usual preservatives used are alcohol or formalin, both of which are toxic. Formalin is also reported to be carcinogenic. Ideally, to preserve a specimen well, it should first be fixed in 10 per cent formalin (1 part commercial formalin in 9 parts water) for at least 48 hours or until effectively fixed, then washed very well in running water or several changes of water for several hours. Once the formalin has been removed, the specimen can be transferred to 70 per cent ethyl alcohol (7 parts ethanol to 3 parts water). If pure alcohol is not available, commercial methylated spirits can be used. Even when diluted to 70 per cent, this can cause hardening and brittleness in specimens in the long term, as can concentrated formalin or long-term preservation in formalin. In an emergency, you can use alcoholic beverages such as gin, whisky or cane spirit to preserve small specimens. Another possible preservative that is not often used is acetone. Ethylene glycol can also be used for short periods. For long-term storage, specimens should be kept submersed in preservative in robust, wide-mouthed storage containers and kept in the dark to avoid the bleaching effects of sunlight or fluorescent light. Many plastic materials deteriorate rapidly when exposed to preservatives, and plastic containers may crack or leak without warning, so the use of glass jars and lids is recommended.

Ensure that your specimen is securely labelled or all your efforts will be in vain, since a specimen without data is useless to science. Your collecting data can be entered in a notebook or on a card, and you must ensure that the specimen can be identified from your notes. You must also label the specimen itself. A field label of strong cardboard tied on with sturdy thread should be sufficient for a short while. Be aware that even strong card can disintegrate very rapidly in wet preservatives. For more permanent labelling, type details onto 'Tyvek' security paper, since the typing

Ensure that your specimen is securely labelled or all your efforts will be in vain, since a specimen without data is useless to science.

embosses the text on the label and it remains readable long after the ink has dissolved. Dymotape is good in the short term (five to eight years). The plastic tags that are fixed around small tree trunks in nurseries are ideal, since they can be cut to the required size. Plastic sheets cut from margarine containers and sanded with fine sandpaper are also excellent. Only waterproof Indian ink or pencil should be used; anything else fades or runs. If the specimen is intended for a museum, the specimen label needs only a serial number and date, both of which should also be recorded in the notebook with the relevant data; but putting all the information on the label is much safer.

The collection or possession of specimens may, however, contravene provincial laws and any would-be collector should ascertain exactly what permits are required for collecting and retaining specimens, whether live or preserved.

Finally, do consider that there is a growing awareness of animal rights and that the kind of collecting that was considered acceptable or even desirable 20 years ago is often now perceived as unethical. Collecting for its own sake is now generally frowned upon, as wildlife is fast approaching the status of a non-renewable resource. However collecting, within reason, for valid research or study must be considered a necessity.

Preserved specimens at the Transvaal Museum in Pretoria. To be of value, such specimens must be housed in the collection of a recognized institution.

adder black mamba common slug-eater boomslang gaboon add
ake eastern congo stiletto snake slender blind snake desert
ng-tailed worm snake forest cobra yellow-bellied house sn
ake berg adder cape cobra anchieta's dwarf python green wat
ake red adder common shield-nose snake. common purple-gloss
ny-horned adder green mamba aurora house snake variegated s
mba common slug-eater boomslang gaboon adder black-necked

ck-necked spitting cobra southern african python ornate gr
tain adder swazi rock snake angola file snake olive whip sna
amibian wolf snake rufous beaked snake southern forest wo
ake eastern st   egel's beaked bli
ake kunene racer vine snake flowerpot snake pungwe worm sna
ater lined olympic snake distant's worm snake puff adder bla
ing cobra southern african python ornate green snake easte

3 SNAKEBITE

*A bite from a
venomous snake
is not necessarily
the same as
snakebite
envenomation*

Although fewer than 10 per cent of snake species in southern Africa are dangerously venomous and the vast majority of bites are inflicted on the extremities (the lower leg, hands, and arms), the realities of a serious snakebite should not be underestimated.

Some years ago a colleague of mine at Assagay Safari Park in KwaZulu-Natal, Crawford Coulsen, was bitten on the leg by a Black Mamba (*Dendroaspis polylepis*). Initially he thought that a rat had bitten him, but fortunately spotted the two metre-long snake slithering away and was familiar enough with southern African snakes to identify it.

He remained as calm as possible while reporting the incident, although the wound was bleeding freely and appeared to be a full bite. My attempts to wrap the affected leg with crêpe bandages before driving him to a hospital were frustrated by the fact that someone had removed the first-aid kit. There was also no one available to notify the nearest hospital to expect us, or to accompany us to assist with artificial respiration, so I decided to proceed straight to Addington Hospital, 45 km away.

Only ten minutes after the bite, Crawford began experiencing the first alarming symptoms. He complained of numbness around his lips, was sweating profusely, and his breathing was shallow. I tried to reassure him as we drove, to minimize the effects of shock. Within 20 minutes of being bitten he had stopped responding and was staring blankly ahead. His breathing was becoming more and more laboured and he had started to lose consciousness. In the half-hour it took us to reach Addington, his condition had deteriorated dangerously.

Crawford was rushed into intensive care where it took four long hours to get him out of danger. He recovered fully within a few days and was back at work within 11 days.

Snakebite statistics in southern Africa indicate that relatively few people are bitten every year and of those bitten, very few actually die. In Mpumalanga and KwaZulu-Natal, for example, between 24 and 34 people in 100 000 are bitten by snakes annually and the mortality rate is only 1 to 2 per cent. Although most snakebites are not fatal, it is nevertheless extremely important to follow the correct procedures in the unlikely event of a serious snakebite.

It is important to follow the correct procedures in the unlikely event of a serious snakebite.

ENVENOMATION

A bite from a venomous snake is not necessarily the same as snakebite envenomation. The former refers to a bite inflicted by a venomous snake, whether or not venom was injected. Most venomous snakes have control over the muscles surrounding the venom glands and can therefore inject venom if and when they want to. They can also control the amount of venom that is injected. A venomous snake may not inject any venom at all when biting. All snakebites are therefore not necessarily dangerous and a bite might even be from a harmless snake.

Snakebite envenomation occurs when a snake bites and injects its venom, i.e. venom poisoning occurs. The vast majority of bites are inflicted on the lower leg, hands or arms. The actual bite may comprise two distinct fang punctures (very rare), several punctures, a deep scratch, or even just a minute scratch. In many cases no puncture wounds can be identified. As it is seldom possible to identify the snake responsible or to judge the severity of the bite simply by looking at the wound, all bites should be considered dangerous until proven otherwise. The outcome of a venomous snakebite will depend on several factors, including the victim's sensitivity to venom and the amount of venom injected relative to the victim's body mass, i.e. the venom : mass ratio. The greater this ratio, the greater the severity of the bite. Owing to their smaller size, children run a higher risk of severe envenomation, which is borne out by the higher mortality rates in children. Juvenile snakes are also capable of injecting lethal quantities of venom.

A small number of herpetologists and individuals who either work with venoms or are exposed to them regularly may develop a syndrome known as venom hypersensitivity. Should such an individual be bitten by a venomous snake, the development of rapid anaphylactic (venom hypersensitivity) reaction is a possibility. Cardio-vascular collapse may ensue within minutes, followed by death if irreversible shock sets in. If the anaphylaxis goes unrecognized, the clinical effects may be attributed to the venom.

It is not possible to give hard and fast rules for how to identify the type of snake responsible for a bite. Most snakebites seen in clinical practice are by unidentified snakes. Some cobra bites produce symptoms similar to those of adder envenomation, and vice versa. However, since many people fear the worst unless reassured, bite victims should be given some idea of what symptoms to expect. Few bites result in severe symptoms within minutes. Immediate symptoms include anxiety, sweating, nausea, a dry mouth and even dizziness. These invariably result from shock and fear of the possible consequences of the bite. The following descriptions of symptoms provide a rough guide.

Cytotoxic venom

Reactions include immediate burning pain at the site of the bite followed by marked local swelling that could continue for the next 48–72 hours. In severe cases, the entire limb may swell. Local tissue necrosis is quite common – especially in bites on digits – and may also lead to secondary bacterial infection. In addition to the above symptoms, some neurotoxic symptoms such as drowsiness may also be experienced. This is typical of the venoms of the Puff Adder (*Bitis arietans*), Gaboon Adder (*Bitis gabonica*), Mozambique Spitting Cobra (*Naja mossambica*), Black-necked Spitting Cobra (*Naja nigricollis nigricollis*), Black Spitting Cobra (*Naja nigricollis*

Few people are bitten by snakes every year and of those, more than 98% survive.

woodi), Zebra Cobra (*Naja nigricollis nigricincta*) and possibly also the Rinkhals (*Hemachatus haemachatus*). Polyvalent antivenom may be required.

Symptoms should be localized and far less severe in the event of a bite by one of the smaller adders such as the Horned Adder (*Bitis caudalis*), Many-horned Adder (*Bitis cornuta*), Night Adder (*Causus rhombeatus*), Berg Adder (*Bitis atropos*), Stiletto Snake (*Atractaspis bibronii*) or even the Natal Black Snake (*Macrelaps microlepidotus*). They could include severe swelling with minimal skin damage. However, in some stiletto snake bites (*Atractaspis* spp.) the tissue damage at the site of the bite could be severe. Polyvalent antivenom is not effective against the venoms of these snakes and is therefore not recommended. Note that the venom of the Berg Adder (*Bitis atropos*) may result in severe neurotoxic symptoms as well as cytotoxic symptoms.

Neurotoxic venom

Reactions to neurotoxic venom include pain at the site of the bite with no or minimal swelling, as well as drowsiness, vomiting and increased sweating within five to 30 minutes. Other neurotoxic symptoms such as blurred vision, ptosis (drooping eyelids), slurred speech, double vision and difficulty with swallowing and breathing could follow within 30 minutes to three hours. Within this period of time the respiratory muscles are gradually paralysed, which may lead to respiratory failure. This is characteristic of Black Mamba (*Dendroaspis polylepis*), Green Mamba (*Dendroaspis angusticeps*), Cape Cobra (*Naja nivea*), Snouted Cobra (*Naja annulifera*), Forest Cobra (*Naja melanoleuca*) and Rinkhals (*Hemachatus haemachatus*) bites. Polyvalent antivenom is effective and may be required in large dosages.

The venom of Coral and Shield-nose snakes is far less toxic than the above and

A Mozambique Spitting Cobra ejects its venom.

the symptoms are usually not that severe. Few cases are known and further studies are required, but antivenom is not effective and not recommended.

The venom of the Berg Adder (*Bitis atropos*) is unusual in that it is neurotoxic and cytotoxic, causing ptosis, loss of eye movement, and the loss of the senses of taste and smell. Such symptoms appear within one to two hours and may become more pronounced over the next day or two. Victims may also experience difficulty in swallowing as well as respiratory distress. Polyvalent antivenom is not effective against the venom of the Berg Adder and is not recommended.

The Yellow-bellied Sea Snake (*Pelamis platurus*) is rarely found along our coast. Its venom may result in minimal local reaction accompanied by numbness and respiratory paralysis caused by damage to the voluntary muscles. Polyvalent antivenom is not effective against the venom of this snake.

Many scorpion stings are inflicted at night on bare feet and may be mistaken for snakebites. A sting from a typical *Parabuthid* scorpion is extremely painful but is not associated with swelling. Instead sweating, abdominal pain and tachycardia (abnormally rapid hearbeat) are experienced. Difficulty urinating is typical of a reasonably severe scorpion sting and does not occur with snakebite. This symptom may be used to differentiate between snakebite and a scorpion sting.

Haemotoxic venom

The symptoms of a haemotoxic venom such as that of the Boomslang (*Dispholidus typus*) or vine snakes (*Thelotornis* spp.) include minimal or no swelling at the site of the bite followed by oozing of blood from the site, headaches, mental confusion, nausea and vomiting as well as increased sweating, usually several hours after the bite. This is followed by bleeding from small cuts, the mucous membranes and, eventually, severe internal bleeding (12–36 hours). A monovalent antivenom is available for the bite of the Boomslang but not for the Vine Snake.

In some instances, you may not be sure whether, in fact, you have been bitten by a snake. Symptoms typical of shock, such as excessive sweating, a thumping heart and difficulty in breathing, must not be confused with the symptoms that would follow envenomation.

Snake venom in the eyes

Spitting snakes do not really spit their venom but rather squirt it. Pressure on the venom glands forces the venom along ducts and down the hollow fangs. Near the tip of the fang an opening, more or less at right angles to the fang, directs the venom out of the snake's mouth. The venom can be ejected as far as 2,5 metres or even further, depending on the size of the snake. Venom is not necessarily aimed at the eyes but rather sprayed in the general direction of danger or movement. Ejecting venom is a defensive mechanism to keep predators at bay. It is also very effective in scaring off humans that venture too close. As well as spitting, these snakes can also bite and would inject the same venom that is normally spat. There are two common spitting snakes within our range, the Rinkhals (*Hemachatus haemachatus*) and the Mozambique Spitting Cobra (*Naja mossambica*). Lesser-known spitters include the Black-necked Spitting Cobra (*Naja nigricollis nigricollis*), the Black Spitting Cobra (*Naja n. woodi*) and the Zebra Cobra (*Naja n. nigricincta*). The Rinkhals only spits from a raised position, while the cobras can spit from almost any position.

THE DEVELOPMENT OF ANTIVENOM

Antivenom was first used in 1886 and the first South African antivenom was produced in 1901 in Pietermaritzburg, though in small quantities. For the next thirty-odd years antivenom was largely imported from the Pasteur Institute in Paris.

During this period, a 10 ml ampoule of cobra or mamba antivenom could be purchased from Mr FW FitzSimons, Director of the Port Elizabeth Museum and Snake Park. A complete first-aid antivenom kit contained a lancet, ligature, syringe and two bottles of serum.

In 1928 the South African Institute for Medical Research (SAIMR) started producing antivenom. They experimented with a variety of domestic animals for serum production but settled on the horse, because a large volume of blood can be tapped in each session. Horses are made immune to snake venom by injecting them with small quantities of snake venom at a time, gradually increasing the dosages as the horse builds up resistance. Once the horse is immune, blood is taken from it and serum is separated from the red blood cells.

Initially, antivenom production was limited to the venoms of the Cape Cobra (*Naja nivea*) and the Puff Adder (*Bitis arietans*) because of the number of bites that were reported. Subsequently, a bivalent antivenom was produced for both snake species but it was not effective against the bite of the Gaboon Adder (*Bitis gabonica*) and many other venomous species. In 1938, Gaboon Adder venom was also introduced into the antivenom process.

During the Second World War, demand for antivenom soared because of the number of soldiers going into remote areas. As many as 46 horses were used at a time by the SAIMR for serum production. It is said that the majority of venomous snakebites suffered during this time were by people collecting snakes to make antivenom!

At this stage the venom of the Rinkhals (*Hemachatus haemachatus*) was added. Various monovalent and trivalent antivenoms for the three southern African mamba species, the Black Mamba (*Dendroaspis polylepis*), the Green Mamba (*D. angusticeps*) and Jameson's Mamba (*D. jamesoni*) were developed in the 1950s and 1960s. These were added to the polyvalent antivenom in 1971. During the 1970s the polyvalent antivenom also included the venoms of the Snouted Cobra (*Naja annulifera*), the Forest Cobra (*N. melanoleuca*) and the spitting cobras (*N. mossambica/nigricollis*).

A monovalent antivenom was produced for the Boomslang (*Dispholidus typus*) in 1940 but not in any quantity. This was largely because of the minute venom yield of this snake as well as the low incidence of bites.

The National Health Laboratory Service currently produces three snake antivenoms: a monovalent Boomslang (*Dispholidus typus*) antivenom, a monovalent Saw-scaled Viper (*Echis* spp.) antivenom and the more popular polyvalent antivenom that is effective against the venoms of the Puff Adder (*Bitis arietans*), the Gaboon Adder (*B. gabonica*), the Rinkhals (*Hemachatus haemachatus*), the Green Mamba (*Dendroaspis angusticeps*), Jameson's Mamba (*D. jamesoni*), the Black Mamba (*D. polylepis*), the Cape Cobra (*Naja nivea*), the Forest Cobra (*N. melanoleuca*), the Snouted Cobra (*N. annulifera*) and the Black-necked Spitting Cobra (*N. nigricollis*) as well as the Mozambique Spitting Cobra (*N. mossambica*).

Snakebite is a rare accident and very few victims die. It is important that you keep your wits about you and obtain help in a logical way. Remember that the snake may even have been harmless.

Snakebite outfits, containing two ampoules (20 ml) of polyvalent antivenom, can be purchased from some snake parks, leading pharmacies and the National Health Laboratory Service. These should ideally be stored at temperatures between 2 °C and 10 °C and should not be frozen. Antivenom eventually loses its clarity and potency if exposed to higher temperatures over an extended period of time. The ampoules do have an expiry date and should not be used thereafter. If you have any intention of using antivenom in an emergency, you should discuss it carefully with your doctor or an authority on snakebite.

TREATMENT GUIDELINES

It is of utmost importance to transport the victim to a proper medical facility as soon as possible. Fortunately, untreated bites by large cobras or mambas seldom kill their victims within the first four hours, while bites by adders usually take much longer to kill their victims. Even without first-aid treatment, more than 98 per cent of all snakebites will not be fatal.

The majority of snakebite victims are bitten on the lower leg, hands, or arms.

First-aid measures

● *EXPOSE THE BITE.* Cut away any clothing and remove constrictive objects such as rings and shoes. Excess venom must be wiped away from the bite with plenty of water or a piece of material.

● *DO NOT CUT OR SQUEEZE.* Never squeeze or cut a snakebite wound and do not resort to outdated measures such as rubbing Condy's crystals (Potassium permanganate) into it.

● *AVOID APPLYING SUCTION.* The benefits of suction are still unknown. Suction at the site of the bite, especially if using a mechanical device, may help if it is done immediately, even if it is only to reassure the victim. Suck through a sheet of rubber or plastic to avoid poisoning yourself, since you may not be aware of scratches in your mouth. Immediately spit out all fluid removed by suction. (Also bear in mind the dangers of HIV/Aids and hepatitis infection and always take measures to protect yourself from contact with the victim's blood or body fluids.)

● *MAINTAIN THE AIRWAY.* In serious Black Mamba (*Dendroaspis polylepis*), Snouted Cobra (*Naja annulifera*) and Cape Cobra (*Naja nivea*) bites, it is particularly important to keep the airway clear and ventilated at all times. Keep the mouth and throat free of saliva and resort to artificial respiration if necessary. Also keep victims warm by wrapping them in blankets or additional clothing.

● *DO NOT APPLY ELECTRIC SHOCK TREATMENT.* This is sometimes applied with a cattle prodder or car battery and should not be used as it is of no benefit whatsoever, no matter what the source of the current.

● *KEEP THE VICTIM STILL.* Discourage any unnecessary movement and keep the victim calm. Stay with the victim and quote snakebite statistics. Also mention that most victims recover fully without treatment and stress the importance of keeping still. Remember that any unnecessary movement could speed up the spread of the venom.

● *IMMOBILIZE THE LIMB.* Use a splint or sling to immobilize the affected limb and, if possible, keep the limb just below the level of the heart.

● *DO NOT GIVE ALCOHOL.* Do not give the victim alcohol or other liquids, or if you must, do so only in very small quantities.

● *APPLY A PRESSURE BANDAGE.* In the event of a suspected or known neurotoxic bite, apply a pressure bandage. (See opposite.) Pressure bandages should not be used for cytotoxic bites. If the victim is bitten high up on the trunk, which seldom happens, apply firm pressure to the site of the bite with your hand to delay the spread of venom.

● *AVOID TOURNIQUETS.* Unless the source of the bite is a Cape Cobra (*Naja nivea*) or Black Mamba (*Dendroaspis polylepis*), avoid using a tourniquet. In such instances, an arterial tourniquet may well be life saving, especially when proper medical help is hours away. The tourniquet, consisting of a belt, a rubber bandage or even some form of clothing, should be applied as soon as possible, above the knee or on the arm above the elbow, depending on the site of the bite. It should not be left on for more than 15 to 30 minutes (or at the very most one hour) at a time without being loosened for a few seconds. In any event, it should never be left on for more than one-and-a-half hours. Tourniquets can cause severe tissue damage and should only be resorted to if absolutely necessary.

● *CONSIDER ANTIVENOM.* In serious snakebite cases, and as a life-saving measure, it may be necessary to administer antivenom. See *Administering antivenom* on page 44. Never inject antivenom in or around the site of the bite.

● *CALL FOR HELP.* With the availability and popularity of cell phones nowadays, make good use of the technology. Inform your closest hospital, doctor or ambulance service that you have a snakebite victim and describe the symptoms. If possible, call one of the poison centres for advice (see page 47).

● *DO NOT ATTEMPT TO KILL THE SNAKE.* A second bite would really complicate matters. If, however, it has been killed and you are not sure what species it is, take it with you to the hospital, as positive identification could simplify treatment. Do not touch the dead snake but rather sweep it into a cardboard box or bucket, as some species play dead.

BE VERY CAREFUL.

PRESSURE BANDAGES

In the event of a bite by one of the non-spitting cobras or mambas, immediately apply a pressure bandage. Please note that this is not a tourniquet. Apply firm pressure to the site of the bite, using your hand. Then wrap a firm bandage over the bitten area (a crêpe bandage is ideal because of its elasticity, otherwise tear up some clothing). You are not aiming to cut off blood circulation, but rather to prevent venom from spreading rapidly though the lymphatic system. The bandage should therefore be as tight as for a sprained ankle. An inflatable splint might be a useful alternative, if available, but take great care not to over-inflate it.

Avoid unnecessary movements, for example in removing clothing, as this may increase the spread of venom. Do remove the victim's shoes or other restrictive clothing.

Now wrap the entire limb in a pressure bandage and then apply splints across major joints to minimize movement. Make sure that you can feel a pulse at the foot or wrist after applying the pressure bandage.

The patient should be carried, if necessary, and immediately transported to a hospital. If you are on your own, walk slowly but do not waste time.

The pressure bandages should stay on until the patient gets to hospital. If the limb swells excessively, loosen the bandage but do not remove it.

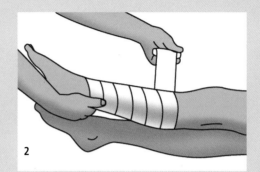

2

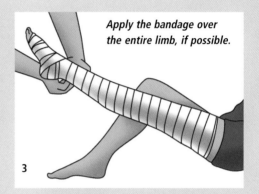

Apply the bandage over the entire limb, if possible.

3

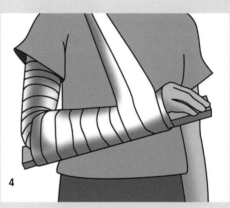

4

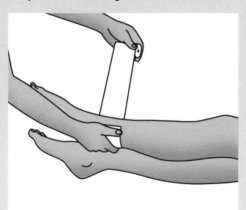

1

1 & 2 Apply firm pressure, then wrap the limb firmly, working towards the heart.

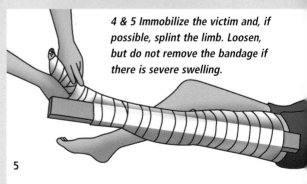

4 & 5 Immobilize the victim and, if possible, splint the limb. Loosen, but do not remove the bandage if there is severe swelling.

5

General medical measures

Snakebite victims should be hospitalized for at least 24 hours and, in the case of a suspected Boomslang (*Dispholidus typus*) or Vine Snake (*Thelotornis* spp.) bite, at least four days. The most effective treatment against severe snakebite envenomation is antivenom. As it is usually administered in conjunction with intravenous cortisone, antihistamines and perhaps adrenaline, it is best to leave this specialized treatment to medical professionals, if you have the choice.

Administering antivenom

Antivenom is most effective if injected intravenously and in fairly large dosages. This has inherent dangers, such as serum sensitivity, and should only be administered by someone who knows how to do it properly and who has the necessary drugs to combat adverse reactions (which may develop more rapidly and be more severe than the snakebite itself). Several deaths have occurred from anaphylaxis caused by antivenom.

Intramuscular or subcutaneous injection of antivenom may be the only route available to the layperson. These routes are much less effective than intravenous administration due to the much slower systemic absorption. They are also far more painful.

Generally you should avoid using antivenom indiscriminately as, more often than not, it will not be required. The antivenom may not be effective against the venom of the snake that inflicted the bite or it may have been a harmless snake. However, in cases of emergency, such procedures may delay serious signs until the victim receives proper medical help. Antivenom should not be injected into or near the site of the bite.

It may be justified to inject antivenom as a life-saving measure in known cases of bites by the mambas (*Dendroaspis* spp.), Cape Cobra (*Naja nivea*), large Snouted Cobra (*N. annulifera*) and the spitting cobras (*N. nigricollis/ mossambica*) (but not the Rinkhals (*Hemachatus haemachatus*)). This should only be carried out where there is definite evidence of progression of signs and symptoms. Early intravenous administration of antivenom (at least 40–60 ml) in these snakebite cases may well save the victim's life. Study the pamphlet in the snakebite kit carefully when it is first purchased and again prior to injecting antivenom.

Remember that polyvalent antivenom is not effective against the bites of the Berg Adder (*Bitis atropos*), the Night Adder (*Causus rhombeatus*), the smaller adders, the Stiletto Snake (*Atractaspis* spp.), the garter snakes (*Elapsoidea* spp.), the Coral Snake (*Aspidelaps lubricus*), the Shield-nose Snake (*Aspidelaps scutatus*), the Yellow-bellied Sea Snake (*Pelamis platurus*), the Boomslang (*Dispholitus typus*) and the Vine Snake (*Thelotornis* spp.) and should not be used in known bites by these snakes.

If you decide that antivenom is required prior to the victim reaching a hospital or a doctor, the two ampoules (20 ml) in the snakebite kit should be injected.

Antivenom should be injected intravenously over a period of about 10 minutes. The alternative, in cases where the veins have collapsed or when the antivenom is being administered by a layperson, is to inject the antivenom intramuscularly. The absorption of intramuscular or subcutaneous antivenom may be minimal in cases where the victim's blood pressure has dropped.

In very severe neurotoxic bites, especially when highly venomous species such as the Black Mamba (*Dendroaspis polylepis*) are responsible, between 80 and 120 ml, or even

The most effective treatment against severe snakebite envenomation is antivenom. It is best to leave this specialized treatment to medical professionals.

as much as 200 ml, of antivenom may be required. Also note that small children require the same dosage as adults. Sufficient quantities of antivenom will be required to neutralize the venom and to counteract the symptoms of severe envenomation.

Antivenom may also be required in cases of severe cytotoxic envenomation and should be administered within six hours of such a bite. The antivenom is effective while the venom is still active and could still be useful after 30 hours. In these cases the contents of the snakebite kit (20 ml) should be injected, preferably intravenously, and additional antivenom may well be required – up to 200 ml in known Gaboon Adder (*Bitis gabonica*) bites.

Allergic reactions to antivenom are a common and ever-present danger and may occur in as many as 20 per cent of cases. It is most likely when the victim has a history of allergies or allergic diseases such as asthma or infantile eczema and, if so, an experienced person rather than a layperson should administer the antivenom, as far as possible. In serious cases of envenomation, the effect of the snake venom far outweighs the potential danger of a severe allergic reaction to the antivenom.

In the past, skin testing for sensitivity was recommended, but can cause anaphylaxis in sensitive persons and is not very reliable. It is, therefore, no longer recommended.

In known Boomslang (*Dispholidus typus*) bites, monovalent Boomslang antivenom is not used in first-aid treatment. The venom is slow in acting (taking anything from 6–36 hours before serious symptoms develop) and so provides sufficient time for victims to be transported to a major hospital. The antivenom is very effective, even if administered quite late. Boomslang antivenom has, however, no effect against Vine Snake (*Thelotornis* spp.) bites.

The same regimes mentioned above apply when treating an animal with antivenom.

It is vital for victims to be hospitalized as soon as possible, especially if antivenom has been administered, so that they can be monitored carefully, particularly in the first hour after administration of antivenom.

In some instances, especially after large dosages of antivenom, serum sickness may occur within 10–14 days, but is seldom life threatening. Symptoms of serum sickness may include itching rashes, nausea, vomiting and joint pains that respond to treatment with antihistamines and steroids.

Antivenom should be used only in life-threatening situations and, ideally, under controlled conditions.

For further advice on the treatment of snakebite and the use of antivenom, readers are referred to *The Diagnosis and Treatment of Envenomation in South Africa* by Leonard Shrire, Gert J Muller and Liron Pantanowitz, published by the South African Institute of Medical Research, Johannesburg.

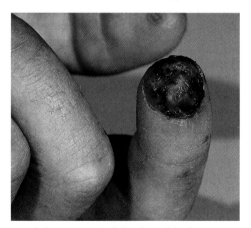

Local tissue necrosis following a bite by a Stiletto Snake.

Large quantities of antivenom (up to 200 ml) may be required in severe Black Mamba or Gaboon Adder bites.

First aid for snake venom in the eyes

On skin, venom will do very little or no damage, unless it enters an open wound. In the eyes, it causes a burning pain and severe inflammation. Rubbing the eyes will do a great deal more harm than good.

Rinse the eyes immediately with large quantities of water or any other harmless fluid such as milk, cold drink, tea, saliva or even beer or urine. Never use Condy's crystals (Potassium permanganate). Do not attempt to neutralize the venom but rather try to flush it from the victim's eyes. Also wipe any venom on the face away from the eyes. Seek medical advice. As a general rule, antibiotic ointments should be used in the victim's eyes for a few days to prevent any secondary bacterial infections from occurring in damaged corneas. The victim's eyes should recover fully within three or four days but, if left untreated, may develop partial blindness from the venom. This is particularly likely where secondary infections have occurred.

Only a trained professional should attempt to handle a dangerous snake. It is always best to leave snakes alone.

PREVENTION OF SNAKEBITE

Many South Africans are outdoor people and spend a great deal of their time fishing, hiking, bird-watching or merely enjoying nature. Confrontations with snakes are therefore rather common. Here are a few suggestions on how to avoid snakes and snakebite:

Precautions to take

● Always leave snakes alone.

● If you are in the veld, wear stout shoes or boots (not sandals) and long trousers, preferably denims. Most victims are bitten on the lower leg or ankle, often when accidentally standing on a snake.

● Do not walk barefoot at night when you are in the veld or camping. If you have to move around in the dark, take along a torch and light your way. Most snakebites occur just before, or within an hour or two of, total darkness. This is when both nocturnal snakes and people are generally very active.

● Keep your eyes open and watch where you are going. When mountain climbing, do not put your hand in places that are out of sight. When collecting firewood, don't reach into holes, burrows or hollow logs.

● Do not step over logs and large rocks, as a snake may be sunning itself on the opposite side. Rather step onto them.

● If you do come across a snake, stand still. No snake will come up and attack you. If you are a fair distance from the snake, approximately four metres or more, retreat slowly. Snakes never chase people.

● Do not try to kill a snake in the wild. Throwing rocks at snakes and shooting at them is looking for trouble.

● Do not tamper with seemingly dead snakes, as some of them feign death. The body may be turned sideways or upside down with the tongue hanging out. *BEWARE*.

● Treat all snakes with respect.

USEFUL CONTACTS

For information on antivenom, or for antivenom kits, call:

National Health Laboratory Services trading as South African Vaccine Producers (Pty) Ltd
Tel: 011 386 6063 office hours
After hours: Contact Dr Blaylock on 083 652 0105 for snakebite emergencies
Website: **www.savp.co.za**

For advice on envenomation, call one of the following Poison Information Centres/Hospitals:

NETCARE 911
24-hour toll-free poison information hot-line: 0800 333 444 countrywide – all hours
Website: **www.netcare.co.za**

Pretoria
Unitas Hospital
Tel: 0800 333 444 all hours

Cape Town
Red Cross Children's Hospital
Tel: 021 689 5227 all hours

Tygerberg Hospital
Tel: 021 931 6129 all hours
021 938 6084 office hours

Durban
St Augustine's Poison Trauma Unit
Tel: 0800 333 444 all hours

Bloemfontein
Universitas Hospital
Tel: 082 410 0160 all hours
051 401 3090 office hours

Port Elizabeth
Livingstone Hospital Paediatric Department
Tel: 041 405 2141 all hours
041 405 9111 all hours
041 392 3385 office hours

East London
Frere Hospital Paediatric Department
Tel: 043 709 1111 all hours

Kimberley
Kimberley Hospital Pharmacy Department
Tel: 053 802 2336 office hours
053 802 2355 office hours

Bruce D Taubert

A professional handling a Black Spitting Cobra, appropriately equipped with a mask and long stick.

Even if a snake
adapts to captive
conditions, it can
never truly be tamed

ff adder black mamba common slug-eater boomslang gaboon add
ake eastern congo stiletto snake slender blind snake desert
ng-tailed worm snake forest cobra yellow-bellied house sr
ake berg adder cape cobra anchieta's dwarf python green wa
ake red adder common shield-nose snake. common purple-gloss
ny-horned adder green mamba aurora house snake variegated s

ck-necked spitting cobra southern african python ornate gre
lain adder swazi rock snake angola file snake olive whip sna
amibian wolf snake rufous beaked snake southern forest wo
ake kunene racer vine snake flowerpot snake pungwe worm sna
ter lined olympic snake distant's worm snake puff adder bla

4 SNAKES IN CAPTIVITY

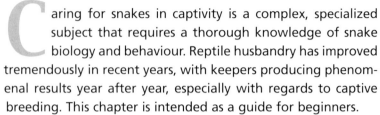

C aring for snakes in captivity is a complex, specialized subject that requires a thorough knowledge of snake biology and behaviour. Reptile husbandry has improved tremendously in recent years, with keepers producing phenomenal results year after year, especially with regards to captive breeding. This chapter is intended as a guide for beginners.

If you are keen on snakes and wish to learn more, you can refer to any of the authoritative books on the subject as well as the many useful articles that appear in specialized snake-keeping magazines. Reading books, visiting snake parks and museum displays and studying snakes under the supervision of someone with experience are all good ways to learn how to identify these reptiles and become fully familiar with their habits.

Dangerously venomous snakes do not belong in home collections. However, should you choose to keep dangerous snakes, always ensure that their cages are lockable and escape-proof and that you have access to the correct medical care in the event of a bite. Do not take any chances with a dangerous snake, no matter how pleasant a disposition it has. Even if a snake adapts to captive conditions, it can never truly be tamed. To handle a dangerous snake freely is foolish and may result in serious injury or even death. Do not assume that it is safe to handle snakes as is done at certain 'snake shows' and on television. Although some handlers are true professionals and know exactly what they are doing, many are simply reckless and take chances to win the admiration of the crowd.

Keeping snakes in captivity has grown in popularity and there are various local and international web sites that cater for beginners, as well as for more advanced keepers. Always bear in mind that there are laws governing the keeping of captive snakes. Should you wish to keep snakes, you must obey all laws at all times and refrain from causing damage to snake populations and to their habitats. Wherever possible, obtain specimens that are bred in captivity and avoid removing more snakes from the wild than is necessary, even if you do have the relevant permits.

Dangerously venomous snakes
do not belong in home collections.

GUIDELINES FOR BEGINNERS

Prior to starting a collection you need to ask yourself the following questions:

● *ARE YOU PERMITTED TO KEEP SNAKES?* In other words, do you have the necessary permits and permission from your local authorities and ruling conservation body? The possession of snakes in a private collection is governed by local authority rules, the ruling conservation body in your area and, in some instances, the State vet. Ensure that you comply with all of the rules and regulations and have the required permits.

● *CAN YOU PROVIDE SUITABLE CONDITIONS FOR THE SNAKE, BOTH IN SUMMER AND IN WINTER?* Snakes require a clean enclosure with shelter and, in many instances, some source of heating. The enclosure must also be escape-proof as snakes are masters of escape.

● *DO YOU HAVE THE TIME TO CARE FOR SNAKES?* Both snakes and their enclosures require a great deal of care. Cages must be cleaned and fresh water supplied regularly. You would have to devote some time to your snakes daily.

● *CAN YOU PROVIDE THE CORRECT FOOD?* This could be difficult for specialized feeders such as the Centipede-eaters or Shovel-snout snakes. Most beginners start off with snakes that eat mice, such as the Brown House Snake. Try to avoid specialized feeders in the beginning and be wary of unscrupulous pet shops that sell snakes without knowing what they eat or what care they need.

● It is vital for the enthusiast to understand snakes. Learn about their biology and habits, reproduction and habitat requirements. By exchanging notes with other enthusiasts and reading specialized literature, you will soon learn a great deal about reptile husbandry. Visit snake parks and private collectors and carefully note how their enclosures are designed and how they care for their snakes. Also note the condition of their snakes.

● All snake-keepers should also join as many snake or reptile organizations and associations as possible. Some of these institutions produce journals and newsletters and such information could be of great benefit. Should you require information about these institutions, please contact me at the e-mail address given on page 15.

OBTAINING SPECIMENS

It is important to ensure that all specimens are obtained legally. Contact your local conservation authority for advice. In the past one had to avoid getting snakes from pet shops as they had little husbandry knowledge and snakes were kept in crowded conditions. Many snakes were infected with diseases and died soon after being purchased. Today there are several pet shops that specialize in keeping and selling snakes and often offer captive-bred specimens. Check all specimens carefully for injuries and mouth infections. Avoid skinny and listless snakes and, if at all possible, see if the snake eats before you purchase it. The best option is to obtain captive-bred individuals from a reputable breeder. These snakes are invariably in good condition and disease free, although they might be a little more expensive.

Always check snakes carefully for mites. They are most visible in the eye sockets and are often found burrowing under overlapping scales, where they are difficult to find. If in any doubt, gently stretch the skin, especially around the eyes, to expose the mites. They are minute and resemble very small specks that move around slowly. Other telltale signs that mites are present are white dots on the body of the snake, caused by the mites defecating. In heavy mite infestations, snakes will lie in their water bowls with just the tip of the snout exposed. A vet can help you to eliminate mites, but it is preferable not to introduce them into your snake's enclosure in the first place.

Minor wounds may heal but could leave unsightly scars. A snake that is alert, with a constantly flickering tongue, can usually be assumed to be in good health.

Choosing a snake species is not easy. Some snakes are dull or particularly secretive and will mostly hide away. Others may have special dietary requirements or be aggressive. Choose a placid species that is fairly colourful and easy to feed.

TRANSPORTING AND HANDLING SNAKES

Snakes can be transported in cloth bags such as pillowcases. Make sure that the bag has no holes in it, especially in the corners, and turn it inside out to prevent the snake from becoming entangled in loose threads. Be very careful if you transport venomous snakes in pillowcases as they can bite through bags.

Once the snake is in a pillowcase, fold the open end over twice and tie it with a rubber band. Leave enough space *above* the rubber band for the bag to be handled safely or carried without any chance of the snake biting through the cloth. Also ensure that you do not injure the snake when applying the rubber band to the bag. Many snakes have been suffocated when they have accidentally been caught with elastic bands. Always handle a pillowcase with a snake in it with great care and place it in a cardboard box or plastic bucket during transportation.

Be careful never to leave a snake in a closed vehicle in the sun or in any other warm spot, for example near a window that gets a lot of light. The heat build-up in a closed vehicle or a plastic container may kill a snake in under 30 minutes.

Many snakes adjust well to a captive environment and soon get used to being handled. Handling should be minimized and unnecessary restraining of a snake should be avoided as far as possible, as most snakes become stressed easily.

ENCLOSURES

An enclosure for snakes such as small egg-eaters or Brown House Snakes should be no smaller than 50 x 30 x 30 cm, though one measuring about 80 x 40 x 40 cm would be more suitable, especially in the longer term. Many snakes spend most of their lives coiled up and it is therefore not necessary for the enclosure to be longer than the length of the snake.

Fish tanks are quite useful and work well if fitted with an escape-proof perforated lid. They are somewhat bulky and difficult to handle but convenient to clean, as an empty fish tank can easily be scrubbed with hot, soapy water.

Wooden cages are popular too. The top, bottom and sides can be made of wood, chipboard or pine panels. The back should be made of pegboard or masonite with small holes drilled for ventilation. The wooden sections should be glued together just before they are screwed together. The front of the enclosure could consist of two bevelled sheets of glass on plastic runners, the latter glued onto the cage after the paint has dried. The sheets of glass must overlap, providing space for a locking device. Use a good-quality paint on all of the wooden surfaces and allow the paint at least two to three days to dry before introducing the snakes, so that it loses any toxic properties.

Be very careful if you transport venomous snakes in pillowcases as they can bite through bags.

Active snakes that have extensive home ranges in nature should be kept in fairly large enclosures. Such enclosures must be escape-proof. Outdoor 'snake pits' are not suitable and should be avoided as they do not provide adequate cover in adverse weather conditions.

CAGE DECORATIONS: A variety of cage decorations may be used, including rocks, cork bark, hollow logs, branches and plastic or live plants. Do not use rocks that could topple over and crush snakes or break the glass. Also provide the snake with a hiding box, either of cardboard or plastic, into which it can fit fairly tightly. Snakes are secretive creatures and it is important for them to be able to hide away.

HEATING: Various methods of heating may be used and with good results. The easiest, and perhaps the most popular method, is a 40-watt light bulb fixed to the roof of the enclosure on one side so that a heat gradient is formed. Use a red light bulb so that you do not confuse the snake about whether it is day or night, as this may adversely affect breeding. Experiment with different wattages in a snakeless enclosure until you reach the ideal temperature range.

You may also build a small wooden box to enclose the light bulb as snakes can burn themselves if they come into contact with a heat source. Leave a small hole in the box so that you can check whether the light is working.

Ambient temperatures between 20 and 29 °C are acceptable to most species. A heat gradient should be created so that the snake can choose a cool or warm spot in the enclosure. If you do provide a retreat or hiding place for the snake, it should be at the cooler end of the cage. If the cage is large enough, provide more than one hiding place so that the snake has a choice.

More sophisticated forms of heating include heating pads or underground heat strips. These accessories are becoming more readily available from specialized pet shops. Never place a snake cage in the sun as the heat build-up in the enclosure may soon kill the snake. Snakes in glass cages do not really benefit from the sun as most of the important ultraviolet rays are filtered by the glass and one has no control over such a heat source.

Snakes have fragile bones and must be handled carefully to avoid injuries.

VENTILATION: Ventilation is important and several small holes should be provided in the sides, on top or at the back of the enclosure. These holes should measure less than 5 mm in diameter, depending on the size of the snake. An old stocking can be stretched over these holes if you are keeping very small snakes. Avoid using wire mesh as snakes often rub their noses against such surfaces while trying to escape, injuring themselves in the process.

WATER: Captive snakes must always have ample fresh water. They may ignore the water bowl but will drink from it the moment fresh water is presented. Use a large dish as most snakes enjoy submerging themselves in water from time to time. The snake should not be able to overturn the water bowl or crawl underneath it. Snakes frequently defecate in their water and, if this happens, the water should be changed immediately.

Enclosures should be kept quite dry as high levels of humidity often cause skin problems and respiratory infections. However, the more specialized tropical snakes require higher humidity and need spraying down at least once a day.

SUBSTRATUM: Sand is not a good choice of floor covering as it harbours bacteria that cause diseases such as mouth rot and provides places for mites to hide. Snake parks all over the world make use of paper towelling or newspapers to keep snake enclosures hygienic. However, newspaper substrate is obviously not ideal for display purposes. Where natural substrate is required, washed river gravel works well and is easy to clean. You can scoop up faecal matter with some of the surrounding gravel using a small plastic spade or aquarium net taped onto the end of a dowel stick. Peat moss, dry leaves, stones and bark can also be used. Many collectors make use of carpet off-cuts, trimmed to size. This ground cover is easy to clean, vacuum or scrub and spare sections of clean carpet can be kept ready for when the old piece needs replacing.

CLEANING: It is best to remove the snakes and place them in a bucket or other similar holding bin when cleaning a cage. Scrub the entire cage every month or two, using hot, soapy water. Faeces should be removed the moment they are observed and if the enclosure has a gravel base, remove some of the gravel with the faeces.

DISINFECTION: Avoid using pine-based disinfectants. Any chlorine-based disinfectant will work well. Ensure that there are no strong odours when you return the snakes to the enclosure. General disinfecting may be necessary from time to time. Thoroughly spray or wet the entire inside surface with disinfectant and leave the empty cage in the sun for a few hours to dry properly.

FEEDING

Most snakes feed on mice or rats, although some prefer frogs, toads, lizards, fish or a variety of other creatures. Other snakes are specialized in their feeding habits in that they feed primarily on one type of food animal. Some water snakes prefer certain frogs and fish while the Green Mamba favours birds and arboreal rodents. Snakes of the genus *Dasypeltis* are highly specialized and feed exclusively on eggs. Snakes have different feeding habits. Some actively hunt their prey and make use of venom to kill their food, while others constrict their prey. A few snakes even eat their prey while it is alive.

Temperature plays an important role in digestion in snakes and they should not be fed during cold spells. If the temperature

Temperature plays an important role in digestion in snakes and they should not be fed during cold spells.

drops suddenly after feeding, snakes may regurgitate their food. After feeding, they usually retire to a suitable hiding spot to digest and should not be handled for a day or two.

Laboratory mice are the most popular food source for captive snakes. Pinks (newborn mice) and weaners can be fed alive but full-grown mice should be killed and fed to the snakes before rigor mortis sets in, since unattended live adult mice may seriously injure a snake. Many keepers freeze mice and then simply thaw them properly as needed. Most snakes are attracted to their food by the prey's movement and it may therefore be necessary to wriggle a dead mouse with a long pair of forceps to get the snake interested.

Always watch the feeding process carefully, especially when you have more than one snake in the enclosure. If two snakes get hold of the same mouse, one of them may eat the mouse and the other snake. By watching them feeding you will know which snakes have eaten and how much. It is advisable to separate snakes when feeding.

If you do decide to use live mice as a food source, watch them carefully, as laboratory mice show little fear of snakes and have been known to bite them, sometimes fatally. A laboratory mouse will sometimes pull large strips of skin from the back of a snake. Never leave live mice or rats in a snake enclosure overnight. Another good reason for feeding snakes dead mice is that a live mouse may bite and blind a snake as it is being caught and constricted.

Hatchlings need to be fed more often than adults, perhaps even once a week. Adults generally require a good meal every two weeks but this varies from species to species and some snakes will be happy with one good meal a month throughout summer. After they have eaten, snakes should

Marius Burger

Some snakes are specialized feeders, preferring certain frogs and fish, while others may prefer birds.

not be offered more food until they have defecated. Also bear in mind that in winter, even if the enclosure is heated, most snakes refuse food for up to six months. Avoid offering too large a meal to a snake and be careful of overfeeding. Most captive snakes are grossly overfed.

Snakes may refuse food for a variety of reasons. They seldom feed prior to shedding and will also refuse food when the weather is too cold. If you experience problems in getting a snake to feed, increase the enclosure temperature by 3 to 4 °C, alter the decorations in the enclosure and provide more hiding places.

Factors that may cause a snake to regurgitate its food are a drop in temperature, prey that is too large, and stress, often from excessive handling. Snakes also refuse food when they are sick.

If a snake persistently refuses to eat, release it rather than let it slowly starve to death, unless it is an exotic snake. Exotics should never be released into the wild and indigenous snakes should only be released into the same areas from which they were captured. Releasing snakes away from their original habitat invariably spells death for these animals. Incorrect introductions into the wild may also cause a variety of problems for scientists, including incorrect distributional data and possible damage to the genetic purity of populations.

Only resort to force-feeding if there is a good reason not to release the snake, for example if it is an exotic or a rare species that is being kept for scientific reasons.

SHEDDING

Snakes shed their skins according to their growth rate. Prior to shedding, while the new skin is forming under the old, the eyes become opaque or milky and the snake is said to be going into 'the blue'. The eyes

The majority of snakes eat rats and mice.

then clear and the snake should shed within two to three weeks. It will rub its nose against a rough surface to loosen the skin and, in most of the smaller snakes, the skin should come off in one piece. This is a sign of good health. If the skin comes off in pieces, it may be necessary to assist.

To aid a shedding snake, soak it in a container half filled with lukewarm water and provide plenty of paper towelling for it to crawl through, so that it can pull the pieces of skin off itself. Leave the snake in the container for a few hours but check it regularly and make sure that it doesn't drown. Remove pieces of skin by hand only if they come off easily. Take care to be gentle during this procedure – the new skin may be delicate and can easily tear.

Always check whether both eye caps are present on a shed skin when you find one in an enclosure. If an eye cap remains on the eye, soak the snake and gently rub the eye with your finger to remove it. If stubborn eye caps refuse to come off, it may be necessary to seek professional assistance.

CAPTIVE BREEDING

All captive snakes should be sexed and, if you intend to breed with them, you should keep males and females as breeding pairs. In many species the males have much longer tails than the females. Furthermore, the base of the tail in males is often visibly distended in the cloacal region. One method of determining sex in snakes is to insert a lubricated metal probe into the cloacal region (i.e. the channel into which the alimentary canal, genital and urinary ducts open) and gently push it towards the tail. In males, the probe usually slides down much further than the fifth or sixth subcaudal scale, whereas in females it seldom extends beyond the third subcaudal scale.

However, the success and ease of this sexing method varies from species to species. This is a rather delicate procedure and should be left strictly to experienced people.

There are various stimuli that may induce mating in snakes. These include reducing the daylight cycle as winter approaches and increasing it towards summer; reducing and increasing temperature; introducing a male or more than one male into an enclosure housing a female, or even spraying down the enclosure with water, to simulate spring rains. Several matings may take place over a few days. Among viviparous snakes, the posterior half of the body in a gravid female may be visibly distended during pregnancy. Most females go off food prior to laying or giving birth. If you suspect that a female is gravid, isolate her and place a plastic ice-cream tub filled with slightly damp peat moss in the enclosure. Cut a small hole in the side so that the snake can enter the tub. Remove the water bowl, as snakes often lay their eggs in water, drowning the embryos. Supply the female with water once a day for no longer than half an hour and make sure that she doesn't lay her eggs in the water bowl. Check the ice-cream tub daily for eggs. It is quite common for gravid females to shed a few days before laying.

Snakes copulating. Mating may occur several times over a number of days.

Warren Schmidt

Eggs and hatchlings

Eggs should be removed as soon as they are laid. If they are stuck together, pull them apart very gently. Place the eggs lengthwise in a container, without turning them. For research purposes, measure the maximum length and width of each egg and record as much information as possible (include the laying date, number of eggs, size and origin of the female, incubation temperature, incubation period, etc.).

Incubating snake eggs can be quite simple. Place them in slightly damp vermiculite, river sand or peat moss (obtainable from nurseries) in a plastic container and keep them in a cupboard. Some keepers prefer slightly damp paper towelling to vermiculite or peat moss. The towelling may have to be changed every three or four days to prevent the growth of mould. The vermiculite, paper or peat moss must not be too dry or too wet. If it is too dry, the eggs will indent and need to be sprayed with water.

Make several small holes in the lid of the container and check the eggs daily.

It is best to incubate most snake eggs at around 28 °C, if you have the choice. Once hatching commences and the baby slits the eggshell from the inside, do not disturb it or attempt to hasten the hatching process. Some snakes take a day or two to emerge from the egg as the remaining yolk is absorbed into the body. Newly hatched snakes or newborn snakes must be kept moist and warm and should be housed individually in plastic containers. Hatchlings need only the tiniest of holes to escape, so an enclosure that contains eggs or a gravid female should be escape-proof. The young are usually full of yolk and will therefore have enough food for at least a week or two. They also shed quite soon after birth and seldom feed before the first shedding. The young of many species have different diets to the adults. For example, young Brown House snakes usually feed on lizards, while adults feed on rodents, birds and bats.

DISEASES

Snakes are susceptible to a variety of diseases and many authoritative books have been published on the subject. In addition to diseases, they are also plagued by both internal and external parasites. Many local veterinarians deal with snake diseases and these should be consulted when necessary.

Atherton de Villiers

Once hatching commences, do not disturb the hatchling or attempt to hasten the hatching process.

common name: Brown House Snake   enclosure no: 23

species: Lamprophis capensis   sex: female

date acquired/born: Hatched 15/01/04; Aquired 20/01/04 card no: 1

locality/source: Captive bred by J. Marias

date	food in (g)	food taken	length (mm)	mass (g)	comments
3/2/04	pink, 4.2	yes	220+45	10.5	taken
					immediately
4/2/04					Shed skin
					(in a single
					piece)

The card above is an example of a simple, effective way of keeping records. Always present a snake's length in two measurements, i.e. snout to vent length (SVL), followed by tail length (220 mm SVL and 45 mm tail length in this example). Record length in millimeters and mass in grams – consistency in data presentation limits confusion. Detailed comments are useful for highlighting health problems.

KEEPING RECORDS

It is important to keep accurate records of your captive snakes: such information may be useful to organizations such as the Herpetological Association of Africa. By keeping a documented record of successful and unsuccessful techniques, keepers learn and benefit more from their experiences than by relying on memory alone. Also bear in mind that none of our snakes has been studied extensively. The Herpetological Association of Africa publishes relevant information in its journal *African Journal of Herpetology* and material that is not quite suitable for the journal may well be published in its newsletter *African Herp News*. Record any behavioural data, mating times and duration, sizes, feeding, growth, shedding and other data that may be of interest. You cannot record too much information. Tape a record card onto each enclosure and fill in the origin of each snake, its common and scientific name, length, sex (if known), shedding dates, feeding dates, diet, and any other useful or relevant information.

It is important to keep accurate records of your captive snakes. You cannot record too much information.

ff adder black mamba common slug-eater boomslang gaboon add
ake eastern congo stiletto snake slender blind snake desert
ng-tailed worm snake forest cobra yellow-bellied house sn
ake berg adder cape cobra anchieta's dwarf python green wat
ake red adder common shield-nose snake. common purple-gloss
ny-horned adder green mamba aurora house snake variegated s

*Southern Africa has a diverse
range of snakes, many of which
have been insufficiently studied
and are poorly understood*

ck-necked spitting cobra southern african python ornate gre
ain adder swazi rock snake angola file snake olive whip sna
mibian wolf snake rufous beaked snake southern forest wo
ke western green snake sand snake sodwana's beaked bli
ke kunene racer vine snake flowerpot snake pungwe worm sna
ter lined olympic snake distant's worm snake puff adder bla

5 SPECIES ACCOUNTS

ADDERS OR VIPERS

Viperidae

Adders are abundant and occur in, or close to, most major cities in southern Africa. They account for many of the snakebites serious enough to require medical attention – the majority, in many regions, the work of the Puff Adder.

Most adders are short and stubby, with large erectile fangs in the front of the mouth. When not in use, the fangs are folded back within their sheaths against the roof of the mouth. They have keeled scales, those on the head and on the body similar in size.

Night adders (*Causus* spp.) are generally less stubby and their heads are not as triangular as those of other adders. They have smooth scales, their head scales larger than their body scales. Night adders have shorter fangs than other adders and the longest venom glands (relative to body size) of all snakes.

Adder venoms are predominantly cytotoxic or cell-destroying, i.e. they are responsible for the destruction of blood vessels and tissue. Symptoms are localized and bites are often extremely painful, followed by severe swelling as a result of internal bleeding and, in some cases, blistering and death of tissue. This, coupled with secondary infection, may even make amputation necessary. Bites from small adder species, although painful and unpleasant, are usually not as serious.

Adders have large, hinged fangs that fold back against the roof of the mouth when not in use.

Most adders (like this Horned Adder) are stubby, with the head distinct from the rest of the body.

Puff Adder

Bitis arietans

OTHER NAMES
Pofadder (A)
Imbululu (Z)
Irhamba (X)

VERY DANGEROUS

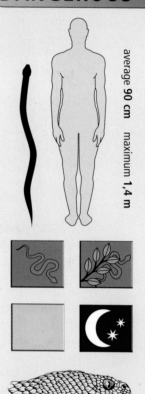

average 90 cm   maximum 1,4 m

Length: Adults average 90 cm in South Africa, but may reach 1,4 m. In Kenya specimens of over 1,8 m have been recorded, making this Africa's largest adder.

Scale count: The dorsal scales are keeled with 29–41 rows at mid-body, 123–147 ventral scales and 14–38 paired subcaudals. The anal shield is entire. There are 12–17 upper labials, no preoculars and 12–16 scales around the eye. There are 13–19 lower labials.

Colour: Above, variable from bright yellow to light yellow, yellow-brown, orange-brown, light brown or grey, with distinct, more or less regular chevron-like dark markings over the back, and dark bands or bars on the tail. A dark blotch on the crown of the head is separated from another blotch above the snout by a light line between the eyes. On the side of the head are 2 dark oblique bands, 1 below and 1 behind the eye. Below, yellowish white to grey with black blotches. Generally, specimens from the drier west (e.g. North West Province) are paler, and those from the wetter east are darker. Specimens are dull just before, and vividly marked after, sloughing of the skin.

Preferred habitat: Puff Adders are common throughout most of southern Africa, except for mountain-tops, true desert and dense forests. This snake does not occur naturally in and around the greater Johannesburg region.

Habits: A slow-moving, bad-tempered and excitable snake that may hiss or puff when disturbed. The Puff Adder is a stout snake with a

A Puff Adder from the Northern Province.

thin neck and triangular head. The eyes are small with a vertical pupil, the snout rounded and the nostrils large, pointing upwards. Usually found on the ground but it may venture onto small shrubs or bushes to sun itself. It hides in thick grass or under bushes, down holes and under any form of ground cover. Mainly active at night but known to bask in the day, especially in the rainy season. It often basks on tarred roads where it may be killed by passing vehicles. It relies on its excellent camouflage to escape detection and prefers to freeze, rather than move off. People frequently step onto or close to Puff Adders and then get bitten. Although it is a sluggish snake it strikes rapidly, often drawing the head back with the body in an S-shape before lunging forward to strike. This snake usually moves forward in a straight line in what has been described as a 'caterpillar-like' motion but, when disturbed, it may move rapidly in the normal serpentine motion. Like most other snakes, it swims well.

Similar species: May be confused with the Gaboon Adder (*Bitis gabonica*) or some of the smaller adders. Note that none of the harmless snakes within our range resembles the Puff Adder.

Enemies: Man, warthogs, birds of prey and other snakes.

Food and feeding: Usually waits in ambush in a spot where it can remain motionless for hours. It feeds on rats and mice, other small terrestrial mammals including hares, ground

A brightly coloured Puff Adder from KwaZulu-Natal.

birds, lizards, toads and, occasionally, other snakes. Large prey are usually bitten and then released and left to die. The Puff Adder then follows its prey's scent with a flickering tongue. The prey is swallowed headfirst. A member of this species is known to have eaten a juvenile tortoise.

Reproduction: Viviparous, giving birth in late summer to 20–40 young, though exceptional broods of 80 have been recorded. The young, measuring 15–20 cm, are born in a fine membranous sac from which they break free soon after birth. A female from Kenya, housed in a Czech zoo, gave birth to 156 young, the largest number of young produced by any snake species in the world. Males are known to engage in wrestling

The Puff Adder has enormous fangs that are folded back against the roof of the mouth when not in use, as is typical of the group.

A dull specimen from Aus in Namibia.

Venom: A potent cytotoxic (cell-destroying) venom that attacks tissue and blood cells. Other than immediate shock, symptoms include extreme pain, excessive swelling and sometimes blistering at the site of the bite. Most victims are bitten on the lower leg. The venom is slow acting, usually taking 24 hours to cause death if not treated or if treatment is unsuccessful. It is uncommon for victims to die in a shorter period, although fatalities within 30 minutes have been recorded. With fatal bites, the victims usually succumb to complications associated with extensive swelling or kidney failure. Less than 10% of Puff Adder bites result in death. Tissue damage may result in the loss of digits or limbs. Antivenom will be required in serious cases.

during the mating season. Females produce a pheromone that attracts males. Several males may follow the scent of a single female.

Danger to man: Because it relies on camouflage to escape detection, this bad-tempered snake with its long fangs (up to 18 mm) and potent venom features prominently in snakebite accidents and is often considered Africa's most dangerous snake. It accounts for most serious snakebites in southern Africa.

Subspecies: Only the typical Puff Adder race (*Bitis arietans arietans*) occurs within our range.

First-aid procedures: See first-aid treatment on page 42.

Although sluggish, the Puff Adder readily snaps back into a striking position and may lunge forward when biting.

Gaboon Adder

Bitis gabonica

OTHER NAMES
Gaboenadder (A)

Length: Adults average 90–120 cm in southern Africa.

Scale count: The dorsal scales are mainly keeled with 33–46 rows at midbody, 124–140 ventrals and 17–33 pairs of subcaudals. The anal shield is entire. There are 13–17 upper labials and 15–21 scales around the eye, with 16–22 lower labials.

Colour: Above, the body is beautifully coloured in various shades of dark and light brown, buff, purple and pink. A broad buff vertebral stripe is broken up by evenly spaced velvety brown hourglass markings, while the flanks are covered in complex buff, purple and brown markings. Jutting from the belly are black-edged purple triangles. The head is buff to chestnut, with a dark brown median line and a dark brown spot above the angle of the jaw. There is a dark brown triangle on either side of the head. The apex of the triangle enters the eye, while the base borders the upper lip. The triangle may be divided into 2 by an oblique light line, which radiates from the eye. Below, this snake is yellowish to buff with dark blotches. The combination of these colours provides excellent camouflage among leaf litter and makes the snake extremely difficult to detect, although it is fairly bulky.

Preferred habitat: In southern Africa it prefers moist, thickly wooded lowland areas in lowland forest and moist savanna on the eastern escarpments of Zimbabwe. It tends to avoid dense forest where food is limited. The Gaboon Adder has a restricted distribution.

Habits: Though mainly active at night, it may be seen basking in the sun. It is a huge, sluggish snake that may remain in a single spot for days. The Gaboon Adder has small eyes with vertical pupils and a

Gaboon Adders prefer a thickly wooded, lowland forest environment.

black, red-tipped tongue. Compared with the Puff Adder (*Bitis arietans*) it is surprisingly placid. When disturbed, it will emit a series of long, drawn-out deep hisses while the forepart of the body is lifted off the ground horizontally. Even then it is reluctant to strike.

Similar species: May be confused with the Puff Adder but is far more colourful and more impressively patterned.

Enemies: Much of this snake's habitat in northern KwaZulu-Natal has been destroyed by squatters. Many individuals are also captured by snake enthusiasts, usually while crossing roads at night. The Gaboon Adder is rare in northern KwaZulu-Natal and is listed as vulnerable in the latest *South African Red Data Book – Reptiles and Amphibians* (Branch, 1988).

Food and feeding: May hunt from dusk onwards, otherwise prefers to ambush its prey. Unlike the Puff Adder, it tends to hang onto its prey while the venom takes effect, except when tackling large prey. Favourite prey includes rodents, hares, ground birds and toads. Small monkeys and duiker are also taken.

Reproduction: Viviparous, giving birth to 16–30 young (in South Africa) in late summer, measuring 25–32 cm. The young are perfect replicas of the adults. Males are known to engage in combat during autumn and early winter. This includes neck wrestling and striking with the mouth closed. This snake is known to hybridize with the Puff Adder. A single hybrid, measuring 1,24 m, was found near Mtubatuba in 1972.

Danger to man: This snake has a potent cytotoxic venom and can inject large quantities in a single bite. It also has enormous fangs that may exceed 40 mm in length. It is extremely dangerous to man but is rarely encountered. Very few bites are reported.

LOOK OUT FOR

- A fat snake with a triangular head that is very distinct from the rest of the body.
- Beautiful colours in various shades of dark and light brown, buff, purple and pink.
- Huffs and puffs a great deal when disturbed.
- Always found on the ground.
- Mainly active at night.
- Has a pale broad head with a dark central line.

Venom: The potently cytotoxic venom is comparable with that of the Puff Adder, but much larger quantities may be injected in a single bite. A full bite from a Gaboon Adder will result in alarming symptoms and early death unless the victim is treated promptly with antivenom. The victim must be treated for shock immediately. Symptoms may include severe pain, swelling and necrosis.

First-aid procedures: See first-aid treatment on page 42.

Colin Tilbury

The Gaboon Adder is far more colourfully marked than the Puff Adder.

Despite its complex coloration, this snake is perfectly camouflaged among leaf litter and can easily be trodden on. It is rare throughout most of its range, and bites are seldom reported.

DANGEROUS

Berg Adder

Bitis atropos

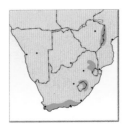

OTHER NAMES
Bergadder (A)
Irhamba lamatye (X)

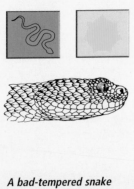

average 40 cm   maximum 60 cm

Length: Adults average 30–40 cm and may reach 60 cm in exceptional cases.

Scale count: The dorsal scales are keeled with 27–33 rows at midbody, 118–144 ventrals and 15–31 paired subcaudals. The anal shield is entire. There are 10–16 scales around the eye, 9–13 upper labials and 10–16 lower labials.

Colour: Above, greyish olive to dark brown or black, with a silvery white dorsolateral line on either side from behind the head to the tail. Above each line is a series of dark subtriangular to semicircular pale-edged markings, and below these a series of similar but smaller markings. The markings form a geometric pattern. The head has a dark arrow-shaped mark on the crown and 2 pale stripes on either side. The underside is off-white to dark grey with dusky infusions, or occasionally slate grey to black. Khaki to reddish brown Berg Adders with faint markings occur near Belfast in Mpumalanga Province.

Preferred habitat: From mountain fynbos in the south to montane grassland and sourveld in the north. The Berg Adder is found from sea level in the Cape Province up to 3 000 m in the Drakensberg.

Habits: A particularly bad-tempered snake that hisses loudly and will strike readily if approached. It is frequently found basking in grass tussocks, on rocky ledges or on footpaths and will quickly seek refuge if disturbed. This snake is endemic to southern Africa.

A bad-tempered snake that hisses loudly and bites readily.

Similar species: May be confused with the Puff Adder (*Bitis arietans*). Its triangular head is distinct from the body and, like the Puff Adder, it hisses when encountered. The Spotted Skaapsteker (*Psammophylax rhombeatus*) and Rhombic Egg-eater (*Dasypeltis scabra*) also have blotched patterns but these snakes have more elongate bodies.

Enemies: Preyed upon by predatory birds and other snakes.

Food and feeding: Mainly lizards and small rodents but also amphibians, including rain frogs. Nestlings of ground-living birds and smaller snakes are also taken. Juveniles, however, feed largely on frogs and other amphibians.

Marius Burger

A vividly marked Berg Adder from the Western Cape.

Berg Adders are usually found on rock ledges or on footpaths.

Reproduction: Mating occurs in autumn and the females give birth to 4–16 young in late summer. The young measure 9–15 cm in length. Females are known to produce more than 1 batch of young from a single mating.

Danger to man: Berg Adders are common, like to bask in the sun and strike readily when encountered. Bites may result in alarming neurological symptoms and signs but no fatalities are known.

Venom: The venom differs from that of most adders in that it is mainly neurotoxic, with a specific action on the optic and facial nerves, causing drooping eyelids, double vision, dizziness and temporary loss of taste and smell. Venom strength may differ between different populations of Berg Adders. Unlike cobra venom, it is not known to cause difficulty in breathing. Most victims recover fully within a few days. Patients should be treated symptomatically. Few bites result in swelling and necrosis. Antivenom does not neutralize the venom of this snake and therefore is not required. Though no deaths have been recorded, bites may be serious and should be treated as such.

First-aid procedures: See first-aid treatment on page 42.

Berg Adders from Mpumalanga may be rather dull in colour and were previously thought to be a subspecies.

DANGEROUS

Many-horned Adder
Bitis cornuta

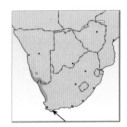

OTHER NAMES
Veelhoringadder (A)
Horingsman (A)
Unompondwana (X)

maximum 54,6 cm

average 40 cm

Length: Adults average 30–40 cm with a maximum of around 54,6 cm. Captive females may reach 75 cm. Females are often larger and bulkier than males.

Scale count: The dorsal scales are in 25–31 rows at midbody, with 127–148 ventral scales. It has 24–37 paired subcaudals, usually not fewer than 27 pairs in males and not more than 32 pairs in females. The anal shield is entire. There are 11–15 upper labials, 12–16 lower labials and 13–18 scales around the eye.

Colour: Above, greyish, occasionally greyish brown to reddish brown, with 3 or 4 rows of 22–31 (usually 25–27) dark angular blotches, which may be pale-edged. The markings on the upper rows are usually bigger than those on the lower rows and sometimes fuse to form larger subrectangular markings. The head has symmetrical dark markings above, which may fuse to form an arrowhead shape. A dark oblique streak radiates from the eye to the angle of the jaw. Below, white to dirty brownish or grey, with or without darker speckling.

Preferred habitat: Found on mountains, rocky outcrops and gravel plains in the Namib Desert and in the Karoo, but enters mountain fynbos in the south.

Habits: Prefers rocky areas on sandy or gravel flats where it can easily shelter from the wind. It does sidewind and can bury itself in

Note the tufts of horns above each eye.

loose sand. It seeks shelter in rock cracks or rodent burrows and is most active at dusk or in the early mornings. When confronted, it will hiss loudly and strike with so much force that most of the body will lift off the ground. This snake is endemic to southern Africa.

Similar species: May be confused with a young Puff Adder (*Bitis arietans*) or some of the smaller adders such as the Horned Adder (*B. caudalis*), but is distinguished by the tuft of 4–7 horns on either side of the head, above each eye.

Enemies: Preyed upon by other snakes. Many individuals are captured for the exotic pet trade and exported illegally. Also, often killed by passing vehicles when crossing roads.

Food and feeding: Feeds mainly on ground-living lizards, small rodents, birds and amphibians.

Reproduction: Viviparous, giving birth to 5–14 young in late summer or early autumn. The young measure 13–16 cm.

Danger to man: The venom is supposedly quite potent, but this snake's venom yield

LOOK OUT FOR

- A tuft of 4–7 horns above each eye.
- Often seen crossing the roads after sunset.
- Most active at dusk or early mornings.
- Will hiss and strike aggressively when confronted.
- Prefers gravel flats where it can shelter from the wind.

is minute. It poses no real threat to man, although it can inflict an extremely painful bite.

Venom: Mildly cytotoxic with much pain and swelling accompanied by necrosis. It is not known to be fatal and antivenom is not required.

First-aid procedures: If you are sure that a Many-horned Adder was responsible for the bite, get the victim to a doctor where the bite must be treated symptomatically. Administer painkillers. Otherwise see first-aid treatment on page 42.

Many-horned Adders inhabit a variety of habitats including gravel plains, rocky outcrops and fynbos.

The Many-horned Adder will hiss loudly and strike viciously when confronted. Boots provide adequate protection against the bite of this snake.

Desert Mountain Adder

Bitis xeropaga

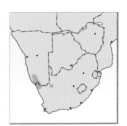

OTHER NAMES
Woestynbergadder (A)

average 40 cm   maximum 61 cm

Length: Adults average 30–40 cm with a maximum length of 61 cm.
Scale count: The dorsal scales are in 25–27 rows at midbody, with 147–155 ventral scales and 22–33 paired subcaudals. The anal shield is entire. There are 13–17 upper labials, 13–16 lower labials and 14–18 scales around the eye.
Colour: Above, ash to dark grey with 16–34 crossbars. Each crossbar consists of a median dark brown to blackish rectangle flanked on either side by a whitish spot and a light brown area. The head does not have any dark markings. The belly is light grey to dusky with darker spots and speckles.
Preferred habitat: This rare snake is found on mountain slopes and sparsely vegetated rocky hillsides.
Habits: This snake appears to be similar to the Many-horned Adder (*Bitis cornuta*) in its habits. It inhabits the driest parts of sparsely veget-ated rocky hillsides and mountain slopes. Captive specimens usually prefer to lie on rocks. Unlike some of the other small adders, it does not sidewind or bury itself in sand. If disturbed, it will hiss and strike in the typical adder fashion. This snake is endemic to southern Africa.
Similar species: Could be confused with some of the other small adders but lacks horns. Might also be confused with the Dwarf

This snake lacks tufts of horns above the eyes.

Beaked Snake (*Dipsina multimaculata*) and the Western Keeled Snake (*Pythonodipsas carinata*) but is not as elongate. Also has a triangular head very distinct from the rest of the body.

Enemies: Unknown. Is sought after in private collections.

Food and feeding: Unknown. Captive specimens have done well on a diet of lizards and mice.

Reproduction: Viviparous, giving birth to 4–5 young in late summer.

Danger to man: Nothing is known of the venom of this snake. It probably poses no real threat to man, but the bite is likely to be painful.

Venom: No human bites have been recorded. The venom is probably similar

LOOK OUT FOR

- Head lacks dark markings.
- Belly has dark spots and speckles.
- Does not have horns.
- Triangular head distinct from the rest of the body.

to that of other small adders, causing pain, local swelling and necrosis.

First-aid procedures: If you are sure that a Desert Mountain Adder was responsible for the bite, get the victim to a doctor where the bite must be treated symptomatically. Administer painkillers. Otherwise see first-aid treatment on page 42.

A rare snake that inhabits sparsely vegetated rocky hillsides and mountain slopes.

Nothing is known of the venom of this snake and no human bites have been recorded.

Plain Mountain Adder

Bitis inornata

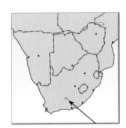

MILDLY VENOMOUS

OTHER NAMES
Ongemerkte bergadder (A)

average 30 cm   maximum 35 cm

Length: Adults average 25–30 cm with a maximum length of 35 cm. Males are much smaller than females.

Scale count: The dorsal scales are in 27–30 rows at midbody, with 126–138 ventrals, and 21–33 pairs of subcaudals. The anal shield is entire. There are 10–14 upper labials, 11–13 lower labials and 11–14 scales around the eye.

Colour: Above, dull yellowish brown to reddish brown, usually with 19–24 faint but darker blotches and occasionally paler spots on the sides. The belly is cream to light brown, sometimes heavily speckled with darker markings.

Preferred habitat: Found under rock slabs and in grass tussocks on mountain slopes in the Sneeuberg from north of Graaff-Reinet to Cradock. It is found between 1 600 and 1 800 m above sea level where both severe frost and snow occur in winter.

Habits: This small adder inhabits montane grassland where winter temperatures plummet during snow and frost. It hibernates during the cold months and is most active in the early mornings and evenings during the warmer months; otherwise it hides under rocks or in grass tussocks. It is seldom encountered and will hiss and strike if disturbed. The Plain Mountain Adder lacks horns above the eyes. This snake is endemic to southern Africa and appears to have become very scarce in recent years. Extensive sheep farming throughout most of its range

This dull, hornless little adder has become very scarce in recent years.

Marius Burger

The Plain Mountain Adder may be confused with small Puff Adders like the one above, but lacks chevron markings.

may have a negative effect on the future survival of this species and this rare snake may well be endangered.

Similar species: May be confused with the Puff Adder (*Bitis arietans*) but lacks chevron markings. Can also easily be confused with other small adders.

Enemies: Unknown.

Food and feeding: Mainly lizards, especially skinks and lacertids, but small mammals are also taken. Little is known of this snake's diet.

Reproduction: Viviparous, giving birth to 5–8 young in late summer. The young are minute, measuring 12,5–15,2 cm.

Danger to man: Nothing is known of the venom of this snake. It probably poses no real threat to man but the bite is likely to be rather painful.

Venom: No human bites have been recorded. The venom is probably similar to

that of other small adders, causing pain, local swelling and necrosis.

First-aid procedures: If you are sure that a Plain Mountain Adder was responsible for the bite, get the victim to a doctor where the bite must be treated symptomatically. Administer painkillers. Otherwise see first-aid treatment on page 42.

> ### LOOK OUT FOR
> - Short, stubby snake with flat snout and triangular head.
> - Dull reddish brown above with faint markings.
> - May hiss and strike when confronted.
> - Found between 1 600 and 1 800 m above sea level.
> - May have 19–24 blotches down the back.

Extensive sheep farming throughout most of its range may threaten the future survival of this rare adder.

MILDLY VENOMOUS

Red Adder
Bitis rubida

OTHER NAMES
Rooiadder (A)

average **30 cm**   maximum **42 cm**

Length: Adults average 25–30 cm with a maximum length of 42 cm. Males are smaller than females.

Scale count: The dorsal scales are usually in 29 (25–29) rows at midbody, with 133–143 ventrals in females and 126–138 in males, 22–28 subcaudals in females and 27–35 in males. The anal shield is entire. There are 12–14 upper labials, 11–14 lower labials and 11–15 scales around the eye.

Colour: Quite variable. Sometimes very red above with virtually no pattern (Cedarberg), or dull brown to reddish brown with 18–30 paired blotches. Stripes radiating from the eye to the lip as well as a rounded dark triangle on the crown of the head may be present. The belly is a dirty cream to grey colour with darker grey-brown infusions.

Preferred habitat: Restricted to rocky mountain fynbos. In the Cedarberg this snake may be found with the Many-horned Adder (*Bitis cornuta*). Elsewhere it is found further inland throughout the foothills of the inland escarpment and into the Little Karoo. To date, specimens have been found between 302 m and 1 380 m above sea level.

Habits: This small adder is often active in the early mornings and evenings when it may be found hiding under shrubs or boulders.

Bill Branch

The Red Adder occurs in rocky mountain fynbos where it may be found with the Many-horned Adder.

Unlike some of the other small adders, it does not scuffle into the sand and does not sidewind. It was only described in 1997 and very little is known of its habits. May have very reduced tufts of horns above each eye.
Similar species: May be confused with several of the other smaller adders.
Enemies: Unknown.
Food and feeding: Mainly lizards, especially geckos, skinks, agamas and lacertids, but small rodents are also taken.
Reproduction: Viviparous, giving birth to up to 10 young in late summer. They measure 12–14 cm.
Danger to man: Nothing is known of the venom of this snake. It probably poses no real threat to man but the bite is likely to be painful.
Venom: No human bites have been recorded. The venom is probably similar to that of other small adders, causing pain, local swelling and necrosis.

LOOK OUT FOR

- Short, stubby snake with a triangular head.
- Dull reddish brown above with faint markings.
- Found between 302 and 1 380 m above sea level.
- The horns above each eye are greatly reduced or, more usually, absent.
- This snake does not bury itself in sand or sidewind.
- May have 18–30 blotches down the back.

First-aid procedures: If you are sure that a Red Adder was responsible for the bite, get the victim to a doctor where the bite must be treated symptomatically. Administer painkillers. Otherwise see first-aid treatment on page 42.

A recently described small adder that feeds largely on lizards. Note that there is great colour variation among Red Adders.

MILDLY VENOMOUS

average 25 cm   maximum 30,2 cm

Albany Adder
Bitis albanica

OTHER NAMES
Albanie-adder (A)

Length: Adults average 25 cm with a maximum of 30,2 cm. Males are smaller than females.

Scale count: The dorsal scales are in 27–29 rows at midbody, with 129–138 ventrals in females and 120–131 in males, 21–23 subcaudals in females and 23–27 in males. The anal shield is entire. There are 12–14 upper labials, 11–14 lower labials and 13–14 scales around the eye.

Colour: A boldly patterned species in grey, white and black with 15–22 dark dorsolateral blotches that may fuse towards the tail. The belly is cream-grey and often has darker infusions.

Preferred habitat: Found in succulent thickets in the Algoa Bay area of the Eastern Cape, occurring between 50 and 500 m above sea level.

Habits: This small adder was first described in 1997 and very little is known of its habits or lifestyle. It may have small tufts of horns above each eye but they are usually absent. Albany Adders are endemic to southern Africa. Only a handful of specimens have been collected and it appears as though much of the former habitat of this snake has been destroyed. Industrial development poses a real threat to the survival of the species.

Similar species: May be confused with several of the other smaller adder species.

Very little is known of the habits or lifestyle of this small adder that was discovered in 1997.

Bill Branch

Enemies: Unknown.

Food and feeding: Unknown but probably lizards and small rodents.

Reproduction: Viviparous.

Danger to man: Nothing is known of the venom of this snake. It probably poses no real threat to man but the bite is likely to be rather painful.

Venom: No human bites have yet been recorded. The venom is probably similar to that of other small adders, causing pain, local swelling and necrosis.

First-aid procedures: If you are sure that an Albany Adder was responsible for the bite, get the victim to a doctor where the bite must be treated symptomatically.

LOOK OUT FOR

- Short, stubby snake with a triangular head.
- Dull grey with dark blotches along the sides of the back.
- May have tufts of small horns above each eye, but they are usually absent.
- Occurs between 50 and 500 m above sea level.
- May have 15–22 dark blotches down the back.

Administer painkillers. Otherwise see first-aid treatment on page 42.

This is an endemic species that inhabits succulent thickets in the Algoa Bay area of the Eastern Cape.

MILDLY VENOMOUS

Southern Adder

Bitis armata

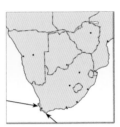

OTHER NAMES
Suidelike adder (A)

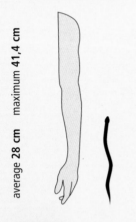

average 28 cm   maximum 41,4 cm

Length: Adults average 25–28 cm with a maximum of 41,4 cm. Males are smaller than females.

Scale count: The dorsal scales are usually in 27 (25–29) rows at mid-body, with 118–128 ventrals in females and 115–125 in males, 19–26 subcaudals in females and 23–31 in males. The anal shield is entire. There are 11–14 upper labials, 11–15 lower labials and 12–16 scales around the eye.

Colour: Above, grey with black stipples and 22–28 dark brown to black and white blotches. There is a dark forward-pointing arrow-shaped mark on the head and dark markings radiate from the eye to the lip. The belly is pale grey-white with dark markings on the sides. The underside of the tail is grey.

Preferred habitat: Restricted to low-lying coastal fynbos not higher than 200 m above sea level in the south-western Cape. Much of its former habitat has been destroyed.

Habits: This small adder was first described in 1997 and very little is known of its habits and lifestyle. It has been found sheltering under limestone rock slabs among thick coastal shrub where it is most active in the early morning and evening. The tufts of horns above each eye are reduced, but always present. This snake is endemic to southern Africa. Urban development poses a real threat to the survival of this

This is a stubby snake, with dark brown and white blotches along the upper body.

Bill Branch

LOOK OUT FOR

- Short, stubby snake with a triangular head.
- 22–28 pairs of dark brown to black and white blotches on the back.
- Reduced tufts of horns above each eye.
- Not found higher than 200 m above sea level.

species. Fortunately, some of the isolated populations of the Southern Adder are situated within protected areas such as Langebaan National Park. Individuals are also collected for the pet trade.

Similar species: May be confused with several of the other smaller adders.

Enemies: Unknown.

Food and feeding: Lizards and small rodents.

Reproduction: Viviparous. Up to 7 young, measuring 12–15,2 cm, are born in late summer.

Danger to man: Nothing is known of the venom of this snake. It probably poses no real threat to man, but the bite is likely to be rather painful.

Venom: No human bites have been recorded. The venom is probably similar to that of other small adders, causing pain, local swelling and necrosis.

First-aid procedures: If you are sure that a Southern Adder was responsible for the bite, get the victim to a doctor where the bite must be treated symptomatically. Administer painkillers. Otherwise see first-aid treatment on page 42.

Much of the low-lying coastal fynbos habitat that this snake prefers has been destroyed.

The Southern Adder has reduced tufts of horns above each eye. Urban development threatens the survival of this species.

DANGEROUS

Horned Adder

Bitis caudalis

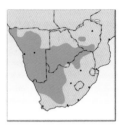

OTHER NAMES
Horingadder (A)
Horingsman (A)

maximum 60 cm

average 40 cm

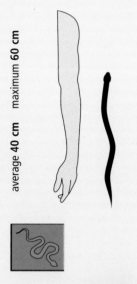

Length: Adults average 25–40 cm, with a maximum length of nearly 60 cm.

Scale count: The dorsal scales are keeled and are in 23–31 rows at midbody (rarely 21 rows), with 120–155 ventral scales and 16–40 paired subcaudals. The anal shield is entire. There are 10–14 upper labials, none entering the eye, 10–16 scales around the eye (rarely 9, 17 or 18) and 10–15 lower labials.

Colour: The coloration of this species is extremely variable, depending on the geographical area. Colour above varies from light sandy grey (specimens from Etosha Pan, Namibia) through buff to reddish (specimens from the Kalahari), greyish, sandy or dark olive brown (specimens from the central Cape). There are 3 series of spots: a median row of dark brown to blackish elongate quadrangular blotches, which may or may not be pale-edged and pale-centred; this is flanked by 2 dorsolateral rows of smaller dark blotches, which are usually pale-centred and sometimes pale-edged. Females are less colourful than males and their markings are often indistinct. The top of the head has a U-shaped or hourglass marking. Dark bars may extend from the eye to the angle of the jaw. Below, it is uniform white to buff or yellowish white, usually with scattered dark markings on the chin and throat.

Preferred habitat: Dry, sandy regions in the Namib Desert, karoo scrub and arid savanna.

Habits: A small adder that may bury itself in loose sand by wriggling or shuffling until concealed. Only the top of the head, the eyes and the little horns are left exposed. Like Péringuey's Adder (*Bitis péringuey*) , this snake may also sidewind on loose sand.

A short, stocky snake with a triangular head.

When disturbed, it usually coils, inflates its body with air and hisses loudly, often striking repeatedly. The Horned Adder is most active at dusk, prior to which it prefers to lie in the shade of shrubs or rocks. The males have much longer tails than the females.

Similar species: The Horned Adder may resemble a small Puff Adder (*Bitis arietans*) but can be distinguished by its small horns, 1 above each eye. May also be confused with other small adders like Many-horned Adders (*B. cornuta*) or Plain Mountain Adders (*B. inornata*). The Many-horned Adder usually has a tuft of 2–4 horns above each eye while the Plain Mountain Adder has no horns. Unlike the Horned Adder, those snakes also have grey bellies that are usually blotched or speckled. May also be confused with the harmless Dwarf Beaked Snake (*Dipsina multi-maculata*) and Rhombic Egg-eater (*Dasypeltis scabra*). These snakes, however, have enlarged shields or scales on the head, while the Horned Adder has only small scales on the head.

Enemies: Predatory birds and other snakes. Also humans, as it is very popular in private collections.

Food and feeding: Feeds mainly on small lizards such as geckos, lacertids and skinks, which it either ambushes during the day or actively hunts at night. Small rodents, birds and frogs are also taken. The Horned Adder reportedly uses the darkened tip of its tail to lure lizards closer when it is buried in loose sand. When it strikes, it hangs onto its prey while its venom takes effect.

Reproduction: Viviparous, giving birth to 3–8 young (although as many as 27 have been recorded), which are born during summer or early autumn, i.e. more or less the same period during which many lizards' eggs hatch.

LOOK OUT FOR

- Short, stocky snake with triangular head distinct from the rest of the body.
- A prominent horn above each eye.
- Coils, inflates its body, hisses and strikes when confronted.
- Most active at dusk.
- May worm itself into loose sand with only parts of the head exposed.

Horned Adders vary greatly in colour, from reddish brown to dark olive brown and sandy grey.

The newborn young measure about 10–15 cm. Females grow much larger than males.

Danger to man: May inflict a painful bite, which causes swelling and some necrosis, but poses no real threat to man.

Venom: The venom is mildly cytotoxic causing swelling and much pain, accompanied by shock and local necrosis. It is not known to be fatal and antivenom is neither effective nor required. Healing may take several weeks.

First-aid procedures: If you are absolutely sure that a Horned Adder was responsible for the bite, get the victim to a doctor or hospital where the bite must be treated symptomatically. Otherwise see first-aid treatment on page 42.

The Horned Adder can usually be identified by the small horns, one above each eye. Hornless specimens are also found, albeit rarely.

Namaqua Dwarf Adder

Bitis schneideri

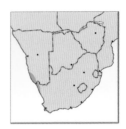

OTHER NAMES
Namakwadwergadder (A)

maximum 28 cm

average 20 cm

Length: Adults average 20 cm with a maximum length of nearly 28 cm.
Scale count: The dorsal scales are strongly keeled in 23–27 rows at midbody (rarely 21 rows), with 104–129 ventrals and 17–27 sub-caudals, paired or single. The anal shield is entire. It has 9–13 upper labials and 9–15 lower labials. There are 14–18 scales around the eye.
Colour: Above, grey to brownish grey with 3 series of dark brown to black but pale-centred blotches right down the back. The back is speckled and the belly greyish to dirty yellow, speckled with black. Where this snake is found on red sand, the body may be orange-red. The tail tip is often dark.
Preferred habitat: Inhabits semi-stable vegetated coastal sand dunes in the Namib Desert and western Karoo.
Habits: This is the smallest adder in the world and it is endemic to southern Africa. Though mainly active in the early evening and at night, it may be seen in the early mornings and often basks during overcast days. Like Péringuey's Adder (*Bitis peringueyi*) it sidewinds and also shuffles itself into soft sand, leaving the head and sometimes part of the body exposed. The track of this snake is very distinctive and individuals may move several hundred metres at a time, shuffling into the sand occasionally as they move along. The tip of the tail is dragged along, leaving a distinctive fine groove in the track. This

Since much of its time is spent burrowed into loose sand, the eyes are situated high up on the sides of the head.

The Namaqua Dwarf Adder is the smallest adder in the world, averaging around 20 cm in length.

LOOK OUT FOR

- Very small snake with rounded, flat head and slightly raised scales.
- Eyes on sides of head and not on top.
- Usually basks on overcast days, otherwise burrows into the sand with the head exposed.

adder may be locally abundant, but is threatened by alluvial diamond mining, which occurs extensively over its range.

Similar species: May be confused with the Horned Adder (*Bitis caudalis*) as the raised scales above each eye may resemble small horns, but this snake has a speckled belly. It can also be confused with Péringuey's Adder, but has eyes on the sides of the head, rather than on top.

Enemies: Greatest threat comes in the form of habitat destruction resulting from alluvial diamond mining.

Food and feeding: Lizards, including skinks and lacertids, nocturnal geckos, small mammals and amphibians.

Reproduction: Viviparous, giving birth to 3–7 young, each measuring 11–13 cm, in the late summer.

Danger to man: As this little adder possesses small quantities of a mild venom, it poses no real threat to man.

Venom: A mild cytotoxic venom that may produce some pain, local swelling and discoloration at the site of the bite. Antivenom is not required.

First-aid procedures: If you are absolutely sure that a Namaqua Dwarf Adder was responsible for the bite, get the victim to a doctor or hospital where the bite must be treated symptomatically. Otherwise see first-aid treatment on page 42.

An endemic snake that shuffles itself into loose sand,
but can also sidewind like Péringuey's Adder.
When buried in loose sand it is very difficult to see.

MILDLY
VENOMOUS

Péringuey's Adder
Bitis peringueyi

OTHER NAMES
Péringuey se adder (A)
Namibduinadder (A)

average **25 cm**   maximum **33 cm**

Length: Adults average 20–25 cm with a maximum length of
nearly 33 cm.
Scale count: The dorsal scales are strongly keeled in 23–31 rows at
midbody. There are 117–144 ventrals and 15–30 paired subcaudals.
The anal shield is entire. There are 10–14 upper labials, 10–13 lower
labials and 10–13 scales around the eye.
Colour: Above, orange-brown to pale sandy or greyish yellow with
3 rows of faint to dark sandy brown or greyish black spots; the spots
on the sides are often pale-centred. Most of the body has faint irregular stippling. The belly is uniform white or white with dark reddish
brown spots on the sides. The tip of the tail may be black.
Preferred habitat: Inhabits the soft wind-blown dunes of the Namib
Desert on the west coast.
Habits: Péringuey's Adder is one of southern Africa's smallest adders.
It is well known for its ability to sidewind, which is the only effective
way to negotiate the soft, unstable dune sand. It usually leaves
S-shaped tracks. It also buries itself in the sand to escape the heat
of the day and to await its prey in ambush. When buried, it usually
leaves the top of its head, its eyes and the tip of its tail exposed. The
tail may be used as a lure to attract lizards – approximately one third

*Habitat destruction,
the use of recre-
ational vehicles like
quad bikes, and
collecting for the pet
trade threaten the
survival of this snake.*

of the population have black-tipped tails. The eyes of this snake are well adapted for survival in the desert and are situated on the top of the head. It drinks water that collects on its body when fog moves in from the cold Atlantic Ocean, otherwise moisture is obtained from its food.

Similar species: Similar to the Namaqua Dwarf Adder (*Bitis schneideri*) in size and appearance but has eyes on the top, and not on the sides, of its head.

Enemies: Habitat destruction and the use of recreational vehicles, including quad bikes. The greatest threat to the survival of this snake may well be over-collecting for the pet trade, although much of its range is in restricted areas.

Food and feeding: Lizards, especially the Sand Lizard (*Meroles anchietae*), which it ambushes during the day. Also geckos, especially the Barking Gecko (*Ptenopus* spp.), which it hunts at night. Captive specimens readily take newborn mice.

Reproduction: Viviparous, giving birth to 3–10 young in late summer. The young measure 8–13,5 cm.

Danger to man: The venom is feebly cytotoxic and of little consequence to man.

Venom: A mild cytotoxin, causing pain and local swelling. Antivenom is not required.

- Very small stubby snake with short flattened head.
- Orange in colour.
- Eyes on top of head and not on sides.
- No horns above the eyes.

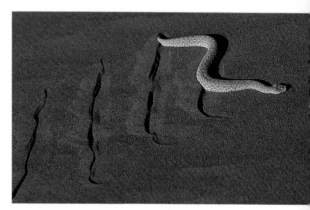

Péringuey's Adder is well known for its ability to sidewind on soft dune sand.

First-aid procedures: If you are sure that a Péringuey's Adder was responsible for the bite, get the victim to a doctor where the bite must be treated symptomatically. Administer painkillers. Otherwise see first-aid treatment on page 42.

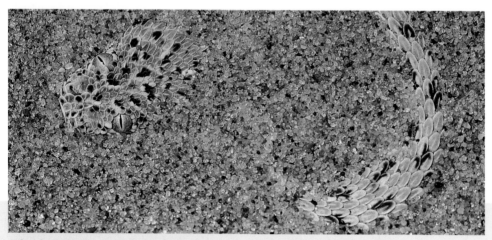

When buried in loose sand, very little of this snake is left exposed. Note that the eyes are situated on the top of the head.

DANGEROUS

Floodplain Viper
Proatheris superciliaris

OTHER NAMES
Eyebrow Viper (E)
Lowland Swamp Viper (E)
Moerasadder (A)

average 45 cm   maximum 60 cm

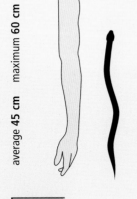

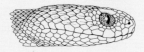

*Large specimens
could inflict a
serious bite.*

Length: Adults average 25–45 cm with a maximum length of just over 60 cm. Males are smaller than females with a maximum length of 55 cm.

Scale count: Scales strongly keeled in 27–29 (rarely 26 or 30) rows at midbody, with 131–156 ventrals. The anal shield is entire. The tail is long with 32–45 pairs of subcaudals. There are 8–9 upper labials (sometimes 10–11) with none of them entering the eye, as well as 8–14 scales around the eye and 11–12 lower labials (sometimes 10 or 13).

Colour: Above, light grey-brown to reddish brown with 3 rows of large blackish spots separated by narrow yellowish bars that form an interrupted stripe down either side of the body. The top of the head has 3 dark chevron markings. The belly is off-white to pale yellow-orange with distinct black spots or blotches. The underside of the tail is dull yellow to orange and more brightly marked in juveniles.

Preferred habitat: Inhabits grasslands bordering swamps and flood plains in lowland forest and moist savanna.

Habits: Very little is known of the habits and behaviour of this slender adder. It is strictly terrestrial and inhabits rodent burrows, often basking at the burrow entrance, especially in the breeding season. Males are known to engage in combat. When threatened, this aggressive snake will coil into a C-shape, rubbing the heavily keeled dorsal scales, which emit a hissing sound, and will then strike out quickly. The young reportedly use their bright yellow tails to lure

Richard Boycott

The young reportedly use their brightly coloured tails to lure prey closer.

LOOK OUT FOR

■ Always found on the ground, often close to rodent burrows.

■ Has a large, elongate head with small, keeled, overlapping scales.

■ The eyes have vertical pupils.

■ There is a large supraocular scale above each eye.

■ Has a heavily blotched belly.

their prey closer. In captivity it is crepuscular and most active in the early evenings.

Similar species: May be confused with the Rhombic Egg-eater (*Dasypeltis scabra*) and Rhombic Night Adder (*Causus rhombeatus*) as it has a similar blotched pattern. This viper has a heavily blotched belly and its head is covered in small, keeled, overlapping scales.

Enemies: Unknown.

Food and feeding: Amphibians, especially Reed Frogs (*Hyperolius* spp.) and small rodents.

Reproduction: Viviparous, with 3–16 young born in summer. They measure 13,2–21 cm.

Danger to man: Very little is known of the venom of this snake and it is thought that large specimens could inflict a serious bite.

Venom: The venom of this snake has not been studied extensively. Snake handlers bitten by this species showed symptoms of immediate pain, swelling and blistering. Antivenom is not effective.

First-aid procedures: In the few recorded case histories, general treatment was adequate and the victims recovered fully. However, bites from large individuals could result in more serious symptoms. See first-aid treatment on page 42.

The Floodplain Viper inhabits grasslands bordering swamps, where it is strictly terrestrial, often basking at a burrow entrance.

Rhombic Night Adder

Causus rhombeatus

**MILDLY
VENOMOUS**

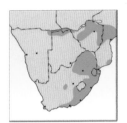

OTHER NAMES
Common Night Adder (E)
Gewone Nagadder (A)
Nyoka yasebusuku (Z)
Unomofuthwana (X)

average 60 cm   maximum 1 m

Length: Adults average 30–60 cm, with a maximum length of about
1 m. In KwaZulu-Natal specimens are generally larger than those
found elsewhere.

Scale count: Midbody scales usually in 17–19 rows (sometimes 15–23)
with 134–155 ventrals, and 20–33 subcaudals, either paired or single.
The anal shield is entire. There are 6 upper labials (rarely 7) that do
not enter the eye, 9 or 10 lower labials (but this is variable), 2–3 preoculars and 1–2 postoculars. Temporals are usually 2 + 3 but may be
2 + 4; 2 + 2 or 3 + 3.

Colour: Above, varying shades of light grey, olive, or light to pinkish
brown with a series of large rhombic markings (sometimes encircled
with white) on the back and tail. The head has a distinct dark brown
or black forward-pointing V-shaped marking, the apex of which
extends to between the eyes. Below, pearly white to yellowish or
light grey, with or without dark mottling. Juveniles are usually
blackish below.

Preferred habitat: Favours damp environments in moist savanna,
lowland forest and fynbos, where it seeks refuge in old termite
mounds, under logs and large flat stones, and among building
rubble. Often found close to dams and rivers and human dwellings.

Habits: The Rhombic Night Adder is a docile snake that moves off if
given the choice. It is largely terrestrial and slow moving. If cornered
or provoked, it will inflate its body with air, coil up and also hiss

*Unlike most other
adders, the Rhombic
Night Adder does not
have a triangular head
that is distinct from
the rest of the body.*

- Medium-sized eyes with round pupils.
- Short head with rounded snout.
- Head covered with large scales.
- Scales slightly keeled, soft and velvety.
- Has distinct dark V-marking on head.
- Coils up and hisses when confronted.
- Prefers damp localities, often close to permanent water.

The Rhombic Night Adder favours damp environments where it hunts for frogs and toads.

aggressively, striking violently at the same time. It is fond of basking during the day and hunts in the evenings. In its search for food, this snake will often venture close to, or even into, farmsteads and houses. It has very long venom glands that extend back into the neck region.

Similar species: May be confused with the harmless Rhombic Egg-eater (*Dasypeltis scabra*), as they have similar markings. The Night Adder, however, has a short, thicker body with a flat head on which black V-shaped markings are clearly visible. The Rhombic Egg-eater may have 2 or 3 fragmented V-shaped markings on the neck behind the head.

Note the V-shaped markings on the head, extending from between the eyes to the back of the head.

Enemies: Preyed upon by a number of other snakes, monitor lizards (*Varanus* spp.), and predatory birds.

Food and feeding: This snake has poor eyesight and relies heavily on smell to locate its prey. It feeds almost exclusively on toads and frogs, including rain frogs (*Breviceps* spp.). Frequents houses to feed on toads that prey on insects attracted by light. The hatchlings are known to feed on tadpoles.

Reproduction: Oviparous, laying 7–26 eggs 2 or 3 times a year. The eggs, measuring 26–37 x 14–20 mm, stick together and form a small bundle. The young measure 13–16 cm. *Causus* is the only egg-laying genus of the adder group.

Danger to man: The venom is only mildly cytotoxic and generally not dangerous to man. No human deaths have been recorded to date.

Venom: Cytotoxic, causing pain and swelling and occasionally local necrosis. May cause acute discomfort in some cases. Though antivenom is effective against the venom of this snake, it is generally not required. In spite of the relatively low toxicity of the venom, bites should not be treated lightly.

First-aid procedures: If you are sure that a Rhombic Night Adder was responsible for the bite, get the victim to a doctor where the bite must be treated symptomatically. Painkillers may be required. Otherwise see first-aid treatment on page 42.

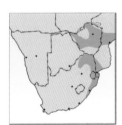

Snouted Night Adder
Causus defilippii

OTHER NAMES
Wipneusnagadder (A)

average 35 cm   maximum 43 cm

Length: A small snake, averaging 20–35 cm with a maximum length of 43 cm.

Scale count: Dorsal scales are in 17 rows at midbody. There are 108–126 ventrals and 10–19 pairs of subcaudals. The anal shield is entire. There are 6 (rarely 7) upper labials that do not enter the eye, and 8 or 9 (rarely 7 or 10) lower labials, with 1–2 preoculars and 1–2 postoculars. Temporals are 2 + 3 (rarely 2 + 4 or 1 + 2).

Colour: Above, pale brown to pinkish brown or mauve with a broad band down the back. The head has a distinct dark brown V-shaped marking, the apex of which extends to between the eyes. There are 20–30 dark brown to black triangular dorsal blotches that extend onto the tail. The belly is pearl-white but blackish to grey in juveniles.

Preferred habitat: Usually found close to water in moist savanna, lowland forest and grassland.

Habits: A smaller species than the Rhombic Night Adder (*Causus rhombeatus*) and distinguished from the latter by its upturned snout. This snake is very similar to the Rhombic Night Adder in behaviour, and also hunts at night, but is often seen during the day. It frequently basks in the sun. Combat has been observed between rival males, during which they entwine and wrestle one another, until the dominant male successfully pushes its adversary to the ground. Footwear, such as boots or even shoes, provides adequate protection against the bite

Note the upturned snout of this snake.

of this snake. When threatened, it will inflate its body, enhancing its markings, and hiss and puff. It strikes very quickly.

Similar species: The Snouted Night Adder and the harmless Rhombic Egg-eater Snake (*Dasypeltis scabra*) have similar markings. The Snouted Night Adder, however, has a shorter and thicker body with a flat head on which the V-shaped marking is clearly visible, whereas the Rhombic Egg-eater usually has 2–3 V-shaped markings on the neck behind the head. Easily confused with the Rhombic Night Adder, but can be distinguished by the upturned snout.

Enemies: Preyed upon by other snakes.

Food and feeding: Feeds almost exclusively on frogs and toads.

Reproduction: Oviparous, laying 3–9 eggs (20–30 mm x 9–16 mm) in summer. The young are just over 10 cm long.

Danger to man: A mild venom that is not considered dangerous to man. Usually associated with pain and rapid swelling and may produce acute discomfort in some cases.

Venom: The venom is feebly cytotoxic and is generally not dangerous, but it causes pain and swelling and may produce acute discomfort in some cases. The swelling usually subsides within 2 or 3 days. Antivenom is not necessary.

Richard Boycott

Although active at night, the Snouted Night Adder also hunts during the day.

First-aid procedures: If you are sure that a Snouted Night Adder was responsible for the bite, get the victim to a doctor where the bite must be treated symptomatically. Painkillers may be required. Otherwise see first-aid treatment on page 42.

> ## LOOK OUT FOR
> ■ Medium-sized eyes with round pupils.
> ■ Tip of snout distinctly upturned.
> ■ Head covered with large scales.
> ■ Has distinct dark V-marking on head.
> ■ Scales slightly keeled, soft and velvety.

The Snouted Night Adder (above) is very similar to the Rhombic Night Adder in appearance.

MAMBAS, COBRAS AND THEIR RELATIVES

Elapidae

Of all the elapids found in southern Africa, only the cobras, Rinkhals, and mambas possess highly dangerous venoms. The remaining elapids are venomous but not all dangerously so, and are seldom encountered by man.

The majority of elapids are long and slender. The Rinkhals and the cobras are easily identified, since they usually rear their heads off the ground and spread a hood in defence. Black Mambas also spread a narrow hood when annoyed.

The venom of most elapids is primarily neurotoxic, affecting the nervous system. The onset of symptoms is often rapid, including dizziness, difficulty with swallowing, slurred speech, blurred vision, convulsions, very shallow or laboured breathing and eventually unconsciousness. Death may follow in under an hour (usually after eight hours or more) as a result of respiratory failure. The venom of a few elapids (e.g. the Black Spitting or Mozambique Spitting cobras) results in symptoms more typical of adder bites.

The Elapidae also include the highly derived sea snakes, which comprise the subfamily Hydrophiidae. Only one species of sea snake, the Yellow-bellied Sea Snake, occasionally washes up off the southern African coast. Sea snakes are easily recognized by their compressed bodies, which form an 'oar' that helps them to move well in water.

The elapids have short, fixed fangs in the front of the mouth.

Many of the elapids, including the cobras, the Rinkhals and, to a lesser degree, the Black Mamba, have the ability to spread a hood.

Black Mamba
Dendroaspis polylepis

OTHER NAMES
Swartmamba (A)
Imamba emnyama (Z)
Imamba (X)

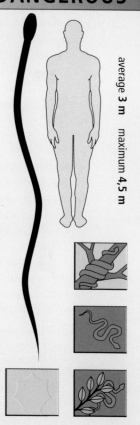

average 3 m   maximum 4,5 m

Length: Adults average 2,4–3 m but may reach 4,5 m.

Scale count: There are 23–25 rows of smooth dorsal scales at midbody (rarely 21 rows), 248–281 ventrals and 109–132 paired sub-caudals. The anal shield is divided. There are 7–10 upper labials, with the 4th (or 3rd and 4th) entering the eye, and 11–13 lower labials (sometimes 10 or 14). There are 3 (sometimes 4) preoculars and 3 or 4 (sometimes 2 or 5) postoculars. Temporals are variable, usually 2 + 3.

Colour: The common name is confusing, as this snake is rarely black. Juveniles are light grey to olive, darkening with age to olive green, dark olive, greyish brown or gunmetal grey, with darker posterior mottling that may form oblique bars. The name is derived from the colour of the inside of the mouth, which is an inky black.

Preferred habitat: Termite mounds, hollow tree trunks, deserted ant bear or porcupine burrows, rock crevices and granite hillocks in both dry and moist savanna, and in lowland forest.

Habits: A graceful, alert and unpredictable snake with deadly venom. It is southern Africa's largest venomous snake. The Black Mamba is active during the day, when it hunts for food. Hunting is usually done from a permanent lair to which it will return regularly if not disturbed. It is also very fond of basking and will return to the same site daily. If it senses danger, it is quick to slither away into dense undergrowth or to disappear down the nearest hole.

The Black Mamba is undoubtedly Africa's largest venomous snake – and the most dangerous.

Equally at home in trees and on the ground, it seems to favour the ground. It is a large snake and can move comfortably with as much as one third of its body off the ground.

The Black Mamba seldom permits a close approach (within 40 m). If cornered or threatened, it will gape, exposing the black inner lining of its mouth, and will spread a narrow hood while waving the tongue slowly up and down. Any sudden movement at this stage will be met with a series of rapid strikes, often with fatal results.

The so-called 'Crested Serpent' of urban legend was probably a large black mamba that did not shed its skin properly, giving the impression of a crest. This snake sup-posedly moves very quickly through long grass, its crest emitting a whistling sound while it moves.

Similar species: People tend to mistake any grey, brown or black snake for the Black Mamba. It may be confused with the larger cobras, female Boomslang (*Dispholidus*

LOOK OUT FOR

- A large, long snake with a long, slender, coffin-shaped head.
- Usually active during the day.
- May form a narrow hood with the mouth open when threatened.
- Inside of the mouth is inky black in colour.
- At home both in trees and on the ground.
- Medium-sized eye with round pupil.
- Usually an overall olive brown to grey colour.
- Can move with up to a third of its body off the ground.

typus), Mole Snake (*Pseudaspis cana*), Olive House Snake (*Lamprophis inornatus*) and some of the grass or sand snakes.

Enemies: Birds of prey and other snakes. Juvenile Black Mambas are extremely nervous

It is often said that the Black Mamba has a coffin-shaped head.

This is one of the deadliest snakes in the world and should be avoided at all costs. If you come across one and retreat slowly and carefully, the snake will do the same.

and are seldom seen. They grow rapidly and can reach 2 m within a year. Adults have very few enemies.

Food and feeding: Actively hunts rodents, squirrels, hyrax (*Procavia capensis*) and other suitably sized mammals, as well as fledgling birds and other snakes. A large specimen has even been recorded eating a young blue duiker (*Philantomba monticola*). Black Mambas prefer warm-blooded prey. The prey is usually bitten once or twice and quickly succumbs to the potent venom.

Reproduction: Oviparous, laying 6–17 eggs (63–91 x 29–35 mm) in summer. The young measure 40–60 cm when they hatch, and grow rapidly, especially in the first year, after which they may reach a length of 2 m. Juveniles are perfect replicas of the adults and are deadly. Males often engage in combat in the spring, twisting around one another in an attempt to wrestle their opponent to the ground.

Danger to man: This is one of the deadliest snakes in the world. It has plenty of potent venom and the ability to inject large quantities in a single bite. Because of its length, it may also bite at chest height.

The Black Mamba's common name is derived from the inky black colour of the mouth lining.

Venom: A potent neurotoxic venom that is absorbed rapidly by the body's tissues. It is responsible primarily for paralysis of nerves, especially those that control breathing and heart rate. The victim experiences increasing difficulty in breathing and eventually suffocates to death. This may take 6–15 hours and is much quicker in serious cases. Large quantities of intravenous antivenom may be required to save the victim's life.

First-aid procedures: See first-aid treatment on page 42.

The Black Mamba is a nervous snake that will try to escape, but won't hesitate to bite if cornered.

Green Mamba

Dendroaspis angusticeps

VERY DANGEROUS

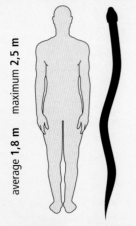

average 1,8 m   maximum 2,5 m

OTHER NAMES
Groenmamba (A)
Imamba eluhlaza (Z)
Imamba (X)

Length: Adults average 1,8 m and seldom, if ever, grow longer than 2,5 m.

Scale count: Dorsal scales in 19 rows at midbody (sometimes 17 or 21), with 201–232 ventral scales, and 99–126 paired subcaudals. The anal shield is divided. There are 7–9 upper labials, the 4th entering the eye, and 9–11 lower labials, as well as 3 preoculars and 3–5 postoculars. Temporals are variable, usually 2 + 3.

Colour: Adults are bright emerald green above, sometimes with a few scattered yellow scales. Below, pale green or yellowish green. Sometimes they may have a dull appearance before sloughing. Hatchlings are often blue-green until they reach a length of 75 cm, at which stage they rapidly assume the colours of the adults. The mouth lining is bluish white, and occasionally dark.

Preferred habitat: Evergreen lowland forest and moist savanna where it favours bamboo thickets, tea, citrus, coconut, cashew nut and mango plantations. In South Africa this snake is usually found in dense coastal vegetation.

Habits: An arboreal species that seldom ventures to the ground, except to bask or chase its prey. It is active during daylight hours, and moves gracefully and effortlessly, quickly disappearing into its leafy background. Although an active snake, it is not often seen. It is also shy, but lacks the nervousness of the Black Mamba (*Dendroaspis*

The Green Mamba is largely arboreal and is extremely well camouflaged in trees.

polylepis) and rarely gapes when threatened. It will, however, strike if provoked. Bites are uncommon.

The Green Mamba sleeps in trees, usually exposed in a coiled-up posture. Holes in trees are seldom used to sleep in. Like many other species, this snake often basks in the morning.

Similar species: People tend to identify all green snakes as Green Mambas. In South Africa, the Green Mamba is only found in coastal forest and does not occur in the Kruger National Park or in Mpumalanga Province. This snake is often confused with the green variety of Boomslang (*Dispholidus typus*) and with the harmless green and bush snakes of the genus *Philothamnus*. The Green Mamba has a much smaller eye than the Boomslang and a green belly as opposed to the white to yellow belly of the Green and Bush snakes. In addition, the harmless green snakes are very slender, seldom thicker than a person's smallest finger.

Enemies: Other snakes. Also humans, as vast tracts of suitable habitat have been destroyed by developers along the KwaZulu-Natal coast.

Food and feeding: Its diet consists mostly of birds, their eggs and fledglings as well as small tree-living mammals, including bats. Chameleons (*Chamaeleo* and *Bradypodion* spp.) may be taken by juveniles but warm-blooded prey is preferred.

Reproduction: Oviparous, laying 6–17 eggs (47–58 x 25–28 mm) in summer. The eggs are usually deposited in a hollow tree trunk among decaying vegetation. Hatchlings measure 30–45 cm. Males are known to engage in combat, intertwining their necks and bodies as they push each other onto the ground. Such combat may last several hours. Mating takes place in trees with the tails of both the males and females hanging down.

Like Black Mambas and cobras, Green Mambas have short, fixed fangs in the front of their mouths.

Danger to man: Even though the Green Mamba possesses deadly venom, it spends most of its life in trees and avoids humans. Bites are rare and are most commonly inflicted on snake handlers.

Venom: Dangerously neurotoxic. Similar to that of the Black Mamba, but not quite as potent. It also injects smaller quantities of venom than the Black Mamba. However, its bite is still serious and must be treated as such.

First-aid procedures: See first-aid treatment on page 42.

The Green Mamba, like the Black Mamba, possesses a potent venom that can easily kill an adult. If given the chance to retreat, however, it will quickly disappear into the closest tree or shrub.

Cape Cobra

Naja nivea

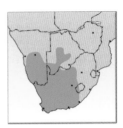

VERY DANGEROUS

OTHER NAMES
Geelslang, Kaapse kobra (A)
Koperkapel (A)

average 1,4 m   maximum 1,6 m

Length: Adults average 1,2 to 1,4 m, seldom exceeding 1,6 m. The largest specimen recorded was from Aus and measured 1,867 m.
Scale count: Midbody scales are in 19–21 rows, with 195–227 ventrals and 50–68 paired subcaudals. The anal shield is entire. There are 7 upper labials with the 3rd and 4th entering the eye, and 9 (sometimes 8 or 10) lower labials, as well as 1 preocular and 3 (sometimes 4) postoculars. Temporals are variable, usually 1 + 3.
Colour: Extremely variable, ranging from yellow through reddish brown to black. Some of the better known varieties, with intermediates, are: (a) bright yellow above – juveniles have a broad dark band on the throat and some specimens may have brown speckles; (b) bright shiny orange-brown to brown above, sometimes with darker or lighter mottles; (c) shiny dark brown to black above and below. The yellow phase is widespread; the black phase restricted to the northwestern parts of the Northern Cape Province. In the Western Cape golden brown, speckled brown and bright yellow specimens are found.
Preferred habitat: Fynbos, karoo scrub, arid savanna and the Namib Desert where it inhabits rodent burrows, disused termite mounds and, in arid regions, rock crevices. It is frequently found near human dwellings on farms, especially in the Karoo. Also inhabits partially developed suburbs and squatter communities where it enters houses to escape the heat of the day. Restricted largely to the Western, Eastern and Northern Cape provinces, but also occurs in the Free State, Botswana and Namibia.

When threatened or cornered, the Cape Cobra is quick to spread a hood, and once it has done so, will not hesitate to bite.

Leonard Hoffmann / SIL

LOOK OUT FOR

- Has a medium-sized eye with a round pupil.
- This cobra is a non-spitter.
- Medium-sized slender cobra with broad head.
- Dorsal scales are smooth and shiny.
- Occurs in the arid parts of southern Africa, especially in the south and west. (Few other cobras occur within this snake's range.)
- Body colour variable, from black to brown, orange, yellow or mottled.
- Stands its ground and spreads a broad hood when confronted.
- Active during the day and early evenings.

Habits: This medium-sized slender cobra with its broad head is active during the day and in the early evenings when it may climb trees in search of food. It is well known for raiding Sociable Weaver (*Philetairus socius*) nests. When attacked this nervous snake invariably faces its enemy, spreading a broad, impressive hood. It cannot spit its venom. Once on the defensive, it strikes readily. If the aggressor remains motionless, the snake will soon drop to the ground and move off, only to snap back into its defensive pose if it detects movement. The Cape Cobra often accounts for stock losses and relatively harmless snakes, like the skaapsteker (*Psammophylax* spp.), are blamed. The Cape Cobra is endemic to southern Africa.

Similar species: Cape Cobras vary considerably in colour and may be confused with other cobras (*Naja* spp.) and with the Mole Snake (*Pseudaspis cana*).

Enemies: Carnivorous mammals, birds of prey and other snakes.

The Cape Cobra possesses a potent venom and accounts for the majority of fatal snakebites in its range.

Food and feeding: Feeds on rodents, birds, other snakes, lizards and toads. Will climb into trees to reach fledgling birds in their nests and to raid Sociable Weavers' nests.

Reproduction: Oviparous, laying 8–20 eggs (60–69 x 24–30 mm) in midsummer. The hatchlings measure 34–40 cm.

Danger to man: This is an extremely dangerous cobra that will stand its ground when confronted. Bites are often fatal, with the victim dying of suffocation due to respiratory collapse.

Venom: A highly neurotoxic venom, most potent of any African cobra. As with Black Mamba (*Dendroaspis polylepis*) bites, artificial respiration could keep the victim alive until sufficient quantities of antivenom have been injected. Bites are often fatal and in the Cape provinces this snake accounts for most human snakebite fatalities.

First-aid procedures: See first-aid treatment on page 42.

Leonard Hoffmann / SIL

Snouted Cobra

Naja annulifera

OTHER NAMES
Previously known as the Egyptian Cobra
Wipneuskobra (A)
Bosveldkapel (A)

VERY DANGEROUS

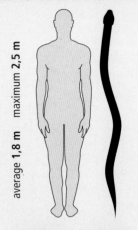

average 1,8 m   maximum 2,5 m

Length: Adults average 1,2–1,8 m but may reach, or exceed, 2,5 m.

Scale count: Midbody scales are in 19 rows (rarely 21) with 175–203 ventrals. There are 51–65 paired subcaudals and the anal shield is entire. There are 7 (sometimes 8) upper labials that do not enter the eye, and 8 or 9 (rarely 10) lower labials, as well as 1 preocular (sometimes 2) and 2 (sometimes 1 or 3) postoculars. Temporals are variable, 1 + 2 or 1 + 3.

Colour: Above, yellowish to greyish brown, dark brown or blue-black. Below, yellow with darker mottles. A banded phase occurs throughout the range and is blue-black with 7–11 yellow to yellow-brown crossbars, the lighter bands being half the width of the darker bands. The latter colour phase is more common in males. Below, yellow mottled with black. A darker throat band is present and is usually more conspicuous in juveniles.

Preferred habitat: Arid and moist savanna; common in lowveld and bushveld areas.

Habits: One of Africa's largest cobras, it often occupies a permanent home in a termite mound where it will reside for years if not disturbed. It is active at night, foraging for food from dusk onwards, often venturing into poultry runs. It likes to bask in the morning sun, usually near its retreat into which it will withdraw if disturbed.
It is not an aggressive snake, but will assume a formidable posture if cornered. Large adults are able to lift as much as half a metre of the body off the ground while spreading a wide, impressive hood. This snake will, however, disappear down the nearest hole or crevice if given the opportunity. Like the Rinkhals (*Hemachatus haemachatus*) it

The banded phase of the Snouted Cobra is found throughout the range of this snake.

may pretend to be dead if threatened, but this is rare. It does not spit its venom.

Similar species: May be confused with other cobras including the Forest Cobra (*Naja melanoleuca*) and the Cape Cobra (*Naja nivea*) (although their distributions differ), the Black Mamba (*Dendroaspis polylepis*), the brown variety of the Boomslang (*Dispholidus typus*), the Mole Snake (*Pseudaspis cana*) and some of the larger grass snakes.

Enemies: Birds of prey and other snakes.

Food and feeding: Toads, rodents, birds and their eggs, lizards and other snakes, especially Puff Adders (*Bitis arietans*). Often raids poultry runs and can become a nuisance.

Reproduction: Oviparous, laying 8–33 eggs (47–60 x 25–35 mm) in early summer. The young average 22–34 cm.

Danger to man: A large cobra with a high venom yield. Bites readily when confronted. Substantial quantities of antivenom may be required in serious cases.

Venom: A potent neurotoxic venom that affects breathing and, in untreated cases, may cause respiratory failure and death. Initial symptoms often include a burning pain and swelling that may result in blistering. Typically, victims are bitten on the lower leg, usually at night.

First-aid procedures: See first-aid treatment on page 42.

LOOK OUT FOR

- Likes to bask near its retreat.
- Not found in forests.
- Does not spit its venom.
- Has a broad head.
- Spreads a broad impressive hood when cornered.
- Most active from dusk onwards.

When cornered or threatened, the Snouted Cobra forms an impressive hood.

The Snouted Cobra was previously referred to as the Egyptian Cobra.

Anchieta's Cobra
Naja anchietae

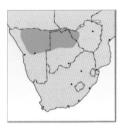

VERY DANGEROUS

OTHER NAMES
Anchieta se kobra (A)

average 1 m   maximum 1,2 m

Length: Adults average less than 1 m and reach a maximum length of 1,2 m.

Scale count: Midbody scales are in 17 rows with 179–200 ventrals. There are 51–56 paired subcaudals and the anal shield is entire. There are 7 (sometimes 8) upper labials that do not enter the eye and 8 or 9 (rarely 10) lower labials, as well as 1 preocular and 2 postoculars. Temporals are variable, 1 + 2 or 1 + 3.

Colour: Both plain and banded phases occur. The plain phase varies from brown through purple-brown to almost black above. Lighter below, but becoming darker and more blotched in the more posterior parts. Becomes darker with age. The banded phase usually has 7 yellowish bands on the body and 2 on the tail. The banded phase is more common in males. In lighter individuals, a darker throat band may be present. The throat band is usually very conspicuous in juveniles.

Preferred habitat: Arid savanna, especially in wooded areas along rivers and wetlands.

Habits: Like its close relative, the Snouted Cobra (*Naja annulifera*), it often takes up residence in the same retreat for years. It is active at night, foraging for food from dusk onwards, often venturing into poultry runs. It is a generalist feeder, taking amphibians, other reptiles, birds and mammals in its diet. It is known to bask in the morning sun, usually near its retreat into which it will withdraw if disturbed.

More aggressive than closely related species such as the Snouted Cobra, but otherwise similar in habits. Although this species will posture in a hostile way when provoked, it will flee when provided with the opportunity. It has been known to play dead, but is not as inclined to display this behaviour as is the Rinkhals (*Hemachatus haemachatus*). It is not able to spit its venom.

Similar species: May be confused with other cobras including the Snouted Cobra and the Cape Cobra (*Naja nivea*), but does not occur in the same areas. Could also be mistaken for a Black Mamba

Colin Tilbury

Like the Snouted Cobra, Anchieta's Cobra forms an impressive hood when cornered or threatened.

Colin Tilbury

LOOK OUT FOR

- Likes to bask near its retreat.
- Often found along wooded river banks.
- Does not spit its venom.
- Has a broad head.
- Spreads a broad impressive hood when it is cornered.
- Most active from dusk onwards.

(*Dendroaspis polylepis*), the brown variety of the Boomslang (*Dispholidus typus*), or the Mole Snake (*Pseudaspis cana*).

Enemies: Birds of prey, mammalian carnivores and other snakes.

Food and feeding: Toads, rodents, birds and their eggs, lizards and other snakes.

Reproduction: Oviparous, laying eggs (47–60 x 25–35 mm) in early summer. The young average 22–34 cm.

Danger to man: Bites readily when confronted. Substantial quantities of antivenom may be required in serious cases.

Venom: A potent neurotoxic venom that affects breathing and, in untreated cases, may cause respiratory failure and death. Initial

Anchieta's Cobra cannot spit its venom.

symptoms often include a burning pain and swelling that may result in blistering. Typically, victims are bitten on the lower leg, usually at night.

First-aid procedures: See first-aid treatment on page 42.

Bill Branch

Anchieta's Cobra tends to be more aggressive than the Snouted Cobra when threatened, but will flee if given the opportunity.

Forest Cobra
Naja melanoleuca

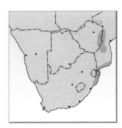

VERY DANGEROUS

OTHER NAMES
Boskobra (A)

maximum 2,7 m

average 2 m

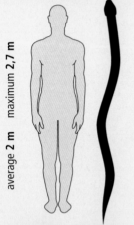

Length: Adults average 1,5–2 m, reaching a maximum length of 2,7 m. This is the largest African cobra.

Scale count: Dorsal scales are in 19 (rarely 17 or 21) rows at midbody, with 201–214 ventrals and 63–72 paired subcaudals. The anal shield is entire. There are 7 (rarely 8) upper labials with the 3rd and 4th entering the eye, and 8 lower labials, as well as 1 preocular (sometimes 2) and 3 (sometimes 2) postoculars. Temporals are variable, either 1 + 2 or 1 + 3.

Colour: The head, neck and forepart of the body are usually yellowish brown, heavily flecked with black, becoming darker to shiny black towards the posterior, sometimes with speckling. Below, creamy white to yellow, often with darker blotches.

Preferred habitat: Lowland forest and moist savanna where it favours coastal thickets.

Habits: A large cobra normally associated with closed-canopy coastal forest in northern KwaZulu-Natal. It is active and alert, climbs well and is equally at home on land and in water. Though primarily active at night, it likes to bask in the sun. It also forages for food on overcast days. If disturbed, it is quick to disappear into dense thickets, but if cornered will spread a narrow hood and bite readily. Males are known to engage in combat in the mating season. This snake is not able to spit its venom.

Similar species: Often mistaken for the Black Mamba (*Dendroaspis polylepis*) but distinguished by its highly polished scales, which give it a shiny appearance. May also be mistaken for some of the larger grass snakes.

This active, alert snake may be found in trees, shrubs, or on the ground.

Colin Tilbury

LOOK OUT FOR

- Slender snake with highly polished scales, giving it a shiny appearance.
- Climbs well and is often found in or near water.
- Spreads a narrow hood if cornered.
- Does not spit its venom.
- Prefers thickly vegetated habitats.

The Forest Cobra is quick to disappear when encountered, but bites readily if threatened.

Enemies: Other snakes.

Food and feeding: Feeds on toads, frogs, small mammals, birds and snakes. Also feeds on fish.

Reproduction: Oviparous, laying 11–26 smooth white eggs in summer (46–61 x 24–31,8 mm) that stick together in a bunch. The young measure 27–40 cm.

Danger to man: Though extremely venomous, this retiring snake seldom features in snakebite accidents.

Venom: Potently neurotoxic but because of this snake's restricted distribution and shy nature, bites are virtually unheard of in South Africa.

Unlike the Black Mamba, the Forest Cobra (above) has a shiny appearance.

First-aid procedures: See first-aid treatment on page 42.

This is a very large cobra that avoids humans, but bites readily when cornered.

VERY DANGEROUS

average 1,2 m   maximum 1,5 m

A common cobra throughout its range.

Mozambique Spitting Cobra

Naja mossambica

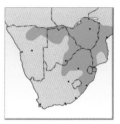

OTHER NAMES
Mosambiekse spoegkobra (A)
M'fezi (Z)

Length: Adults average 1–1,2 m, rarely exceeding 1,5 m.

Scale count: Dorsal scales are in 23–25 (rarely 21 or 27) rows at mid-body, with 177–205 ventrals and 52–71 paired subcaudals. The anal shield is entire. There are 6 (rarely 7) upper labials with the 3rd (sometimes 3rd and 4th) entering the eye, and 9 (sometimes 8, 10 or 11) lower labials, as well as 2 preoculars (sometimes 1) and 3 (sometimes 2) postoculars. Temporals are variable.

Colour: Above, slate grey to olive brown, with each scale dark-edged. Below, salmon pink or sometimes yellowish with black cross-bars and blotches on the throat – sometimes forming a band across the ventral scales.

Preferred habitat: The most common of the region's cobras, found largely in moist savanna and lowland forest where it favours broken rocky country, hollow logs, termite mounds and animal holes, often close to permanent water.

Habits: May bask near a retreat or forage on overcast days, otherwise it is more active at night. Juveniles, however, are quite active in the day. It is a retiring snake that seldom stands its ground. If cornered it may spread a hood, but will not hold the pose for long. Its main defence, other than going into hiding, is to eject or spit its venom.

The fangs are specially modified for spitting: the venom canal openings at the tips are directed forwards and at right angles to the

Colin Tilbury

This snake always has black crossbars and blotches on the throat.

LOOK OUT FOR

- May spread a hood when cornered and can spit its venom.
- Underside usually salmon pink or yellowish in colour.
- Has irregular black markings in the throat region that are visible when it spreads a hood.
- Has medium-sized eyes with round pupils.
- May play dead.

fangs, enabling the snake to eject its venom to a distance greater than 2 m. This snake does not always spread its hood before spitting and may only open its mouth slightly before doing so. It can spit effectively from a concealed position within a rock crevice. The venom supply is seemingly inexhaustible. If venom lands on the hair, face or arms it poses no threat, but in the eyes it causes an immediate burning sensation and should be washed out immediately with large quantities of water or any other bland liquid.

Similar species: May be confused with other cobras, the Mole Snake (*Pseudaspis cana*) and the Rinkhals (*Hemachatus haemachatus*).

Enemies: Preyed upon by snakes.

Food and feeding: Preys on toads, small mammals, birds, lizards, insects and snakes, including the Puff Adder (*Bitis arietans*). May be found searching for food in poultry runs and in the vicinity of houses.

Reproduction: Oviparous, laying 10–22 eggs (35 x 20 mm) in midsummer. Hatchlings measure 23–25 cm.

Danger to man: A common snake with a potent venom. Accounts for many bites in KwaZulu-Natal and Mpumalanga.

Venom: Predominantly cytotoxic, causing serious local tissue damage that often requires skin grafts. Only slight neurotoxic symptoms, such as drowsiness, may occur and fatalities are rare. The early administration of antivenom may reduce the extent of tissue damage.

First-aid procedures: See first-aid treatment on page 42.

The Mozambique Spitting Cobra spits its venom from a reared or normal position and can spit from within a rock crevice.

VERY DANGEROUS

maximum 2 m   average 1,5 m

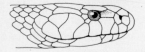

Black-necked Spitting Cobra

Naja nigricollis

Naja nigricollis nigricollis

OTHER NAMES
Swartkeelspoegkobra (A)

Length: This is the largest of the African spitting cobras, averaging 1,2–1,5 m but reaching lengths of 2 m.

Scale count: Dorsal scales are in 17–23 rows at midbody, with 176–228 ventrals and 54–74 paired subcaudals. The anal shield is entire. There are 6 upper labials (rarely 7) with the 3rd (rarely the 4th) entering the eye, and 9 (rarely 8 or 10) lower labials, as well as 2 preoculars and 3 postoculars. Temporals are 2 + 4 or 2 + 5.

Colour: Highly variable, depending on locality (and subspecies – see subspecies section below). The typical form is similar in appearance to the Mozambique Spitting Cobra (*Naja mossambica*) and is uniform dark olive brown to grey-brown or black above, with a yellow to red belly. The throat has a broad black band.

A barred phase occurs in the arid western parts of the range. In these individuals, there are between 50 and 85 vivid black crossbars on a brown or pinkish background colour on the body, and up to 32 crossbars on the tail. These crossbars usually encircle the body. The head is a uniform black, both above and below. Individuals with this colour scheme belong to the Zebra Cobra (*Naja nigricollis nigricincta*) subspecies (see subspecies section below)

All black individuals occur in the south-western parts of their range. These individuals generally belong to the subspecies *Naja nigricollis woodi*.

Preferred habitat: Variable. Moist and arid savanna, arid rocky outcrops, dry watercourses, desert and the Karoo.

Habits: May be locally abundant in certain areas. Often shelters in

The Zebra Cobra has between 50 and 85 vivid black crossbars that usually encircle the body.

The Black Spitting Cobra readily eats other snakes, including Puff Adders.

LOOK OUT FOR

■ Has a broad head with a round snout.
■ Readily spreads its hood and spits.
■ Often stands its ground when threatened.

disused termite mounds, down rodent burrows, in hollow tree trunks or in hollows among tree roots. It is fond of basking but is largely nocturnal, actively foraging for food. Juveniles, however, are active during the day. Though terrestrial, it is a good climber and is frequently found near human habitations. It often raids fowl runs. When threatened, this nervous snake readily spreads a narrow, rudimentary hood. Its main defence, other than going into hiding, is to spit its venom. The fangs are specially modified for spitting, with venom canal openings at the tips directed forward at right angles to the fangs, enabling the snake to eject its venom for 2 m or more, depending on the size of the snake. On the hair, face or arms it poses no threat,

but in the eyes it causes an immediate burning sensation and should be washed out at once with large quantities of water or any other bland liquid. The venom of the Black-necked Spitting Cobra is known to have caused permanent blindness in humans. (See 'First aid for snake venom in the eyes' on page 46.)

Similar species: May be confused with the Snouted Cobra (*Naja annulifera*), but the Black-necked Spitting Cobra is able to spit its venom, and may do so with little provocation.

Enemies: Preyed upon by other snakes.

Food and feeding: A generalized feeder that raids fowl runs for eggs, often killing distressed fowls in the process. Snakes, lizards and amphibians are preferred, but small fish, birds and rodents are also taken. A Zebra Cobra has been observed eating mopane worms (*Imbrasia belina*) from leaves close to the ground.

Reproduction: Oviparous, laying 10–15 but as many as 22 eggs (29–37 x 17–24 mm). Hatchling Black Spitting Cobras (*Naja nigricollis woodi*) measure 36–37 cm.

Danger to man: A common snake with potent venom. In addition to biting it also spits its venom.

Subspecies: There are 3 subspecies, the Black-necked Spitting Cobra, the Black Spitting Cobra and the Zebra Cobra.

The Black-necked Spitting Cobra (*Naja nigricollis nigricollis*), discussed above, is the largest of the three subspecies and is found

Very few of our snakes, including cobras, have the ability to spit their venom.

in the northern parts of the range. It also occurs extensively north of southern Africa and is similar to the Mozambique Spitting Cobra (*Naja mossambica*) in coloration and general habits.

The Black Spitting Cobra

(*Naja nigricollis woodi*) averages 1,2–1,5 m but may grow to 2 m. It has 223–228 ventrals. For many years it was believed to be a black variety of the Cape Cobra (*Naja nivea*). This rare snake is sometimes seen on the road at Aninauspas between Port Nolloth and Steinkopf and is also often seen near Springbok. The Black Spitting Cobra appears to be very effective at ejecting large quantities of venom when spitting. It may be confused with dark varieties of the Cape Cobra and the Mole Snake (*Pseudaspis cana*). Its diet includes snakes, such as the Puff Adder (*Bitis arietans*), as well as a wide variety of lizards, amphibians and rodents. This subspecies is listed as rare in the latest *South African Red Data Book – Reptiles and Amphibians* (Branch 1988).

The Zebra Cobra (*Naja nigri-collis nigricincta*) averages

only 1–1,2 m and rarely exceeds 1,5 m. It has 192–226 ventrals. This subspecies inhabits the Namib Desert and regions of karoo scrub in central and northern Namibia, extending into the southern reaches of Angola. It is a nocturnal snake that is often found on tarred roads. It is shy, choosing to escape if it has the choice but, if cornered, will spread a hood and spit its venom. Because of its barred markings, it may be confused with the harmless Tiger Snake (*Telescopus spp.*) and the Coral Snake (*Aspidelaps lubricus*). The Zebra Cobra feeds on other snakes, lizards, amphibians and

small mammals. It is oviparous, laying 10–22 eggs. This snake is common where it occurs, and accounts for many bites among humans. Its venom is dangerously cytotoxic.

The Mozambique Spitting Cobra and the Black-necked, Black Spitting and Zebra cobras can spit venom from virtually any position, even when concealed in a rock crevice.

Note that the taxonomical status of both the Zebra Cobra (*Naja nigricollis nigricincta*) and the Black Spitting Cobra (*Naja nigricollis woodi*) is uncertain and presently under review.

Venom: Predominantly cytotoxic, causing serious local tissue damage. Only minor neurological symptoms, such as drowsiness, sometimes occur. This snake has inflicted many serious bites on humans.

First-aid procedures: See first-aid treatment on page 42.

Andrew Turner & S Davies

The Black-necked Spitting Cobra (right) may be confused with the dark phase of the Cape Cobra. However, the latter cannot spit its venom.

Rinkhals

Hemachatus haemachatus

OTHER NAMES
Rinkhals (A)
Uphempthwane (Z)
Iphimpi (X)

VERY DANGEROUS

Length: Adults average 1 m but may reach, or exceed, 1,5 m.

Scale count: Dorsal scales in 17–19 rows at midbody, with 116–150 ventrals and 30–47 paired subcaudals. The anal shield is entire. There are 7 upper labials with the 3rd and 4th entering the eye, and 8 or 9 (rarely 7) lower labials, as well as 1 preocular (sometimes 2) and 3 postoculars. Temporals are 2 + 3, 2 + 2 or 2 + 4.

Colour: Variable, but normally olive to dark brown or dull black above and below with 1 or 2 (rarely 3) white crossbars on the throat, which are more conspicuous when the hood is displayed (specimens from the Witwatersrand). Otherwise olive to dark brown or black, with irregular crossbars of creamy white or yellow to yellow-orange. These specimens also have white crossbars on the throat. Below, dark brown to black. Specimens from KwaZulu-Natal, the Eastern Cape and Zimbabwe have crossbars on the back that do not extend onto the belly.

Preferred habitat: Grassland, moist savanna, lowland forest and fynbos; often encountered on smallholdings in and around Johannesburg.

Habits: Common throughout most of its range, especially the grasslands of the higher-lying areas. In spite of urban development, it is still common around parts of Johannesburg, especially near vleis, dams, compost heaps, stables and rockeries. It is very effective at regulating its body temperature in a temperate climate, and can

average 1 m maximum 1,5 m

The banded phase of the Rinkhals from the KwaZulu-Natal Midlands.

Specimens from the Highveld are usually dull grey to black with white markings on the throat.

Peter Dawson

LOOK OUT FOR

- Scales on body and tail are strongly keeled.
- Often has a black belly with white bars on the throat.
- Lifts up to half of its body off the ground and spreads a broad hood.
- Can spit its venom.
- May sham death.
- Likes to bask in the sun.

It is a good climber and may climb into hedges and even trees, especially when making its escape.

Like the Mozambique Spitting Cobra (*Naja mossambica*) it spits its venom, but only from an upright or reared position, while exposing its hood. When spitting, it draws its head backward and throws the raised part of its body forward, often hissing at the same time. It spits effectively for 2–3 m, not aiming accurately, but rather spraying 2 jets of venom in the general direction of its attacker.

maintain body temperatures of more than 30 °C during the day, even in winter.

Mainly diurnal, basking in sunny areas in the morning, moving into partially shaded areas as its body temperature approaches 32 °C. Forages actively by day, but may also be encountered on the hunt at night in the summer months. The Rinkhals disappears quickly when disturbed, unless cornered, when it will lift as much as half its body off the ground, with its hood spread and the 2 or 3 white bars on the throat clearly visible.

If approached closely, the Rinkhals may drop to the ground, twist the anterior portion of the body sideways or upside down, and play dead. The tongue is often left hanging out of a partially opened mouth. If it is picked up while playing dead, it may hang limply, but could equally strike out at any time.

Like some other snakes, the Rinkhals may sham death when threatened.

The Rinkhals only spits from a reared position.

Envenomation is rare and it is usually dogs and horses that are bitten. Despite its cobra-like appearance, the Rinkhals is not a true cobra. It has keeled dorsal scales and gives birth to live young (true cobras lay eggs). There are also some important skeletal differences between this snake and cobras.

Similar species: May be confused with the Mole Snake (*Pseudaspis cana*). Farmers often incorrectly refer to the Mozambique Spitting Cobra and the Snouted Cobra (*Naja annulifera*) as the Rinkhals.

Enemies: Other snakes and predatory birds are important predators. Yellow Mongooses (*Cynictis penicillata*) have been recorded preying on Rinkhals. Bullfrogs (*Pyxicephalus adspersus*) also eat the young. Urban development appears to be this snake's biggest threat as more and more of its habitat is being destroyed.

Food and feeding: Very partial to toads but also feeds on lizards, rodents, snakes, birds and their eggs. The eggs are swallowed whole.

Reproduction: Viviparous, giving birth to 20–30 young, but as many as 63 in late summer. The young, averaging 16–22 cm, are perfect replicas of the adult.

Danger to man: Although this snake's venom is potentially deadly, it is not as potent as that of most cobras. Human fatalities are rare.

Venom: A dangerous neurotoxic venom that affects breathing and, in untreated cases, may cause respiratory failure and death. Antivenom is effective against this snake's venom. Bites are rare and fatalities virtually unheard of.

First-aid procedures: See first-aid treatment on page 42.

Should one attempt to pick up a Rinkhals shamming death, the snake may bite suddenly.

DANGEROUS

maximum 75 cm

average 60 cm

Coral Snake

Aspidelaps lubricus

Aspidelaps lubricus lubricus

OTHER NAMES
Koraalslang (A)
Inkamela (X)

Length: Adults average 30–60 cm, but may reach lengths of 75 cm.

Scale count: Dorsal scales in 19 rows at midbody, with 149–168 ventrals and 20–28 pairs of subcaudals. The anal shield is entire. There are 6 (sometimes 7) upper labials with the 3rd and 4th entering the eye, and 8 lower labials, as well as 1 preocular and 3 (sometimes 2) postoculars. Temporals are 2 + 3, 2 + 4 or 2 + 2.

Colour: Variable, depending largely on the subspecies. In the southern parts of the range, individuals tend to be orange-yellow to coral red above, with 20–47 narrow, well-defined black crossbars, which may encircle the body and tail. A short, vertical black stripe runs across each eye to the mouth. The underside is usually yellowish white with black crossbars. These individuals belong to the Cape Coral Snake (*Aspidelaps lubricus lubricus*) subspecies.

Further north, Coral Snakes tend to have black heads and a grey to brown body with crossbars that range from distinct to barely visible. These are Western Coral Snakes (*A. l. infuscatus*).

At the northern extremes of its range, individuals with a pale brown head and body, darker neck and very faint crossbars predominate. These individuals belong to the Angolan Coral Snake (*A. l. cowlesi.*) subspecies.

Preferred habitat: Rocky outcrops, stony and dry sandy regions in the Namib Desert, arid savanna, karoo scrub and fynbos.

Habits: Spends much of its life underground, emerging at night to forage for food. Very active after rains, when many individuals are killed on roads by vehicles. It is a bad-tempered snake that spreads a narrow hood when cornered. It will strike repeatedly while hissing and lunging forward.

Similar species: The tiger snakes (*Telescopus* spp.) and the Zebra Cobra (*Naja nigricollis nigricincta*).

Enemies: Other snake species.

Food and feeding: Feeds on lizards, small snakes and rodents.

Reproduction: Oviparous, laying 3–11 eggs (45–54 x 14–15 mm) in the summer months. The young

When threatened, the Cape Coral Snake lifts its head well off the ground and may spread a narrow hood.

LOOK OUT FOR

- An orange-yellow to coral red snake with 20-47 black crossbars.
- Usually only active at night.
- Has an enlarged rostral scale.
- When threatened, it rears up with a narrow hood.
- Specimens from Namibia have a distinct black head.

The Cape Coral Snake may hiss and strike repeatedly.

The Angolan Coral Snake inhabits karoo scrub and the Namib Desert.

measure 17–18 cm. Captive females produce more than 1 batch of eggs in a season.

Danger to man: In South Africa bites from this snake have not resulted in life-threatening symptoms, but in Namibia the Western Coral Snake (*Aspidelaps lubricus infuscatus*) has reportedly killed 2 children.

Subspecies: There are 3 subspecies.

The Cape Coral Snake (*Aspidelaps lubricus lubricus*), discussed above, usually doesn't grow larger than 40 cm and occurs on rocky outcrops and in fynbos in the south.

The Western Coral Snake (*Aspidelaps lubricus infuscatus*) grows to 60 cm. It occurs in arid savanna, karoo scrub and the Namib Desert.

The Angolan Coral Snake (*Aspidelaps lubricus cowlesi*) is found from north-western Namibia and northwards into Angola, where it inhabits karoo scrub and the Namib Desert.

Venom: Very little is known about this snake's venom, but it is believed to be dangerously neurotoxic, and victims must be treated promptly.

First-aid procedures: See first-aid treatment on page 42.

The Western Coral Snake may also spread a narrow hood.

DANGEROUS

Shield-nose Snake

Aspidelaps scutatus

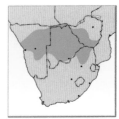

Aspidelaps scutatus scutatus

OTHER NAMES
Skildneusslang (A)

maximum 75 cm   average 45 cm

Length: Adults average 40–45 cm, with a maximum length of 75 cm. The females grow much larger than the males.

Scale count: Dorsal scales in 21–25 rows at midbody, with 108–125 ventrals and 20–35 pairs of subcaudals. The anal shield is entire. The rostral scale is obviously enlarged and prominent. There are 6 (sometimes 5 or 7) upper labials, with the 4th entering the eye, 8 lower labials (the first 3 or 4 in contact with the anterior chin scales). There is 1 preocular and 3 (sometimes 2 or 4) postoculars. Temporals are usually 2 + 4, but occasionally 2 + 5, 2 + 6 or 3 + 5.

Colour: Variable, but usually pale grey-brown, salmon pink or orange-brown to reddish brown above, with a series of liver-brown blotches over the back and tail. Most of the head and neck is black, the markings extending onto the throat region and sometimes encircling the neck. Below, uniform white to yellowish.

Preferred habitat: Sandy and stony regions in the Namib Desert, and moist and arid savanna.

Habits: Hides during the day and forages for food at night. This snake has a large rostral scale, which it uses as a bulldozer to push through sandy soil. It may play dead, like the Rinkhals (*Hemachatus haemachatus*), but when molested it performs like a Coral Snake (*Aspidelaps lubricus*), raising its head while hissing and striking repeatedly. It does not spread a hood. This snake is endemic to southern Africa.

Similar species: May be confused with coral snakes (*Aspidelaps lubricus* subsp.), tiger snakes (*Telescopus* spp.) or the Zebra Cobra (*Naja nigricollis nigricincta*).

Enemies: Other snakes.

Food and feeding: Feeds at night, eating amphibians, snakes, lizards and small mammals.

When threatend, the Shield-nose Snake lifts its head off the ground, but doesn't spread a hood.

Wulf Haacke

Reproduction: Oviparous, laying 4–14 eggs. The female may coil around her eggs to protect them. The young measure 16–18 cm.

Danger to man: Bites from this snake seldom result in serious symptoms but at least 1 death has been reported.

Subspecies: There are 3 subspecies.

The **Common Shield-nose Snake** (*Aspidelaps. scutatus scutatus*), discussed above, occurs in moist savanna in Mpumalanga Province.

The **Intermediate Shield-nose Snake** (*A. s. intermedius*) is very similar to the Common Shield-nose Snake in coloration.

The **Eastern Shield-nose Snake** (*A. s. fulafula*) is a larger snake with large, distinct blackish blotches on the back and sides. It occurs in moist savanna and lowland forest in Mozambique.

Venom: Little is known of this snake's venom. Mild neurological symptoms may result, accompanied by much pain. Symptoms have also included severe pain and swelling with no neurological symptoms whatsoever. The symptoms may persist for several days.

Note the distinct large scale on the nose from which it derives its common name.

First-aid procedures: See first-aid treatment on page 42.

The Intermediate Shield-nose Snake is similar to the Common Shield-nose Snake in coloration.

Günther's Garter Snake

Elapsoidea guentheri

DANGEROUS

OTHER NAMES
Günther se kousbandslang (A)

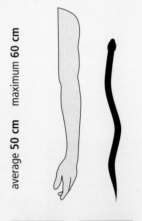

average 50 cm   maximum 60 cm

Length: Adults average 40–50 cm with a maximum length of just over 60 cm.

Scale count: Dorsal scales are in 15 rows at midbody, with 131–173 ventrals, and 49–60 subcaudals. The anal shield is entire. There are 6 (rarely 5) upper labials, with the 3rd and 4th (sometimes 2nd and 3rd) entering the eye, and 5 (sometimes 6) lower labials, as well as 1 preocular and 1 postocular. Temporals are 0 + 1 + 1 or 1 + 1.

Colour: Juveniles are black with 16–20 light crossbars on the back and 2–4 crossbars on the tail. In adults (from about 30–40 cm) the bands fade and the dorsal colour becomes grey-black to black and paler below.

Preferred habitat: Found in moist savanna.

Habits: A shy and secretive nocturnal snake that spends its days hiding under stones and in burrows. It is associated with *miombo* woodland on the central watershed in Zimbabwe. It is front-fanged and venomous but nothing is known of its venom.

Similar species: Could be confused with a number of other grey to black snakes, but has clear crossbars on the back and tail that fade with age. Banded specimens cannot easily be confused with other snakes.

This is a young Günther's Garter Snake. In adults, the bands on the back fade.

Bill Branch

Enemies: Unknown.

Food and feeding: Feeds on small snakes, skinks, amphibians and termite alates.

Reproduction: Oviparous, laying up to 10 eggs in summer.

Danger to man: A very docile snake that is reluctant to bite, but may carry dangerous venom.

Venom: Nothing is known about the venom of this snake. No human bites have ever been recorded. Antivenom is unlikely to be effective in treating bites.

First-aid procedures: If you are sure that a

> ### LOOK OUT FOR
>
> ■ Medium-sized snake with rounded snout.
> ■ Juveniles have 16–20 crossbars on the back and 2–4 crossbars on the tail.
> ■ Usually concealed during the day.

Günther's Garter Snake was responsible for the bite, get the victim to a doctor where the bite must be treated symptomatically. Painkillers may be required. Otherwise see first-aid treatment on page 42.

Colin Tilbury

Günther's Garter Snake may be confused with the Zambezi Garter Snake (above), which may also have light bands on the body that fade with age.

Ian Michler / SIL

Moist savanna is the preferred habitat of Günther's Garter Snake.

DANGEROUS

Angolan Garter Snake

Elapsoidea semiannulata

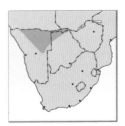

OTHER NAMES
Angolakousbandslang (A)

average 50 cm   maximum 60 cm

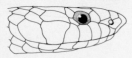

This snake inhabits arid and moist savanna.

Length: Adults average 50 cm with a maximum of nearly 60 cm.
Scale count: Midbody scales in 13 rows, with 136–161 ventrals and 13–28 paired subcaudals. The anal shield is entire. There are 7 upper labials, the 3rd and 4th entering the eye, and 7 lower labials, as well as 1 preocular and 2 postoculars. Temporals are 1 + 2.
Colour: Adults are blackish above with narrower white crossbars that fade with age. Juveniles have a largely white head, and a black back with between 12 and 19 white bands on the body and 2–3 white bands on the tail. The belly is uniformly white.
Preferred habitat: Arid savanna and moist savanna in northern Namibia extending into Angola and further northwards, usually at an altitude of between 900 and 2 000 m.
Habits: A rare, slow-moving and inoffensive snake.
Similar species: Quite easily recognized as it has narrow white crossbars across its body. These markings fade with age.
Enemies: Other snakes.
Food and feeding: Skinks, geckos, amphibians and small snakes.
Reproduction: Oviparous, laying up to 10 small eggs (20 x 8–10 mm).
Danger to man: Reluctant to bite. Venom may be dangerous.
Venom: The venom of this snake has not been studied and few bites have been recorded. Known bites have resulted in immediate pain and swelling that subsided within a few days. Severe symptoms have not been recorded to date.
Subspecies: Only the typical race of Angolan Garter Snake (*Elapsoidea semiannulata semiannulata*) occurs within our range.
First-aid procedures: If you are sure that an Angolan Garter Snake was responsible for the bite, get the victim to a doctor where the bite must be treated symptomatically. Painkillers may be required. Otherwise see first-aid treatment on page 42.

Steve Spawls

LOOK OUT FOR

- ■ Medium-sized snake with rounded snout.
- ■ Has a uniform white belly.
- ■ Slow-moving and docile snake.

Zambezi Garter Snake
Elapsoidea boulengeri

DANGEROUS

OTHER NAMES
Previously known as Boulenger's Garter Snake
Zambesikousbandslang (A)

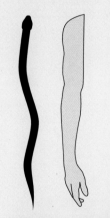

average 60 cm   maximum 77 cm

Length: Adults average 50–60 cm with a maximum length of 77 cm.
Scale count: Midbody scales are in 13 rows, with 138–161 ventrals and 14–27 paired subcaudals. The anal shield is entire. There are 7 upper labials with the 3rd, 4th and 5th (sometimes the 3rd and 4th) entering the eye, and 7 lower labials, as well as 1 preocular and 2 postoculars. Temporals are 1 + 2.
Colour: Above, dark chocolate brown to black with 8–17 narrow white bands on the back and up to 3 white bands on the tail. These markings usually disappear in older specimens. Juveniles have a white head and are black above with 12–17 white to pale yellow bands on the body and tail. The yellow bands are about half to one-third the width of the black bands. The belly is usually dark grey or brown, but may occasionally be white.
Preferred habitat: Found in a variety of habitats from lowland forest through moist savanna, karoo scrub, grassland and arid savanna, from sea level to an altitude of 1 500 m.
Habits: This nocturnal fossorial snake is seldom encountered as it spends most of its life underground, often in termite mounds. It is sluggish and reluctant to bite, even when first handled. If molested, it will coil up and hiss but does not form a hood like a cobra.
Similar species: As this snake gets older and its colours fade, it becomes more and more difficult to identify and may then be confused with a variety of other snakes.

Bill Branch

Juvenile Zambezi Garter Snakes are vividly marked, but these markings fade with age.

A nocturnal snake that spends much of its life underground and is, therefore, seldom encountered.

LOOK OUT FOR

- A medium-sized snake with rounded snout.
- May coil up and hiss if confronted but does not spread a hood.
- A quiet, sluggish snake that is reluctant to bite.

First-aid procedures: If you are sure that a Zambezi Garter Snake was responsible for the bite, get the victim to a doctor where the bite must be treated symptomatically. Painkillers may be required. Otherwise see first-aid treatment on page 42.

Enemies: Other snakes.

Food and feeding: Small reptiles, especially snakes, and amphibians. Newborn mice are taken in captivity.

Reproduction: Oviparous, laying 4–10 eggs (20–40 x 8–16 mm).

Danger to man: Very docile and reluctant to bite, but may carry dangerous venom.

Venom: A cobra-type venom that may cause immediate pain and stiffness of the affected limb. The symptoms are usually short-lived and severe effects have not been recorded.

The venom of this snake may cause immediate pain, but is not thought to be very dangerous.

This sluggish snake is reluctant to bite, even when first handled. It may coil up and hiss if threatened.

Elapsoidea s.sundevalli

Sundevall's Garter Snake

Elapsoidea sundevalli

OTHER NAMES
Sundevall se kousbandslang (A)

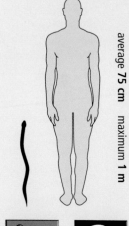

average 75 cm   maximum 1 m

Length: Adults average about 75 cm with a maximum length of just under 1 m.

Scale count: Midbody scales are in 13 rows, with 147–181 ventrals. Subcaudals are paired (sometimes single) and number 13–33. The anal shield is entire. There are 7 upper labials, the 3rd and 4th entering the eye, and 7 lower labials, as well as 1 preocular (sometimes 2) and 2 postoculars. Temporals are 1 + 2 or 1 + 1.

Colour: Adults are slate grey with a reddish brown tinge and have 19–34 pale bands on the body and 2–4 pale bands on the tail. The belly and scales on the outer flanks are yellowish and may have darker mottling. In juveniles, the head and belly are pale and the body and tail distinctly banded with chocolate brown to black, and white to cream bands. The white bands fade with age.

Preferred habitat: Found in a variety of habitats from karoo scrub to arid savanna, moist savanna, grassland and lowland forest.

Habits: Because of its nocturnal habits and fossorial existence, this snake is seldom encountered. It shelters underground, especially in disused termite mounds, under rocks and logs and among leaf litter. Individuals are sometimes encountered while crossing roads at night. It is a sluggish, inoffensive snake that seldom bites, even when first handled.

A Sundevall's Garter Snake eating a mouse.

Similar species: As the markings fade with age this snake becomes more and more difficult to distinguish from similarly marked snakes. Banded juveniles cannot easily be mistaken for any other snake.

Enemies: Other snakes.

Food and feeding: Varied, including snakes, lizards and their eggs, amphibians, especially rain frogs (*Breviceps* spp.), small rodents and moles.

Reproduction: Oviparous, laying up to 10 eggs (20 x 8–10 mm).

Danger to man: Larger individuals may inflict serious bites, but few bites have been recorded.

Subspecies: There are 5 subspecies.

Sundevall's Garter Snake (*Elapsoidea sundevalli sundevalli*), discussed above, is the largest and is found in KwaZulu-Natal and Mpumalanga Province.

The Highveld Garter Snake (*Elapsoidea sundevalli media*) occurs in the extreme Northern Cape, the Free State, North West Province and Gauteng. Juveniles have 16–23 distinct pink bands on the tail. These bands fade with age. The belly and scales on the lower flanks are pale brown. This snake has 13–23 subcaudals and 140–168 ventrals.

The Kalahari Garter Snake (*Elapsoidea sundevalli fitzsimonsi*) is found in the Northern Cape, Botswana and northern Namibia, where it is restricted to sandveld areas in arid savanna and karoo scrub. Juveniles have

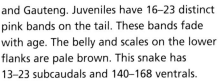

De Coster's Garter Snake.

LOOK OUT FOR

■ A medium to large snake with a pointed snout.
■ Slow moving and reluctant to bite.
■ Usually found under rocks, logs and in disused termite mounds.

A brightly marked Highveld Garter Snake from Lydenburg.

18–21 white bands on a black background on the body and 2–3 white bands on the tail. The belly and scales on the lower flanks are white. The dorsal band only appears when the snake reaches a length of about 37 cm. Until then it is dark slate grey with a reddish brown tinge and a creamy white belly. The dorsal bands fade with age. This snake also has 13–23 subcaudals and 156–180 ventrals.

The Long-tailed Garter Snake (*Elapsoidea sundevalli longicauda*) occurs from southern Mozambique northwards into the Limpopo Province and south-east Zimbabwe. Juveniles have 17–20 buff bands on a black background on the body and 2–3 buff bands on the tail. The belly is uniform white. The bands fade with age and the adults are uniform black above with a white belly and pink on the lower flanks. This is the largest race and has 22–33 ventrals and 138–159 subcaudals.

The Long-tailed Garter Snake is the largest of the subspecies.

De Coster's Garter Snake (*Elapsoidea sundevalli decosteri*) has a limited distribution from northern KwaZulu-Natal into southern Mozambique. Juvenile specimens have 19–21 white-edged pale brown bands on a darker background on the body. There are also 3–4 of these bands on the tail. The belly and scales on the lower flanks are white. These bands fade with age and eventually disappear completely. It has 148–179 ventrals and 22–33 subcaudals.

Venom: The venom has been little studied and only a few case histories have been documented. Known symptoms include nausea, vomiting, pain, swelling, blurred vision and loss of consciousness. The Long-tailed Garter Snake grows in excess of 1 m and may be capable of inflicting a serious bite.

First-aid procedures: If you are sure that a Sundevall's Garter Snake was responsible for the bite, get the victim to a doctor where the bite must be treated symptomatically. Painkillers may be required. Otherwise see first-aid treatment on page 42.

A Highveld Garter Snake. The tail bands fade with age.

Spotted Harlequin Snake

Homoroselaps lacteus

MILDLY VENOMOUS

OTHER NAMES
Gevlekte kousbandjie (A)

average 40 cm   maximum 65 cm

Length: Adults average 30–40 cm but may reach a length of 65 cm.
Scale count: Midbody scales in 15 rows with 160–209 ventrals and 24–43 paired subcaudals. The anal shield is divided. There are 6 upper labials, the 3rd and 4th entering the eye, and 6 lower labials, as well as 1 preocular and 1 postocular. Temporals are 0 + 1 or 1 + 1.
Colour: Variable, including the following: (a) yellowish white with regular black bars and blotches and a wide, bright orange vertebral stripe; (b) black above with irregular yellow-white to white crossbars and red to orange spots down the vertebrae that usually form a streak from head to tail; (c) black above with a yellow dot on each scale and a bright orange to orange-yellow streak down the centre of the back; (d) black with hollow diamond-shaped markings (yellow to whitish yellow) and a dorsal orange stripe. The belly is never plain but usually has black or dark brown markings on a lighter background.
Preferred habitat: Occurs in fynbos, lowland forest, moist savanna and grassland.
Habits: A brightly coloured little snake that inhabits a wide range of habitats. It is quite common in some areas and is usually found in deserted termite mounds or under rocks. Although it spends most of its time underground, especially in termite mounds, it is not a burrower. When disturbed it wriggles violently to escape. The Spotted Harlequin Snake seldom attempts to bite and, because of its small head, has a rather narrow gape.

A Spotted Harlequin Snake from Port Elizabeth.

Richard Boycott

A somewhat striped phase of the Spotted Harlequin Snake.

Similar species: This snake may be confused with the Aurora House Snake (*Lamprophis aurora*).

Enemies: Other snakes.

Food and feeding: Feeds on legless skinks, blind snakes and other snakes as well as other small lizards.

Reproduction: Oviparous, laying 6–9 but as many as 16 eggs in summer. The eggs vary in size from 22–28 x 8–10 mm and 14–18 x 11–12 mm. Hatchlings measure 13–15 cm.

Danger to man: Not considered dangerous.

Venom: Its venom has not been studied in detail and may cause mild to severe swelling, mild haemorrhage and painful glands. Severe headaches that ease within a day have also been reported. Swelling usually subsides within 2–3 days. Anti-venom is not effective and is certainly not required.

First-aid procedures: If you are sure that a Spotted Harlequin Snake was responsible for the bite, get the victim to a doctor where the bite must be treated symptomatically. Painkillers may be required. Otherwise see first-aid treatment on page 42.

The Spotted Harlequin Snake feeds on a variety of reptiles.

A secretive snake that spends most of its time underground and may be found in deserted termite mounds or under rocks.

MILDLY VENOMOUS

Striped Harlequin Snake

Homoroselaps dorsalis

OTHER NAMES
Gestreepte kousbandjie (A)

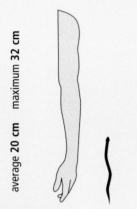

average 20 cm　maximum 32 cm

Length: Very small, averaging 20 cm with a maximum of nearly 32 cm.
Scale count: Midbody scales are in 15 rows, with 210–239 ventrals and 22–33 paired subcaudals. The anal shield is divided. There are 6 upper labials, the 3rd and 4th entering the eye, and 5 lower labials, as well as 1 preocular and 1 postocular. Temporals are 0 + 1.
Colour: Black above, with a conspicuous yellow vertebral stripe from the tip of the nose to the tip of the tail. The lips, belly and outer scales on the flanks are creamy white to yellowish white.
Preferred habitat: Found mainly in moist savanna and grassland.
Habits: A small, slender snake that is rare and seldom seen. It inhabits deserted termite mounds and is probably very similar to the Spotted Harlequin Snake (*Homoroselaps lacteus*) in habits and behaviour. It is listed in the most recent *South African Red Data Book – Reptiles and Amphibians* (Branch 1988) as rare.
Similar species: Quite distinct and not easily confused with other species.
Enemies: Other snakes.
Food and feeding: Feeds on worm snakes of the genus *Leptotyphlops*.
Reproduction: Oviparous, laying 2–4 minute elongate eggs.
Danger to man: Harmless, owing to a very small gape, small venom yield and short fangs.

A small, slender snake that is seldom seen.

Venom: Its venom has not been studied but is considered to have very little effect on man. The venom yield of this snake is minute.

First-aid procedures: If you are sure that a Striped Harlequin Snake was responsible for the bite, get the victim to a doctor where the bite must be treated symptomatically. Painkillers may be required. Otherwise see first-aid treatment on page 42.

see first-aid treatment on page 42.

LOOK OUT FOR

■ A small, slender snake.
■ Has a distinct yellow vertebral stripe from its head to the tip of its tail. The body is black.

Deserted termite mounds are a favourite habitat of the Striped Harlequin Snake.

Nigel Dennis / SIL

Bill Branch

The Highveld Garter Snake (above) may prey on Striped Harlequin Snakes.

Yellow-bellied Sea Snake

Pelamis platurus

maximum 1 m

average 60 cm

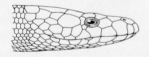

OTHER NAMES
Pelagic Sea Snake (E)
Swart-en-geel seeslang (A)

Length: Adults average 40–60 cm. Males may reach 75 cm but females sometimes attain a length of as much as 1 m.

Scale count: Midbody scales are in 49–67 rows, with 264–406 ventrals and 36 or more subcaudals. The anal shield is divided. There are 7 or 8 upper labials with the 4th and 5th entering the eye, and 10 or 11 lower labials, as well as 1 or 2 preoculars and 2 or 3 postoculars. Temporals are variable.

Colour: Variable, but usually black above and yellow to yellow-brown below, sometimes with black blotches. The darker and lighter colours are clearly demarcated on the sides. The oar-shaped tail has distinct reticulated markings in black and yellow.

Preferred habitat: This is the most widely distributed sea snake in the world and it is found throughout the warmer waters of the Indian and Pacific oceans, but doesn't occur in most of the Atlantic. In fact, this is probably the most widely distributed and common snake in the world. It has been recorded at various places along southern Africa's eastern and southern coasts, as individuals occasionally wash up on KwaZulu-Natal and Cape beaches. Snakes that are washed ashore are usually sick or injured.

Habits: This truly pelagic sea snake is largely surface dwelling and tends to float motionlessly, moving with the sea currents. It is

Little is known of the venom of the Yellow-bellied Sea Snake other than that it is neurotoxic and potentially lethal.

Bill Branch

an accomplished diver (it can dive deeper than 50 m and stay underwater for longer than 3 hours), but spends most of its time on the surface. It is an excellent swimmer and can swim forwards or backwards. It is associated with slicks that have been described as 'rivers within the ocean', where it hides among seaweed, floating branches, coconuts, logs and foam. The floating debris also attracts a variety of small fish, upon which the snake preys. It sheds its skin by knotting itself, using friction against its own body to rid itself of the old skin. It often occurs in large numbers and at great densities.

The Yellow-bellied Sea Snake is specially adapted to its aquatic existence. With its laterally compressed body and paddle-shaped tail, it is often mistaken for an eel. Ventral scales are largely reduced as they serve no purpose in the sea, and most sea snakes are therefore awkward and helpless on land. It swims using lateral undulations that are very similar to the movements of many terrestrial snakes. It is not an aggressive snake but will fend for itself if molested. This snake appears to have few enemies.

Similar species: Cannot be confused with any other snake. Some people mistake it for an eel.

Enemies: Unknown.

LOOK OUT FOR

- Black above and yellow to yellow-brown below.
- Has a paddle-shaped tail with black and yellow markings.
- May be found washed up on beaches, especially after bad weather.

Food and feeding: Ambushes suitably sized fish that frequent the floating debris where this snake is found.

Reproduction: Viviparous, giving birth to between 2 and 8 young, which measure about 25 cm.

Danger to man: Very few bites have been recorded in South Africa, and beach-goers are at very low risk. Usually, snakes washed ashore are injured or sick and are often nearly dead.

Venom: Little is known about the venom of this snake other than that it is neurotoxic and potentially lethal, but recorded bites are rare. It is often incorrectly stated that the venom is largely myotoxic, causing paralysis of skeletal muscles. In the unlikely event of a bite, first-aiders may need to help the victim breathe. No antivenom is available in South Africa.

First-aid procedures: See first-aid treatment on page 42.

Bill Branch

The Yellow-bellied Sea Snake is sometimes found on beaches, usually only after severe storms.

BACK-FANGED AND OTHER VENOMOUS SNAKES

Of all the back-fanged snakes only the Boomslang (*Dispholidus typus*) and the twig or vine snakes (*Thelotornis* spp.) have caused fatal bites in the past.

The venom of these snakes is primarily haemotoxic and affects the blood-clotting mechanism, causing severe headaches, bleeding from the mucous membranes, nausea, vomiting and eventually bleeding from all internal organs. Blood may also ooze from the fang punctures. It may take more than eight hours before the first symptoms are detected, and 24 hours or more before serious symptoms develop.

Antivenom for the bite of the Boomslang is only available from the National Health Laboratory Service (formerly the South African Institute of Medical Research) in Johannesburg. No antivenom exists for vine snake venom. Fortunately, bites from these snakes are rare and fatalities seldom heard of. The venom of the Natal Black Snake (*Macrelaps microlepidotus*) has not been studied thoroughly and should be regarded as potentially dangerous. Bibron's Stiletto Snake (*Atractaspis bibronii*) has also been included in this group and is capable of inflicting an extremely painful bite that has, in the past, resulted in the loss of limbs. Polyvalent antivenom is not effective against the venom of this snake and is therefore not recommended.

Back-fanged snakes have small fangs that are situated quite far back in the mouth.

The majority of back-fanged snakes, like this Crossed Whip Snake, have mild venoms.

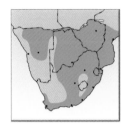

Boomslang
Dispholidus typus

OTHER NAMES
Boomslang (A)

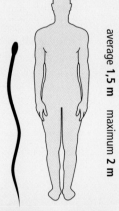

VERY DANGEROUS

average 1,5 m   maximum 2 m

Length: Adults average 1,2–1,5 m, with a maximum length of nearly 2 m.

Scale count: Midbody scales are in 19 rows (rarely 17 or 21), with 164–201 ventrals and 104–142 paired subcaudals. The anal shield is divided. There are 7 (rarely 6 or 8) upper labials, the 3rd and 4th (sometimes 4th and 5th) entering the eye, and 8–13 lower labials, as well as 1 preocular (sometimes 2) and 3 (sometimes 2 or 4) postoculars. Temporals are 1 + 2, but variable.

Colour: Colour variation is far greater than in any other South African snake. Juveniles are light grey to brown above with a fine stippling of blue, especially on the anterior parts. The head is brown to grey above, while the throat may be vivid yellow to orange. Below, white to yellowish with dark speckles. The enormous eyes are brilliant emerald green. When the snake is about 1 m long the colour changes to that of the adult.

Most females are light to olive brown with dirty white to brown bellies, whereas males might have the following coloration: (a) green to olive green with or without black interstitial skin, the belly a similar but lighter colour; (b) bright green with black-edged scales, giving the snake a crossbarred appearance; (c) dark brown to black with bright yellow belly; (d) black above with dark grey belly scales that are black-edged. Brick-red specimens are found in some areas.

The Boomslang has the largest eyes of any African snake.

Richard Boycott

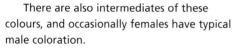

LOOK OUT FOR

- Strongly keeled dorsal scales.
- Has enormous eyes and a short stubby head.
- May inflate the neck and most of the body under severe provocation.
- Spends most of its life in trees and shrubs.
- Active during the day.

Most females are light brown to olive in colour.

There are also intermediates of these colours, and occasionally females have typical male coloration.

Preferred habitat: Found in a variety of habitats throughout southern Africa including karoo scrub, arid savanna, moist savanna, lowland forest, grassland and fynbos. It is absent from much of the drier western parts of South Africa and is also not found on the central Highveld and most of Lesotho.

Habits: A notably unobtrusive, shy and diurnal snake that spends most of its time in trees and shrubs. It may also descend to the ground to hunt or bask, only to disappear into the leafy concealment of the closest shrub or tree when disturbed, where it is well camouflaged and difficult to detect. Most of its hunting is done in trees and shrubs, but it does descend to the ground to

feed, especially along streams. With its superior vision, the Boomslang has no difficulty in locating prey. When it does, it freezes with its head cocked, the only movement being lateral waves that sweep the neck. It then swoops onto its prey, which is held firmly in its jaw while the fangs move with a chewing motion. The victim soon succumbs to the venom and is swallowed from the side, head first, or even from the back, if it is small enough.

If provoked, the Boomslang will inflate the neck region to more than twice the normal size, displaying the vividly marked skin. Eventually, the entire body is inflated, at which stage the snake will strike sideways and forward with a jerky motion. Most victims are snake park attendants or snake collectors. It is a widespread fallacy that the

The male Boomslang is usually more colourful than the female.

The juvenile Boomslang has enormous emerald eyes.

The likelihood of being bitten by this snake is extremely remote, unless one actually handles it. Never handle any small snakes, especially if brought into the house by a cat.

Boomslang will drop from a tree onto any-one who risks walking beneath it, and then strike the moment it makes contact.

Although the fangs are situated far back in the mouth, the Boomslang can open its mouth as wide as 170 degrees and, contrary to popular belief, can easily deliver an effective bite on an arm or leg.

Similar species: Often confused with the Black and Green mambas (*Dendroaspis* spp.) and with the harmless green snakes of the genus *Philothamnus*.

Enemies: Predatory birds and other snakes. Birds such as bulbuls often mob it.

Food and feeding: Actively hunts cha-meleons and other tree-living lizards, birds, nestlings, eggs (swallowed whole) and frogs. Small mammals are seldom taken.

Reproduction: Oviparous, usually laying 8–14, but as many as 27 eggs (27--53 x 18–37 mm) in hollow tree trunks, rotting logs or among leaf litter in late spring to mid-summer. The young measure 29–38 cm.

Danger to man: Though its venom is deadly, this shy snake very seldom bites. Most victims have been snake handlers and park attendants.

A male Boomslang from KwaZulu-Natal.

Venom: Potently haemotoxic, causing severe internal bleeding and bleeding from the mucous membranes. May result in fatal haemorrhage if untreated. Although the venom is extremely potent, it is slow acting and may take more than 24–48 hours to produce serious symptoms. An effective antivenom is available from the National Health Laboratory Service in Johannesburg. Victims should be hospitalized for at least 48 hours.

Subspecies: Only the typical race of Boomslang (*Dispholidus typus typus*) is found within our range.

First-aid procedures: See first-aid treatment on page 42.

Males often have bright green, black-edged scales, but brick-red specimens are also found in some areas.

VERY DANGEROUS

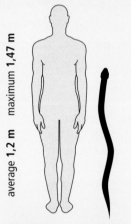

Vine Snake
Thelotornis capensis

Thelotornis capensis capensis

OTHER NAMES
Twig Snake (E)
Bird Snake (E)
Savannevoëlslang (A)
Ukhokhothi (Z)

Length: Adults average 80 cm to 1,2 m and reach a maximum length of 1,47 m.

Scale count: Midbody scales are in 19 rows (rarely 17), with 144–162 ventrals and 127–155 paired subcaudals. The anal shield is divided. There are 8 (sometimes 7 or 9) upper labials, the 4th and 5th (rarely the 3rd and 4th, 5th and 6th or 3rd, 4th and 5th) entering the eye (variable), and 9 or 13 lower labials. There is 1 preocular and 3 (rarely 2 or 4) postoculars. Temporals are 1 + 2 (very rarely 1 + 1 or 1 + 3).

Colour: These snakes are cryptically coloured and, when motionless in a tree, they resemble branches or twigs. Above, ash grey or grey-brown with darker and lighter blotches and flecks of black, orange and/or pink. On the sides of the neck there are usually 1 or 2 dark blotches. The head above is pale blue-green, heavily speckled with dark brown, black and sometimes pink. A wide pinkish white black-speckled band runs along the upper lip from the snout to the back of the head, passing across the lower half of the eye. A dark, oblique band radiates from each eye to the upper lip. Both chin and throat are white, speckled with black. Below, pinkish white to light grey, speckled and streaked with brownish black. The tongue is bright yellow to orange-red and black-tipped.

Preferred habitat: Trees and shrubs in lowland forest to moist savanna and arid savanna.

Like the Boomslang, the Vine Snake is thought to have very good vision.

The Vine Snake is very well camouflaged and extremely difficult to see in shrubs and trees.

Habits: A slender, mostly tree-living snake that prefers low shrubs, bushes and trees where its cryptic coloration blends so well with the background that it is seldom seen. It moves gracefully and swiftly when disturbed. It may remain in the same position for several days if not disturbed.

Though timid and retiring, it will inflate its neck to display the bright skin between the scales when threatened. Lunging strikes usually follow this, while the bright tongue flickers in a wavy motion.

It actively hunts for food during the day, first approaching its prey in short spurts, then darting forward to seize it. The prey is held firmly in the jaws while the venom takes effect. Terrestrial prey is hunted from low shrubs.

Males engage in combat, intertwining their bodies while attempting to push one another's heads down. Snakes of this genus are sexually dimorphic in that the males have much longer tails than the females and the latter are more heavy-bodied than males.

The common name 'Bird Snake' appears to be inappropriate, as birds do not make up the bulk of this snake's diet, probably because they are not easy to capture. Previous reports

LOOK OUT FOR

- Lance-shaped head with keyhole-shaped pupil.
- Superbly camouflaged as a branch or twig.
- Inflates the neck showing the skin colours when confronted.
- Spends most of its life in trees and in shrubs.
- Top of the head is green or blue-green.
- Red and black tongue is held out when threatened.

of this snake using its brightly coloured tongue to lure birds closer seem unlikely to be true.

Similar species: Some of the whip, grass or sand snakes (*Psammophis* spp.). Vine Snakes, however, are usually found in shrubs and trees and have unique cryptic coloration.

Enemies: Birds of prey and other snakes.

Food and feeding: Lizards, including chameleons (*Chamaeleo* and *Bradypodion* spp.), and frogs. Snakes and birds are also taken on occasion. This snake usually strikes from above and often swallows its prey

Though timid by nature, this snake may react viciously if handled.

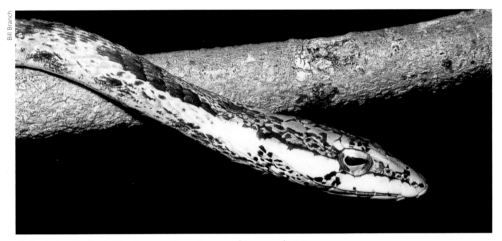

Oates' Vine Snake is the larger subspecies, reaching nearly 1,7 m.

with the anterior part of its body hanging downwards.

Reproduction: Oviparous, laying 4–18 eggs (25–41 x 12–17 mm) in summer. The young measure 22–37 cm. Females may produce more than 1 clutch of eggs in a season.

Danger to man: Like the Boomslang, the Vine Snake is very shy and the chance of being bitten by it is remote.

Subspecies: There are 2 subspecies.

The Southern Vine Snake (*Thelotornis capensis capensis*), discussed above, is the smaller, reaching a maximum length of less than 1,5 m. It occurs in the southern parts of the range, usually has fewer than 160 ventrals and has speckling on the head.

Oates' Vine or Twig Snake (*Thelotornis capensis oatesii*) is the larger subspecies, reaching nearly 1,7 m and usually has more than 160 ventrals. The top of its head is blue-green and generally lacks speckling, except for a dark Y-shaped marking. It occurs in northern Namibia, northern Botswana, Zimbabwe, western Mozambique and elsewhere.

Venom: Dangerously haemotoxic and very similar in effect to the venom of the Boomslang (*Dispholidus typus*). Bites are rare, which is fortunate because at present there is no antivenom (the monovalent Boomslang antivenom does not neutralize the venom of this snake). Victims must be hospitalized as soon as possible. Human fatalities are rare.

First-aid procedures: See first-aid treatment on page 42.

The Southern Vine Snake is the smaller subspecies, reaching less than 1,5 m in length.

Vine Snake bites are rare, which is fortunate because at present there is no antivenom.

Eastern Vine Snake
Thelotornis mossambicanus

OTHER NAMES
Eastern Bird Snake (E)
Oostelike voëlslang (A)

VERY DANGEROUS

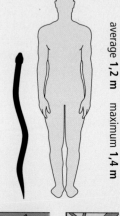

Length: Adults average 80 cm to 1,2 m and reach a maximum length of just over 1,4 m.

Scale count: Midbody scales are in 19 rows (rarely 17, 21 or 23), with 144–172 ventrals and 123–168 paired subcaudals. The anal shield is divided. There are 8 (sometimes 6, 7 or 9) upper labials, the 4th and 5th (rarely the 5th and 6th, 3rd and 4th, 3rd or 5th only) entering the eye (variable), and 9–13 lower labials. There is 1 preocular and 3 (rarely 2 or 4) postoculars. Temporals are 1 + 2 (very rarely 1 + 1 or 1 + 3 or 2 + 2).

Colour: The head above is plain green with a dark speckled Y-marking, or brown speckled with black. Both chin and throat are white, speckled with black. Below, light grey speckled and streaked with brownish black. Body ash grey or grey-brown above with darker and lighter blotches and flecks of black, orange and/or pink. On the sides of the neck there are usually 1 or 2 dark blotches.

Preferred habitat: Trees and shrubs in lowland forest to moist savanna in Mozambique and eastern Zimbabwe.

Habits: Very similar to the Southern Vine Snake (*Thelotornis capensis capensis*) in habits and behaviour but very versatile, inhabiting both forest and the drier savanna habitats. Males engage in wrestling, intertwining their bodies, while each attempts to push the other's head down.

Similar species: Some of the whip, grass or sand snakes (*Psammophis* spp.). Vine Snakes, however, are usually found in shrubs and trees.

average 1,2 m   maximum 1,4 m

Bill Branch

This snake spends most of its life in trees and shrubs.

Enemies: Birds of prey and other snakes.
Food and feeding: Lizards and frogs, while small mammals, fledgling birds and other snakes are also taken. The snake usually strikes from above and swallows its prey while the anterior part of the body hangs downwards.
Reproduction: Oviparous, laying up to 18 eggs.
Danger to man: Like the Boomslang (*Dispholidus typus*), the Vine Snake is very shy and the chance of being bitten is remote.
Venom: Dangerously haemotoxic and very similar in effect to the venom of the Boomslang. Bites are rare, which is fortunate because at present there is no Vine Snake antivenom (the monovalent Boomslang antivenom does not neutralize the venom

of this snake). Victims must be hospitalized as soon as possible. Human fatalities are rare.
First-aid procedures: See first-aid treatment on page 42.

LOOK OUT FOR

- Lance-shaped head with keyhole-shaped pupil.
- Superbly camouflaged as a branch or twig.
- Inflates the neck showing the skin colours when confronted.
- Spends most of its life in trees and shrubs.
- Top of the head is usually green.

Richard Boycott

Like the Boomslang, this snake is shy and seldom bites.

Males are known to engage in combat,
wrestling with their bodies intertwined.

Southern Stiletto Snake

Atractaspis bibronii

OTHER NAMES
Bibron's Stiletto Snake (E)
Southern or Bibron's Burrowing Asp (E)
Side-stabbing Snake (E)
Previously known as Mole Viper
or Burrowing Adder (E)
Suidelike sypikslang (A)

DANGEROUS

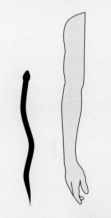

average 40 cm   maximum 70 cm

Length: Adults average 30–40 cm but may grow to 70 cm.

Scale count: Midbody scales are in 21–23 rows (rarely 19 or 25), with 196–260 ventrals and 18–28 single subcaudals. The anal shield is entire. There are 5 upper labials with the 3rd and 4th (sometimes only the 4th) entering the eye, and 5 or 6 lower labials, as well as 1 preocular and 1 postocular (sometimes 2). Temporals are 1 + 2 or 2 + 2.

Colour: Above, uniform purple-brown to black, except before sloughing, when it may have a bluish appearance. Below, creamy white or dark brown to black, with or without dusky or light mottling.

Preferred habitat: Found in a wide variety of habitats including fynbos, the Namib Desert, karoo scrub, grassland, arid savanna, moist savanna and lowland forest.

A burrowing species usually found in deserted termite mounds, under rotting logs or beneath sun-warmed rocks.

An insignificant looking snake with a potent venom that causes extreme pain.

Habits: Previously called the Mole Viper or Burrowing Adder, this nocturnal snake usually emerges on warm, wet summer evenings, especially after heavy rains. Individuals are often exposed during excavations. An irascible snake that bites readily. The fangs are positioned horizontally, facing towards the back of the upper jaw, and are not movable as are adder fangs. This makes it impossible for this snake to be held in the usual way. If gripped behind the head, it merely twists its head sideways to pierce a finger. It may also press the sharp tip of its tail against a person holding it, creating the impression that it is biting. To inject venom into its prey, it protrudes a fang, then moves its head over its prey while stabbing downwards.

Similar species: Often confused with a variety of other inconspicuous species including the purple-glossed snakes (*Amblyodipsas* spp.), the Natal Black Snake (*Macrelaps microlepidotus*) and the harmless wolf snakes (*Lycophidion* spp.).

Enemies: Other snakes.

Food and feeding: Preys upon a variety of burrowing reptiles, frogs and small rodents, most of which are taken while in their burrows.

Reproduction: Oviparous, laying 3–7 eggs (27–36 x 10–12 mm) in midsummer. The young measure 15 cm.

Danger to man: No fatalities have been recorded. However, this snake delivers an extremely painful bite and envenomation has led to the loss of fingers. Most victims are snake handlers. Bites are quite common in KwaZulu-Natal and Mpumalanga Province. People often incorrectly assume that because a snake is small and somewhat drab in colour, it is harmless. Be very careful.

Venom: Bite victims experience intense local pain, swelling and often necrosis. In the early

LOOK OUT FOR

- ◼ A fairly inconspicuous snake with small eyes.
- ◼ Tail ends in a spine.
- ◼ Active on warm wet nights.
- ◼ Often found under rocks or logs.
- ◼ Usually nocturnal.
- ◼ Uniform purple-brown to black in colour.
- ◼ Neck arches just behind the head so that the head points downwards at an angle.

stages mild neurotoxic symptoms such as nausea and a dry throat may be present. Antivenom is not effective against the venom of this snake and should therefore not be administered.

First-aid procedure: If you are certain that a Southern Stiletto Snake was responsible for the bite, get the victim to a doctor or hospital where the bite must be treated symptomatically. Administer painkillers. Otherwise see first-aid treatment on page 42. This snake cannot be held safely and you will, in all likelihood, get bitten if you attempt to hold one.

Because of its fang position, the Southern Stiletto Snake cannot be handled safely.

This snake is often mistaken for a harmless Mole Snake, resulting in many painful bites, sometimes with the loss of a finger.

Beaked Stiletto Snake
Atractaspis duerdeni

OTHER NAMES
Duerden's Stiletto Snake (E)
Duerden's or Beaked Burrowing Asp (E)
Side-stabbing Snake (E)
Haakneussypikslang (A)

Length: Adults average 30–40 cm with a maximum length of 55 cm.

Scale count: Midbody scales are in 23–25 rows, with 193–225 ventrals and 19–27 single subcaudals. The anal shield is entire. There are 5 or 6 upper labials, the 3rd and 4th entering the eye, and 6 (sometimes 5 or 7) lower labials, as well as 1 preocular and 1 or 2 post-oculars. Temporals are variable.

Colour: Above, uniform grey to black. The belly is uniform white, and this colour extends onto the flanks.

Preferred habitat: Isolated populations are thought to occur in central Namibia and south-eastern Botswana in karoo scrub and arid savanna.

Habits: A nocturnal snake known largely from individuals found on roads at night. Specimens from Namibia have been found in the Eastern National Water Carrier Canal. This species appears to be less aggressive than the Southern Bibron's Stiletto Snake (*Atractaspis bibronii*). It is known to jerk into a coil when agitated and will conceal its head under the coils.

Similar species: Can be confused with a variety of other inconspicuous species.

Enemies: Other snakes.

Food and feeding: Lizards, especially lacertids, and snakes.

average 40 cm maximum 55 cm

Wulf Haacke

A secretive, nocturnal snake that may be found crossing roads, especially after rain.

Reproduction: Unknown but probably egg-laying like other snakes in the genus.

Danger to man: Unknown, but not thought to be extremely dangerous. Probably inflicts a very painful bite, similar to that of the Southern Bibron's Stiletto Snake. These snakes look harmless, but must never be handled.

Venom: Little is known of this snake's venom but if it is similar to the venom of the Southern Bibron's Stiletto Snake, it will cause intense local pain, swelling and, in some instances, necrosis.

First-aid procedures: If you are certain that a Beaked Stiletto Snake was responsible for the bite, get the victim to a doctor or hospital, where the bite must be treated symptomatically. Administer painkillers. Otherwise see first-aid treatment on page 42.

This snake cannot be held safely and you will, in all likelihood, get bitten if you attempt to hold one.

see first-aid treatment on page 42.

LOOK OUT FOR

- Short, stocky, inconspicuous snake with small eyes.
- Tail ends in a terminal spine.
- Neck arches just behind the head so that the head points downwards at an angle.

The Southern Stiletto Snake (above) is very similar to the Beaked Stiletto Snake.

The Southern Stiletto Snake on the left and the Beaked Stiletto Snake on the right look harmless, but must never be handled.

This snake is known to jerk into a coil when agitated and will conceal its head under the coils.

Eastern Congo Stiletto Snake

Atractaspis congica

OTHER NAMES
Eastern Congo Burrowing Asp (E)
Side-stabbing Snake (E)
Oos-Kongolese sypikslang (A)

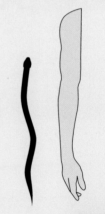

average 45 cm   maximum 55 cm

Length: Adults average 30–45 cm with a maximum length of 55 cm.
Scale count: Midbody scales in 19–21 rows, with 193–225 ventrals and 18–25 paired subcaudals. The anal shield may be entire or divided. There are 5 upper labials with the 3rd and 4th entering the eye, 5 lower labials, 1 preocular and 1 postocular. Temporals are 1 + 2.
Colour: Uniform glossy purple-brown to black above and below.
Preferred habitat: Found in moist savanna in the Caprivi strip and elsewhere further north.
Habits: Virtually nothing is known of this snake. Its venom has not been studied and should be regarded as dangerous to man. Members of this genus readily bite if handled.
Similar species: Can be confused with a number of other inconspicuous species.
Enemies: Other snakes.
Food and feeding: Unknown, but probably preys on lizards and other snakes.
Reproduction: Oviparous, laying 3–6 elongate eggs (62 x 12 mm).
Danger to man: Unknown but not thought to be extremely dangerous. Probably inflicts a very painful bite, similar to that of the Southern Stiletto Snake.
Subspecies: Only 1 of 3 subspecies, the Eastern Congo Stiletto Snake (*Atractaspis congica orientalis*), is found within our range.
Venom: Little is known of this snake's venom but if it is similar to the venom of the Southern Stiletto Snake, it will cause intense local pain, swelling and, in some instances, necrosis.
First-aid procedures: If you are certain that an Eastern Congo Stiletto Snake was responsible for the bite, get the victim to a doctor or hospital where the bite must be treated symptomatically. Administer painkillers. Otherwise see first-aid treatment on page 42. This snake cannot be held safely and you will, in all likelihood, get bitten if you hold one.

Moist savanna habitats are preferred by the Eastern Congo Stiletto Snake.

Adrian Bailey

LOOK OUT FOR

- Short, stocky, inconspicuous snake with small eyes.
- Tail ends in a terminal spine.
- Neck arches just behind the head so that the head points downwards at an angle.

MILDLY VENOMOUS

Natal Black Snake

Macrelaps microlepidotus

OTHER NAMES
Natalse swartslang (A)

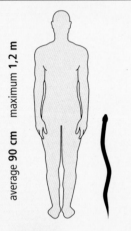

maximum 1,2 m

average 90 cm

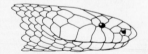

Length: Adults average 60–90 cm and attain a maximum length of nearly 1,2 m.

Scale count: Smooth midbody scales in 25–27 rows (rarely 23), but faintly keeled towards the anus, with 158–172 ventrals and 35–50 single subcaudals. The anal shield is entire. There are 7 upper labials with the 3rd and 4th entering the eye, and 8 lower labials. No preoculars and 1 postocular. Temporals are 1 + 2 or 0 + 1 + 1.

Colour: Uniform inky black to jet black above and below. Becomes dull silvery grey before sloughing.

Preferred habitat: Damp localities in lowland forest and along streams in coastal bush. Also found in urban gardens.

Habits: Usually found beneath rotting logs or under stones, in leaf litter, animal burrows and in stormwater drains. It may be seen moving about on warm overcast days, or it may surface on warm, damp nights. It is a docile snake that is very reluctant to bite. The Natal Black Snake is a good swimmer and has been observed swimming in forest streams. It burrows through leaf litter in search of food.

Similar species: May be confused with the Southern Stiletto Snake (*Atractaspis bibronii*) and the purple-glossed snakes (*Amblyodipsas* spp.).

A slow-moving snake that is reluctant to bite.

Enemies: Other snakes.

Food and feeding: Feeds on frogs, especially rain frogs (*Breviceps* spp.), legless lizards, snakes and small rodents. It grabs a prey item, wraps a few coils around it and then chews to enable the venom to penetrate.

Reproduction: Oviparous, laying 3–10 eggs (38–56 x 23–31 mm) in summer. The young measure 20–29 cm.

Danger to man: The venom of this snake has not been well studied. Bites are very rare.

Venom: This snake does not often feature in snakebite accidents but one recorded bite did result in the loss of consciousness for

LOOK OUT FOR
■ Stout snake with small blunt head and minute eyes.
■ Eyes have round pupils.
■ Usually uniform black to jet black above and below.
■ Movement slow and deliberate.

approximately 30 minutes. Antivenom is not required as it has no effect in neutralizing the venom of this snake.

First-aid procedures: See first-aid treatment on page 42.

This snake may be found beneath rotting logs and in leaf litter, where it searches for food.

*This burrowing snake seldom comes to the surface except
on hot, damp nights and on hot, overcast days.*

Rufous Beaked Snake
Rhamphiophis rostratus

OTHER NAMES
Haakneusslang (A)

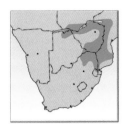

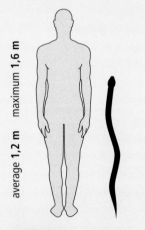

average 1,2 m   maximum 1,6 m

Length: Adults average 1–1,2 m, reaching a maximum length of 1,6 m.
Scale count: Midbody scales are in 17–19 rows, with 148–194 ventrals and 87–118 pairs of subcaudals. The anal shield is divided. There are 7–9 upper labials with the 5th (sometimes the 4th or 4th and 5th) entering the eye, and 10–11 (sometimes 12) lower labials, as well as 3 (sometimes 2 or 4) preoculars and 2 (sometimes 3 or 4) postoculars. Temporals are variable, 2 + 3 or 3 + 3.
Colour: Above, yellowish brown to pale red-brown, with each scale dark-edged. The head has a dark streak on either side, extending from the nostril and running across each eye. The underside is usually creamy white, sometimes edged with reddish brown.
Preferred habitat: Bushveld or thorny sandveld areas in moist savanna.
Habits: A slow-moving, diurnal snake that spends much of its time in rodent burrows and termite mounds searching for food. It has the peculiar habit of jerking its elevated head from side to side. This snake may hiss, but seldom attempts to bite.
Similar species: The female Boomslang (*Dispholidus typus*) and the Olive Whip Snake (*Psammophis mossambicus*).
Enemies: Predatory birds and other snakes.
Food and feeding: Rodents, lizards, small snakes, frogs and small birds. Juveniles also feed on insects.
Reproduction: Oviparous, laying 7–18 eggs (34–42 x 22–24 mm) in midsummer. The young measure 30 cm.
Danger to man: No danger to man.
Venom: Has virtually no effect on man.

LOOK OUT FOR

■ Has a prominent hooked snout.
■ Large eyes with round pupils.
■ The head has a prominent dark stripe on either side.

The Rufous Beaked Snake may be confused with the Boomslang, but has a dark streak running through each eye.

Dwarf Beaked Snake
Dipsina multimaculata

OTHER NAMES
Dwerghaakneusslang (A)

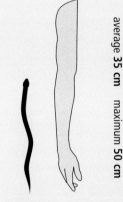

average 35 cm   maximum 50 cm

MILDLY VENOMOUS

Length: Adults average 30–35 cm, but may reach 50 cm.
Scale count: Midbody scales are in 17 rows, with 144–170 ventrals and 28–45 subcaudals, usually paired but sometimes single. The anal shield is divided. There are 8 upper labials (sometimes 7 or 9) with the 4th and 5th entering the eye but this is variable, and 10 (sometimes 9 or 11) lower labials, as well as 1 preocular (sometimes 2 or 3) and 2 or 3 (sometimes 4 or 5) postoculars. Temporals are variable, 2 + 3.
Colour: Variable, from pale buff to ash grey or light greyish brown to pinkish brown above with darker blotches or spots that may be pale-centred and sometimes fuse to form distinct crossbars. The neck has a dark V-shaped marking, and a similar coloured stripe extends from the back of the eye to the angle of the jaw on either side of the head. The belly is pinkish-cream to white with dark spots.
Preferred habitat: Found in rocky, sandy areas in the Namib Desert, karoo scrub and arid savanna.
Habits: A small diurnal snake that inhabits dry stony and sandy habitats where it hides under stones or in loose sand under shrubs and bushes. From there it waits to ambush small lizards. The Dwarf Beaked Snake is very docile but may assume a coiled position when threatened, mimicking the Horned Adder (*Bitis caudalis*).
Similar species: May be confused with the Horned Adder, Rhombic Egg-eater (*Dasypeltis scabra*), a young Mole Snake (*Pseudaspis cana*) and the rare Fisk's House Snake (*Lamprophis fiskii*).
Enemies: Snakes, predatory birds and small mammalian carnivores.
Food and feeding: Mainly lizards.
Reproduction: Oviparous, laying 2–4 eggs (22–28 x 8–9 mm) in midsummer. A 37,3 cm specimen from Lekuru Pan in Botswana contained 4 eggs. The young measure 11–13 cm.
Danger to man: No danger to man.
Venom: A mild venom that is virtually harmless to man.

This mildly venomous snake may coil up and mimic the Horned Adder.

LOOK OUT FOR

■ A small, slender snake with a distinct head.
■ Has a prominent hooked snout.
■ Has large eyes with round pupils.
■ May assume a coiled position, mimicking the Horned Adder.

MILDLY VENOMOUS

Lined Olympic Snake
Dromophis lineatus

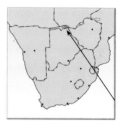

OTHER NAMES
Gestreepte moerasslang (A)

maximum 1 m

average 80 cm

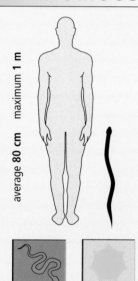

Length: Adults average 70–80 cm with a maximum length of just over 1 m.

Scale count: Midbody scales are in 15–17 rows, with 138–159 ventrals and 83–105 paired subcaudals. The anal shield is divided. There are 8 upper labials, the 4th and 5th entering the eye, and 9 lower labials, as well as 1 preocular and 2 (sometimes 1 or 3) postoculars. Temporals are variable, 1 + 1 or 1 + 2.

Colour: Above, olive with black-edged scales. There are 3 distinct greenish yellow stripes over the back and tail. The belly is greenish yellow to pale green with black dots or bars on the outer edges of the ventral scales.

Preferred habitat: Inhabits waterside vegetation in extreme western Zimbabwe, the Caprivi Strip and elsewhere further northwards.

Habits: An active diurnal snake that forages for food. Although sometimes found far from water, it appears to be largely aquatic, inhabiting swamps and marshland. It is well camouflaged and rather docile when first captured, seldom attempting to bite. Many adults have truncated tails, indicating high rates of predation, probably by birds.

Similar species: May be confused with some of the whip, grass and sand snakes of the genus *Psammophis*.

Enemies: Other snakes and predatory birds.

Food and feeding: Largely frogs but small mammals are also taken. A captive specimen has been seen eating another snake.

Reproduction: Oviparous, laying 6–9 eggs (23–27 mm x 12–18 mm).

Danger to man: None.

Venom: The venom of this snake is thought to have very little effect on man.

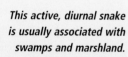

This active, diurnal snake is usually associated with swamps and marshland.

John Visser

LOOK OUT FOR

■ Has medium-sized eyes with round pupils.
■ Is active during the day.
■ Usually found very close to water.
■ Has 3 greenish yellow stripes down the back and tail.

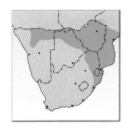

Olive Whip Snake

Psammophis mossambicus

OTHER NAMES
Olive Grass Snake (E)
Olyfsweepslang (A)

MILDLY VENOMOUS

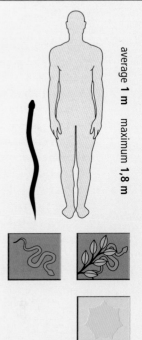

average 1 m   maximum 1,8 m

Length: Adults average 1 m, but may reach nearly 1,8 m.

Scale count: Midbody scales are in 17 rows, with 150–180 ventrals and 82–121 paired subcaudals. The anal shield is divided. There are 8 (sometimes 6, 7 or 9) upper labials with the 4th and 5th entering the eye, though this varies, and 10 (sometimes 9 or 11) lower labials, as well as 1 preocular and 2 postoculars. Temporals are 1 + 3 or 2 + 3.

Colour: Above, uniform olive brown or with black-edged scales on the back that may form longitudinal dark lines, and often with scattered black scales on the neck and chin. The lips are pale with finely black-edged reddish brown spots or blotches. The underside is white to yellowish, sometimes with darker spots and mottling.

Preferred habitat: An inhabitant of moist savanna and lowland forest. Often found in the vicinity of water where it is fond of foraging in marshes.

Habits: A robust, active and alert diurnal snake that hastens for cover when disturbed. It will remain hidden until flushed out. Like the Black Mamba (*Dendroaspis polylepis*), it lifts the front third of its body well off the ground. This snake has a very nervous disposition and retreats before one can approach closely.

Although mainly a ground-dwelling snake, the Olive Whip Snake may climb onto shrubs and bushes to bask. Many individuals have truncated tails – the result of injuries sustained during encounters with predators.

An alert, diurnal snake that actively hunts its prey.

Similar species: May be mistaken for the Black Mamba, the Rufous Beaked Snake (*Rhamphiophis rostratus*), the Short-snouted Whip Snake (*Psammophis brevirostris*) and the Boomslang (*Dispholidus typus*).

Enemies: Other snakes, predatory birds and mammalian carnivores such as mongooses. This fast-moving snake is often killed by vehicles when crossing roads.

Food and feeding: Feeds on lizards, small mammals, frogs and snakes, including the Black Mamba and the Puff Adder (*Bitis arietans*). Small birds are also taken.

Reproduction: Oviparous, laying 10–30 eggs (28–40 x 10–20 mm) in midsummer. The young average 27–30 cm.

Danger to man: This snake is not thought to pose great danger to humans, although large specimens can deliver a painful bite.

> ## LOOK OUT FOR
> - A fairly large, robust snake.
> - Active during the day.
> - Bites readily.
> - Eye has a round pupil.
> - Has dark speckling on the upper lip.
> - Longitudinal stripes down the body.

Venom: A mild venom that may cause local pain, swelling and occasionally nausea.

First-aid procedures: If you are certain that an Olive Whip Snake was responsible for the bite, get the victim to a doctor or hospital where the bite must be treated symptomatically. Painkillers may be required. Otherwise see first-aid treatment on page 42.

This is one of the largest whip snakes, reaching nearly 1,8 m in length.

The Olive Whip Snake is quick to retreat, but bites readily if handled. Its venom is mild and is not considered dangerous to man.

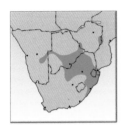

Short-snouted Whip Snake

Psammophis brevirostris

OTHER NAMES
Short-snouted Grass Snake (E)
Kortsnoetsweepslang (A)

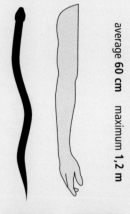

average 60 cm   maximum 1,2 m

Length: Adults average 60 cm with a maximum length of about 1,2 m.

Scale count: Midbody scales are in 17 rows, with 146–167 ventrals and 79–108 paired subcaudals. The anal shield is divided. There are 8 (sometimes 7 or 9) upper labials, the 4th and 5th entering the eye, though this varies, and 10 (sometimes 9 or 11) lower labials, as well as 1 preocular and 2 postoculars. Temporals are 1 + 3 or 2 + 3.

Colour: Above, olive brown with a pale dashed median line flanked on either side by up to 3 rows of black-edged scales, which may form narrow black lines. A narrow lighter line borders these lines dorso-laterally on each side. The sides are usually light to red-brown. Below, white or yellow, sometimes with a line of black spots at each side.

Preferred habitat: Grassland, moist savanna and lowland forest in the east, and karoo scrub and Namib Desert in the west.

Habits: An alert, fast-moving snake that dashes for cover when disturbed and will remain motionless until flushed out. May also venture into low shrubs to bask. Like the Olive Whip Snake (*Psammophis mossambicus*), it is quick to bite if handled.

Similar species: Resembles other whip, grass and sand snakes (*Psammophis* spp.) and may be mistaken for a small Black Mamba (*Dendroaspis polylepis*) or a female Boomslang (*Dispholidus typus*).

Enemies: Other snakes, birds of prey and small mammalian carnivores.

Food and feeding: Snakes, lizards, rodents and small birds.

Reproduction: Oviparous, laying 4–15 eggs (23–40 x 10–20 mm) in summer. The young measure 19–27 cm. Females may produce 2 clutches of eggs in a season.

Danger to man: No danger to man.

Venom: Not thought to have any harmful effect on humans.

This fast-moving snake is often seen crossing tarred roads.

LOOK OUT FOR

- An active, alert snake.
- Has stripes down the body.
- Bites readily if handled.
- Has fairly large eyes with round pupils.
- Dashes for the closest cover when disturbed.

Richard Boycott

MILDLY VENOMOUS

maximum 1,4 m

average 80 cm

When disturbed, the Leopard Whip Snake dashes for cover, where it freezes to escape detection.

Leopard Whip Snake
Psammophis leopardinus

OTHER NAMES
Leopard Grass Snake (E)
Luiperdsweepslang (A)

Length: Adults average 80 cm with a maximum length of about 1,4 m.
Scale count: Midbody scales are in 17 rows, with 149–174 ventrals and 79–108 paired subcaudals. The anal shield is divided. There are 8 upper labials, the 4th and 5th entering the eye, and 10 (rarely 8, 9 or 11) lower labials, as well as 1 preocular and 2 postoculars. Temporals are 2 + 2 + 3, but variable.
Colour: A light red-brown, grey-brown or olive above, with a lighter black-edged median stripe extending the length of the body. Median line flanked on either side by up to 3 rows of black-edged scales, which may form narrow black lines. A narrow lighter line borders these lines dorsolaterally on each side. Some specimens lack the typical patterning and may be uniform grey. The chin and throat may have blotches on each scale and a series of stripes forms an intricate pattern on the head.
Preferred habitat: Namib Desert to karoo scrub, below an altitude of 1500 m.
Habits: An alert, fast-moving snake that is difficult to catch owing to its speed. It is quick to dash for cover when disturbed and will remain motionless until flushed out. Although primarily a ground-dweller, it often ventures into low shrubs to bask. Like the Olive Whip Snake (*Psammophis mossambicus*), it is quick to bite if handled.
Similar species: Resembles other whip, grass and sand snakes (*Psammophis* spp.).
Enemies: Other snakes, birds of prey and small mammalian carnivores.
Food and feeding: Snakes, lizards, rodents and small birds.
Reproduction: Oviparous.
Danger to man: No danger to man.
Venom: Not thought to have any harmful effect on humans.

LOOK OUT FOR

- An active, alert snake.
- Has stripes down the body.
- Bites readily if handled.
- Has fairly large eyes with round pupils.
- Dashes for the closest cover when disturbed.

Western Whip Snake

Psammophis trigrammus

OTHER NAMES
Western Sand Snake (E)
Westelike sweepslang (A)

MILDLY VENOMOUS

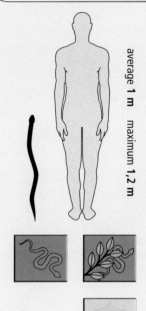

average 1 m   maximum 1,2 m

An active and alert snake that chases lizards during the day.

Length: Adults average 90 cm to 1 m but may reach 1,2 m.

Scale count: Midbody scales are in 17 rows, with 182–201 ventrals and 132–156 paired subcaudals. The anal shield is divided. There are 9 (sometimes 8 or 10) upper labials, the 5th and 6th entering the eye, though this may vary, and 10–11 lower labials, as well as 2 (some-times 1) preoculars and 2 postoculars. Temporals variable, but are usually 2 + 2 + 3.

Colour: Above, pale olive to greyish brown becoming reddish to yel-lowish towards the rear. There may be black-edged scales along the back that form a dorsal stripe, which is often flanked by a yellowish to creamy white stripe. The belly is white to creamy white or yellow-ish white with a well-defined light grey to olive median band, while the chin and throat are white.

Preferred habitat: Arid scrub in the Namib Desert, karoo scrub, arid savanna and moist savanna to the north.

Habits: A slim snake that moves very quickly and chases after lizards during the day. It is well camouflaged in its arid surroundings and will seek refuge in a shrub if disturbed.

Similar species: May be confused with other grass, whip and sand snakes (*Psammophis* spp.).

Enemies: Snakes and birds of prey.

Food and feeding: Mainly lizards, especially skinks and lacertids.

Reproduction: Oviparous, the number of eggs laid is not known.

Danger to man: None.

Venom: The venom of this snake is mild and is not considered dangerous to man.

LOOK OUT FOR

- A slender snake.
- Very fast moving and will chase lizards in the heat of the day.
- Its body is striped from the back of the head to the tail.
- White to creamy white or yellowish white belly.

Wulf Haacke

MILDLY VENOMOUS

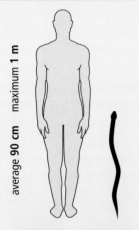

maximum 1 m

average 90 cm

Karoo Whip Snake

Psammophis notostictus

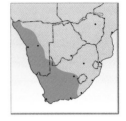

OTHER NAMES
Karoo Sand Snake (E)
Karoo-sweepslang (A)

Length: Adults average 75–90 cm with a maximum length of just over 1 m.

Scale count: Midbody scales are in 17 rows, with 155–183 ventrals and 76–107 paired subcaudals. The anal shield is usually entire, but might be divided. There are 8 (sometimes 7 or 9) upper labials, the 4th and 5th (sometimes the 3rd and 4th) entering the eye, and 9–12 lower labials (usually 10). There are 2 (sometimes 1) preoculars and 2 (sometimes 3) postoculars. Temporals are variable, usually 2 + 2 + 3.

Colour: Above, light to olive grey, sandy to reddish or dark brown with darker flanks. The snake may have a pale stripe made up of spots along the vertebrae, and pale stripes on the sides. The centre of the belly is off-white to yellowish with greyish tinges and with white and grey stripes on the sides.

Preferred habitat: Found in fynbos, grassland, arid savanna, karoo scrub and the Namib Desert.

Habits: An alert and quick-moving snake that chases after lizards in the heat of the day. It is the most abundant snake in many parts of the Karoo and prefers hard, stony ground. Specimens are often found in deserted termite mounds or under rocks. Many of these snakes are killed by vehicles while crossing roads.

Similar species: Easily confused with other grass, whip and sand snakes (*Psammophis* spp.).

Enemies: Snakes and birds of prey.

Food and feeding: Mainly lizards, including skinks, lacertids, agamids and geckos. Mice and other small rodents are also taken.

Reproduction: Oviparous. A gravid female collected in October (mid-spring) contained 3 eggs (28 x 6 mm). Between 3 and 8 eggs are laid in summer.

Danger to man: None.

Venom: The venom of this snake is thought to have no effect on man.

The venom of the Karoo Whip Snake is of no consequence to man.

Randall D Babb

LOOK OUT FOR

- Very slender snake.
- Has large eyes with round pupils.
- Quick-moving and active during the day.

Cape Whip Snake
Psammophis leightoni

OTHER NAMES
Cape Sand Snake (E)
Kaapse sweepslang (A)

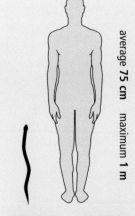

MILDLY VENOMOUS

average 75 cm   maximum 1 m

Length: Adults average about 75 cm with a maximum length of just over 1 m.

Scale count: Midbody scales are in 17 rows, with 155–169 ventrals and 92–112 paired subcaudals. The anal shield is divided. There are 8 upper labials, the 4th and 5th entering the eye, and 10 (sometimes 9) lower labials, as well as 1 preocular and 2 postoculars. Temporals are 2 + 2 + 3.

Colour: Above, dark brown with 2 yellow stripes and barring on the head. A series of fine yellow spots form a vertebral line with a narrow yellow dorsolateral line on either side. The belly has a mottled grey median band. There is a series of bars or spots on the top of the head.

Preferred habitat: This snake is found in West Coast renosterveld and the sand-plain fynbos of the western Cape.

Habits: An alert, diurnal snake that actively hunts its prey. When disturbed it will disappear into the closest bush or shrub where it will freeze, relying on its camouflage to escape detection.

Similar species: Easily confused with other grass, whip and sand snakes (*Psammophis* spp.).

Enemies: Other snakes and birds of prey. Habitat destruction poses a real threat to the Cape Whip Snake.

Food and feeding: Ground-living lizards, especially lacertids and skinks. Small rodents and snakes are also taken.

Reproduction: Oviparous. A gravid female collected in October (mid-spring) contained 8 well-developed eggs, each measuring 25 x 9 mm. The young measure 22–24 cm.

Danger to man: None.

Venom: Not thought to have any effect on man.

LOOK OUT FOR

- Very slender snake.
- Has large eyes with round pupils.
- Active during the day.

The Cape Whip Snake is threatened by habitat destruction.

Wulf Haacke

MILDLY VENOMOUS

maximum 1,1 m

average 75 cm

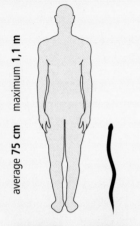

Kalahari Sand Snake
Psammophis trinasalis

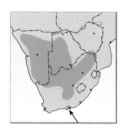

OTHER NAMES
Kalaharisandslang (A)

Length: Adults average about 75 cm with a maximum length of just over 1,1 m.

Scale count: Midbody scales are in 17 rows, with 150–175 ventrals and 84–128 paired subcaudals. The anal shield is divided. There are 8 upper labials (rarely 7 or 9), the 4th and 5th entering the eye, and 10 (sometimes 9 or 11) lower labials, as well as 1 preocular (rarely 2) and 2 postoculars. Temporals are 2 + 2 + 3.

Colour: Dark brown to light grey-brown above, with yellow stripes and barring on the head. A series of fine yellow spots form a vertebral line with a narrow yellow dorsolateral line on either side. The flanks are lighter than the dorsal parts. The belly has a mottled grey median band.

Preferred habitat: Mainly found in Kalahari thornveld, but may also occur in savanna and grassland.

Habits: An alert diurnal snake that actively hunts its prey. In the morning, will often bask near a favourite retreat. When disturbed, it will disappear into the retreat or into the closest bush, where it will freeze, relying on its camouflage to escape detection.

Similar species: Easily confused with other grass, whip and sand snakes (*Psammophis* spp.).

Enemies: Other snakes and birds of prey.

Food and feeding: Ground-living lizards, especially lacertids and skinks. Small rodents and snakes are also taken.

Reproduction: Oviparous. A female from the Free State contained 8 eggs, while another contained only 1.

Danger to man: None.

Venom: The venom of this snake is not thought to have any effect on man.

LOOK OUT FOR

- A very slender snake.
- Has large eyes with round pupils.
- Active during the day.

The Kalahari Sand Snake feeds on lizards and small rodents.

Namib Sand Snake
Psammophis namibensis

OTHER NAMES
Namibsandslang (A)

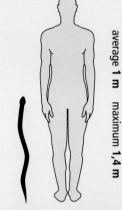

average 1 m   maximum 1,4 m

Length: Adults average 75 cm to 1 m, with a maximum length of nearly 1,4 m.

Scale count: Midbody scales are in 17 rows, with 167–188 ventrals and 90–116 paired subcaudals. The anal shield is divided. There are 8 upper labials, the 4th and 5th entering the eye, and 10 (sometimes 9 or 11) lower labials, as well as 1 preocular and 2 postoculars. Temporals are 2 + 2 + 3.

Colour: Above, dark brown with yellow stripes and barring on the head. A series of fine yellow spots form a vertebral line with a narrow yellow dorsolateral line on either side. The belly has a mottled grey median band. The head has a series of stripes and spots. In the northern parts of its range, this species has a black and yellow speckled pattern.

Preferred habitat: Namib Desert and karoo vegetation, usually below an altitude of 1 500 m.

Habits: An alert diurnal snake that actively hunts its prey. Often lifts the first quarter of its body into the air to gain a better view of its surroundings. When disturbed, it will disappear into the closest bush or shrub, where it will freeze, relying on its camouflage to escape detection.

Similar species: Easily confused with other grass, whip and sand snakes (*Psammophis* spp.).

Enemies: Birds of prey and small mammalian carnivores.

Food and feeding: Ground-living lizards, especially lacertids (including *Meroles anchietae*) and skinks. Small rodents and snakes are also taken.

Reproduction: Oviparous. Details are unknown.

Danger to man: None.

Venom: The venom of this snake is not thought to have any effect on man.

The Namib Sand Snake often lifts the front quarter of its body off the ground for a better view.

LOOK OUT FOR

- A very slender snake.
- Has large eyes with round pupils.
- Active during the day.
- Lifts anterior part of body when alert.

Richard Boycott

MILDLY VENOMOUS

average 90 cm   maximum 1,2 m

This rare, fast-moving snake seldom attempts to bite, even when handled for the first time.

Jalla's Sand Snake
Psammophis jallae

OTHER NAMES
Jalla se sandslang (A)

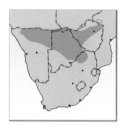

Length: Adults average 80–90 cm but may reach 1,2 m.
Scale count: Midbody scales are in 15 rows, with 154–175 ventrals and 84–112 paired subcaudals. The anal shield is divided. There are 7 (sometimes 6 or 8) upper labials with the 3rd and 4th entering the eye, though this may vary, and 9 (sometimes 8 or 10) lower labials, as well as 1 preocular and 2 postoculars. Temporals are 2 + 2 or 2 + 3.
Colour: Above, light grey to grey-brown or olive brown with a broad black-edged band (it may have a vertebral row of paler spots) bordered by a narrow off-white to yellow streak on either side. The flanks are reddish brown while the upper lip is white to creamy yellow. The belly has a broad yellow to olive yellow central stripe, with or without darker edging. The outer edges of the ventrals are white to cream.
Preferred habitat: Arid savanna, moist savanna, open woodlands and grasslands at an altitude of between 750 and 1 500 m.
Habits: A rare, fast-moving diurnal snake that inhabits open sandy savanna or grassland areas. It is shy and quick to seek refuge in shrubs or in holes in the ground. Like most other sand snakes, this snake lifts its head well off the ground, probably to gain a better vantage. It is not inclined to bite, even when captured.
Similar species: May be confused with other grass snakes, whip snakes and sand snakes (*Psammophis* spp.).
Enemies: Other snakes and birds of prey.
Food and feeding: Lizards, especially skinks, lacertids and agamids.
Reproduction: Oviparous. The number of eggs laid is not known.
Danger to man: None.
Venom: The venom of this snake is thought to have very little effect on man.

Niels Jacobsen

LOOK OUT FOR

- A very slender snake.
- Has large eyes with round pupils.
- Active during the day.
- Is striped from head to tail.
- Fast-moving.

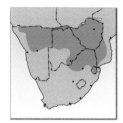

Western Stripe-bellied Sand Snake

Psammophis subtaeniatus

OTHER NAMES
Westelike gestreepte sandslang (A)
Umhlwazi (X)

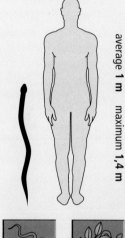

MILDLY VENOMOUS

average 1 m   maximum 1,4 m

Length: Adults average 1 m, with a maximum length of nearly 1,4 m.
Scale count: Midbody scales are in 17 rows, with 155–181 ventrals and 106–132 paired subcaudals. The anal shield is divided. There are 9 (sometimes 8 or 10) upper labials, the 4th, 5th and 6th entering the eye, though this may vary, and 10 (sometimes 9 or 11) lower labials, as well as 1 preocular (sometimes 2) and 2 postoculars. Temporals are 2 + 2 + 3, but this is variable.
Colour: Above, greyish brown to olive grey or dark brown with a broad black-edged stripe down the back. This is bordered by a narrow cream to yellow stripe on either side, then by a dark lateral stripe with a black line on the lower edge. The head has pale dark-edged markings that form transverse bars. The middle of the belly is bright lemon yellow, bordered on either side by a black hairline; the outer portions of the belly on either side of the yellow stripe are pure white.
Preferred habitat: Arid savanna, especially in mopane and acacia veld. Very common in the Zambezi and Limpopo valleys.
Habits: This is probably southern Africa's fastest snake. It is common throughout most of its range. Like many of the other sand snakes, it is active during the day, often during the hottest hours. This snake moves off rapidly when disturbed, only to freeze when it gets into

The Western Stripe-bellied Sand Snake has a broad, yellow band right down the centre of the belly.

the nearest bush or shrub. It relies on excellent camouflage to escape detection. Though ground-dwelling, it may bask or seek food in shrubs and low bushes.

Similar species: Easily confused with the other sand snakes, whip snakes and grass snakes (*Psammophis* spp.) and the equally harmless Striped Skaapsteker (*Psammophylax tritaeniatus*).

Enemies: Other snakes and predatory birds.

Food and feeding: Prefers lizards but also eats frogs, rodents and small birds.

Reproduction: Oviparous, laying 4–10 eggs in summer (32 x 12 mm). The young are about 20 cm long.

LOOK OUT FOR

- A long, slender snake.
- A pointed head with large eyes and round pupils.
- Usually striped from head to tail.
- Very fast-moving snake.
- Active during the day.
- A lemon-yellow belly.

Danger to man: No danger to man.

Venom: The venom of this snake is not thought to have any harmful effect on humans.

Warren Schmidt

Feeds largely on lizards, but also takes rodents and small birds.

The Western Stripe-bellied Sand Snake is common where it occurs, often seeking streams or still water to drink.

Eastern Stripe-bellied Sand Snake

Psammophis orientalis

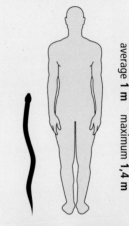

MILDLY VENOMOUS

OTHER NAMES
Oostelike gestreepte sandslang (A)

Length: Adults average 1 m, with a maximum length of nearly 1,4 m.
Scale count: Midbody scales are in 17 rows, with 146–170 ventrals and 91–118 paired subcaudals. The anal shield is divided. There are 8 (sometimes 7 or 9) upper labials, the 4th and 5th entering the eye, and 10 (sometimes 9 or 11) lower labials, as well as 1 preocular (sometimes 2) and 2 postoculars. Temporals are 2 + 2 + 3, but variable.
Colour: Above, greyish brown to olive grey or dark brown with a broad black-edged stripe down the back. This is bordered by a narrow cream to yellow stripe on either side, then by a dark lateral stripe with a black line on the lower edge. The head has pale, dark-edged markings that form transverse bars. The head and body markings are not as vivid as in the Western Stripe-bellied Sand Snake (*Psammophis subtaeniatus*). The middle of the belly is bright lemon yellow, bordered on either side by a black hairline. The outer portions of the belly on either side of the yellow stripe are pure white.
Preferred habitat: Lowland forest and moist savanna.
Habits: Like many of the other sand snakes and whip snakes, it is diurnal, and may be active during the hottest hours. The Eastern Stripe-bellied Sand Snake is often found near water.

This snake moves off rapidly when disturbed, only to freeze when it gets into the nearest bush or shrub. There it relies on its excellent

average 1 m   maximum 1,4 m

Bill Branch

This active and alert diurnal snake is extremely well camouflaged in shrubs.

The Eastern Stripe-bellied Sand Snake prefers lowland forest and moist savanna habitats.

LOOK OUT FOR

- A long, slender snake.
- A pointed head with large eyes and round pupils.
- Usually striped from head to tail.
- Very fast-moving snake.
- Active during the day.
- Frequents water when available.
- A lemon-yellow belly.

camouflage to escape detection. Though a ground-dweller, it ventures into shrubs and low bushes either to bask or to seek out food.
Similar species: Easily confused with the other sand snakes, whip snakes and grass snakes (*Psammophis* spp.) and the equally harmless Striped Skaapsteker (*Psammophylax tritaeniatus*).
Enemies: Predatory birds and other snakes.
Food and feeding: Prefers lizards, but also eats frogs, rodents and small birds.
Reproduction: Oviparous. Details unknown.
Danger to man: No danger to man.
Venom: Not thought to have any harmful effect on humans.

May be confused with the Olive Whip Snake (above), but the latter lacks the distinctive stripes.

A fast-moving, diurnal snake that dashes into the closest shrub when disturbed, where it will freeze.

Crossed Whip Snake

Psammophis crucifer

OTHER NAMES
Cross-marked Sand Snake (E)
Montane Grass Snake (E)
Kruismerksweepslang (A)

MILDLY VENOMOUS

average 60 cm   maximum 82,2 cm

Length: A small species that seldom exceeds 60 cm. Maximum length 82,2 cm.

Scale count: Midbody scales are in 15 rows (rarely 17), with 134–165 ventrals and 61–82 paired subcaudals. The anal shield is divided. There are 8 (sometimes 7 or 9) upper labials, the 4th and 5th (sometimes the 3rd and 4th or 5th and 6th) entering the eye, and 9 (sometimes 10) lower labials, as well as 1 preocular and 2 (sometimes 3) postoculars. Temporals are variable, usually 2 + 2 + 3.

Colour: Above, silvery grey to greyish olive or olive brown with a well-defined, broad dark-edged stripe down the back. On either side of the body there is a similar dark stripe with a white lower border. The head has 1 or 2 cream-coloured dark-edged bars or blotches with a similar stripe on the nose. The 1 or 2 dark, transverse bars on the nape produce a cross-like dorsal marking, hence the common name. These markings are not always present, however, and the common name of this snake may thus be misleading. The belly is yellow to orange-yellow, either uniform or with grey lateral streaks. Some specimens, however, are uniform olive grey above with an off-white belly.

Preferred habitat: Found largely in lowland forest, moist savanna, montane forest, grassland and fynbos with relict populations in eastern Zimbabwe and Namaqualand.

Habits: This fast-moving diurnal snake is very common along the sandy scrub-covered areas of the Cape coast and the mountain

Marius Burger

This specimen lacks the characteristic markings on the side of the head, as well as other markings on the body.

Note the dark, broad band down the back.

LOOK OUT FOR

■ Usually striped from head to tail.
■ Active during the day.
■ Has large eyes with round pupils.

An active, alert snake that seldom attempts to bite.

plateau of Mpumalanga. If disturbed, it moves off very quickly, seeking refuge under a stone or in any other suitable spot. Deserted termite mounds are well utilized by this snake. Though it wriggles when captured, it seldom attempts to bite. This snake is endemic to southern Africa.

Similar species: May be confused with other grass snakes, whip snakes and sand snakes (*Psammophis* spp.).

Enemies: Other snakes and birds of prey.

Food and feeding: Small lizards, especially skinks and geckos, as well as frogs.

Reproduction: Oviparous, laying 3–13 eggs. The eggs measure 18–21 mm x 9–10 mm but may be as long as 36,1 mm. The young are 18–20 cm long.

Danger to man: None.

Venom: The venom of this snake has virtually no effect on man.

The Crossed Whip Snake is often found in deserted termite mounds.

Dwarf Whip Snake
Psammophis angolensis

OTHER NAMES
Dwarf Sand Snake (E)
Pygmy Sand Snake (E)
Dwergsweepslang (A)
Dwergsandslang (A)

MILDLY VENOMOUS

average 30 cm   maximum 50 cm

Length: Adults average 25–30 cm with a maximum length of 50 cm.
Scale count: Midbody scales are in 11 rows, with 133–157 ventrals
and 58–80 paired subcaudals. The anal shield is divided. There are
8 (sometimes 6, 7 or 9) upper labials, the 4th and 5th entering the
eye, though this may vary, and 8 (sometimes 7 or 9) lower labials.
1 preocular and 2 postoculars. Temporals usually 1 + 2.
Colour: Above, grey to yellowish with a broad dark brown stripe
down the centre of the back. There is a thin, dark broken dorsolateral
stripe on either side. The head is dark brown with 3 narrow pale
crossbars, whereas the neck has 1 or 2 dark collars. The lips, throat
and belly are white to yellowish or caramel-coloured.
Preferred habitat: Found mostly in moist savanna.
Habits: A beautifully marked little snake that is diurnal, actively
hunting its prey. It forages among grass tussocks and fallen logs and,
if disturbed, will dart off and freeze in the typical whip snake fashion.
It is a secretive snake and seldom attempts to bite, even when
first handled. The Dwarf Whip Snake tends to be rare over most
of its range.
Similar species: May be confused with other sand snakes, whip
snakes and grass snakes (*Psammophis* spp.), although the head
markings are quite distinct.
Enemies: Other snakes and birds of prey.
Food and feeding: Small lizards, especially skinks, and frogs.
Reproduction: Oviparous, laying 3–5 eggs (15–24 x 5–8 mm).
Danger to man: None.
Venom: Has virtually no effect on man.

LOOK OUT FOR

- Active during the day.
- Has fairly large eyes with
  round pupils.
- Body striped from behind
  the head to the tail.

*This small snake is rare
throughout most of its range.*

MILDLY VENOMOUS

average 85 cm   maximum 1,4 m

Spotted Skaapsteker

Psammophylax rhombeatus

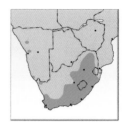

OTHER NAMES
Rhombic skaapsteker (E)
Gevlekte skaapsteker (A)

Length: Adults average 45–85 cm but may reach, or exceed, 1,4 m.
Scale count: Midbody scales are in 17 rows, with 143–177 ventrals and 60–84 paired subcaudals. The anal shield is divided. There are 8 (sometimes 7, 9 or 10) upper labials, the 4th and 5th entering the eye, though this may vary, and 10–11 (sometimes 9 or 12) lower labials, as well as 1 preocular (sometimes 2) and 2 (sometimes 3) postoculars. Temporals are variable, 2 + 3.
Colour: Above, yellowish brown to pale olive with 3 (occasionally 4) rows of dark-edged markings, 1 row down the centre of the back and 1 on either side. These markings may form zigzag or longitudinal lines along the body, or may even coalesce to form jagged lines. A few KwaZulu-Natal specimens are regularly striped, like *Psammophis* spp. The underside is usually yellowish with spots and blotches, and is sometimes colourful.
Preferred habitats: Found from the coast to mountaintops where it inhabits fynbos, grassland and moist savanna.
Habits: A diurnal snake that actively hunts its prey. It is nervous and quick moving, disappearing into grass when disturbed. There it freezes and will usually coil around a tuft of grass. It is well camouflaged and difficult to find. Like the Rinkhals (*Hemachatus haemachatus*) this snake is known to play dead when threatened, but this behaviour is not common in this species.
Similar species: May be confused with some of the equally harmless sand, whip and grass snakes.

A Spotted Skaapsteker from the KwaZulu-Natal midlands.

■ Active during the day.
■ Fairly large eyes with round pupils.
■ Dashes for cover where it is well camouflaged.
■ Nervous and quick moving.

Enemies: Predatory birds and other snakes.
Food and feeding: Mostly feeds on rodents, lizards, birds, frogs and snakes.

Reproduction: Oviparous, laying 8–30 eggs (20–35 x 12–18 mm) in summer. Females have been found coiled around their eggs. Embryos are partially developed when the eggs are laid, resulting in reduced incubation periods of approximately 6 weeks. The young measure 15,5–24 cm.
Danger to man: No danger to man.
Subspecies: Only the typical race of Spotted Skaapsteker (*Psammophylax rhombeatus rhombeatus*) is found within our range.
Venom: Not thought to be harmful to man.

A Spotted Skaapsteker from the Southern KwaZulu-Natal Drakensberg.

Females lay between 8 and 30 eggs in summer, which hatch within about 6 weeks.

A Spotted Skaapsteker from the Western Cape.

MILDLY VENOMOUS

maximum 93 cm

average 65 cm

This back-fanged snake has a mild venom and is not considered dangerous to man.

Striped Skaapsteker
Psammophylax tritaeniatus

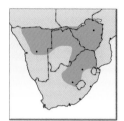

OTHER NAMES
Gestreepte skaapsteker (A)

Length: Adults average 60–65 cm with a maximum length of 93 cm.
Scale count: Midbody scales are in 17 rows, with 139–176 ventrals and 49–69 paired subcaudals. The anal shield is divided. There are 8 upper labials, the 4th and 5th entering the eye, and 9–11 lower labials, as well as 1 preocular and 2 postoculars. Temporals are 2 + 3.
Colour: Above, grey to pale olive grey or brown with 3 well-defined black-edged dark brown stripes that extend along the entire body. The narrowest of the 3 stripes forms a vertebral stripe that may be divided down the middle by a fine yellowish line. The 2 lateral stripes extend onto the head, passing through the eyes. The upper lip and belly are white to cream or yellowish white. The middle of the belly sometimes has a pale lime green or yellowish stripe.
Preferred habitat: Open grassland, arid savanna, moist savanna and karoo scrub.
Habits: A common diurnal snake that favours vlei-areas and open grassland where it actively hunts its prey. It is also commonly found under building rubble and other debris near towns. The Striped Skaapsteker is quick to dash into grass when disturbed, where it will either coil around a tuft or remain perfectly still, relying on its excellent camouflage to escape detection. If captured, it may struggle vigorously but seldom attempts to bite. It is back-fanged and venomous but is not considered dangerous to man.

Similar species: May be confused with several of the equally harmless whip snakes, grass snakes and sand snakes.

Enemies: Predatory birds and other snakes.

Food and feeding: Adults feed largely on rodents and occasionally on nestling birds; the young take frogs and lizards, especially skinks.

Reproduction: Oviparous, laying 5–18 eggs (20–29 x 10–16 mm) in summer. The female does not coil around her eggs like the Spotted Skaapsteker (*Psammophylax rhombeatus*) does. The young measure 13–22 cm.

LOOK OUT FOR

- Has a small head with pointed snout and small eyes.
- The pupils are round.
- Active during the day.
- Has stripes from head to tail.

Danger to man: None.

Venom: A mild venom that has virtually no effect on man.

With its striped appearance, it is easily confused with the grass and sand snakes.

The Striped Skaapsteker feeds largely on rodents, which are actively hunted during the day.

Grey-bellied Grass Snake

Psammophylax variabilis

OTHER NAMES
Gryspensgrasslang (A)

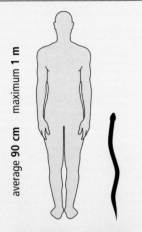

average 90 cm　maximum 1 m

Length: Adults average 70–90 cm with a maximum length of just over 1 m.

Scale count: Midbody scales are in 17 rows, with 149–167 ventrals and 49–61 paired subcaudals. The anal shield is divided. There are 8 upper labials with the 4th and 5th entering the eye, and 9–11 lower labials, as well as 1 preocular and 2 postoculars. Temporals are variable, usually 1 + 2.

Colour: Above, plain grey to olive brown or with 3 thin dark lines that may be flecked with white. The upper lip is dirty white to grey and the belly uniform grey.

Preferred habitat: In southern Africa, restricted to flood plain grasslands along the Chobe river, just above 1000 m. However, north of southern Africa this snake also inhabits montane grasslands above 1 800 m.

Habits: It is active mainly during the day. Seeks refuge under logs or in vegetation on the ground and is known to bask.

Similar species: May be confused with equally harmless grass snakes, whip snakes and sand snakes.

Enemies: Other snakes.

Food and feeding: Rodents, shrews, fledgling birds, lizards, frogs and small fish.

Reproduction: Viviparous, giving birth to 4 young in summer, each measuring 15–15,5 cm. Up to 8 eggs have, however, been removed from a dissected specimen. Eggs removed from a Malawian specimen measured 21 x 10 mm.

Danger to man: None.

Subspecies: Only the typical race of Grey-bellied Grass Snake (*Psammophylax variabilis variabilis*) occurs within our range.

Venom: The venom of this snake has virtually no effect on man.

The range of the Grey-bellied Grass Snake enters the southern African region along the Chobe River.

Colin Tilbury

LOOK OUT FOR

- Medium-sized snake with small head and rounded snout.
- Has average-sized eyes with round pupils.
- Plain grey to olive brown above

Eastern Bark Snake

Hemirhagerrhis nototaenia

OTHER NAMES
Mopane Snake (E)
Oostelike basslang (A)
Mopanieslang (A)

MILDLY VENOMOUS

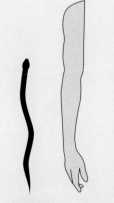

average 30 cm   maximum 50 cm

Length: Adults average 30 cm with a maximum length of about 50 cm (in East Africa). The largest specimen from southern Africa, a female, was 43,2 cm long.

Scale count: Midbody scales are in 17 rows, with 156–183 ventrals and 68–98 paired subcaudals. The anal shield is divided. There are 8 (sometimes 7) upper labials, the 4th and 5th (sometimes 3rd and 4th) entering the eye, and 9 or 10 lower labials, as well as 1 preocular and 2 postoculars. Temporals are variable: 1 + 2, 1 + 3, 2 + 2 or 2 + 3.

Colour: Above, ash grey to grey-brown with a darker vertebral stripe or band. This stripe is flanked by a series of blackish spots that may unite with the vertebral stripe, forming crossbars or a zigzag pattern. The stripes and spots become paler towards the posterior. The head is blackish and the belly a dirty white to pale brownish colour, with darker mottles. The last third of the tail is usually yellow to orange or salmon pink.

Preferred habitat: Found in moist and arid savanna as well as lowland forest.

Habits: Found under the bark of trees and in rotting logs. It is arboreal and mildly venomous. Captured specimens are very docile and seldom attempt to bite. Individuals are sometimes flushed from cracks in dry wood when people make campfires.

Eastern Bark Snakes are arboreal. Individuals are sometimes flushed from cracks in dry wood when people make campfires.

Similar species: The zigzag pattern down the back is unique for the genus and makes it difficult to confuse this snake with other species, apart from the Viperine Bark Snake (*Hemirhagerrhis viperinus*).

Enemies: Other snakes.

- ■ Has a zigzag pattern on its back.
- ■ A small, slender snake with a flattened head.
- ■ Largely arboreal.
- ■ Has small eyes with vertical pupils.

Eastern Bark Snakes inhabit moist savanna, where they are fond of hiding under bark.

Food and feeding: Small lizards, especially skinks and day geckos, and occasionally frogs. Like the vine snakes, the Eastern Bark Snake often swallows its prey while hanging its head down.

Reproduction: Oviparous, laying 2–8 eggs (24 x 6 mm).

Danger to man: None.

Venom: The venom of this snake is thought to have virtually no effect on man.

Wulf Haacke

The Eastern Bark Snake feeds on lizards and frogs.

The zigzag pattern down the back of this snake is unique, making identification easy.

Viperine Bark Snake
Hemirhagerrhis viperinus

OTHER NAMES
Westelike basslang (A)

MILDLY VENOMOUS

average 28 cm   maximum 30 cm

Length: Adults average 28 cm with a maximum length of just over 30 cm.

Scale count: Midbody scales are in 17 rows, with 154–177 ventrals and 52–75 paired subcaudals. The anal shield is divided. There are 8 (sometimes 7) upper labials, the 4th and 5th (sometimes 3rd and 4th) entering the eye, and 9 or 10 lower labials.

Colour: Above, the back is boldly patterned with triangular dark markings, flanked by ash grey to grey-brown. The dark triangular markings usually form crossbars or a zigzag pattern. The head is greyish to grey-brown. The last half of the tail is usually yellow to orange.

Preferred habitat: Karoo vegetation and arid savanna in Namibia and further northwards.

Habits: Found in deep rock cracks where it hunts for lizards, especially diurnal geckos at rest.

Similar species: The zigzag pattern down the back is unique for the genus and makes it difficult to confuse this snake with other species, apart from the Eastern Bark Snake (*Hemirhagerrhis nototaenia*).

Enemies: Other snakes.

Food and feeding: Feeds on lizards, especially day geckos (*Lygodactylus* spp.).

Reproduction: Unknown, but thought to be oviparous.

Danger to man: None.

Venom: The venom of this snake is thought to have virtually no effect on man.

LOOK OUT FOR

- Has a zigzag pattern on its back.
- A small, slender snake with a flattened head.
- Has small eyes.

Unlike the Eastern Bark Snake, this snake is found in deep rock cracks.

Bill Branch

MILDLY VENOMOUS

Western Keeled Snake
Pythonodipsas carinata

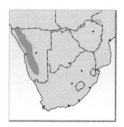

OTHER NAMES
Westelike gekielde slang (A)

maximum 80 cm

average 50 cm

Length: Adults average 50 cm with a maximum of around 80 cm.
Scale count: Midbody scales are in 21 rows, with 182–208 ventrals, and 41–55 subcaudals (not paired). The anal shield is entire. There are 9–10 upper labials that do not enter the eye, as well as 1 preocular and 3 postoculars. Temporals are numerous and variable.
Colour: Above, light orange-yellow to pale buff or greyish with a double series of grey-brown to dark grey blotches that form crossbars or a zigzag pattern down the back. The sides have smaller, less pronounced spots or bars while the underside is uniform white, sometimes with dark spots on the sides. The eye has a dark vertical pupil.
Preferred habitat: Rocky desert areas in the Namib Desert and northwards into Angola.
Habits: A terrestrial nocturnal snake that occurs in rocky desert areas. It has large back fangs and bites readily. This snake settles down well in captivity and will feed on laboratory mice. It is rarely seen. One specimen, found in the Kuiseb Canyon, inhabited riverine bush close to semi-permanent water, but most individuals have been found in dry, rocky areas. Females grow much larger than males.
Similar species: Resembles an adder in colour and habits but has a distinctive, somewhat triangular head with small, irregular head shields. This snake may mimic the Horned Adder (*Bitis caudalis*).
Enemies: Unknown.
Food and feeding: Lizards, especially geckos and skinks, and rodents. Once captured, the prey is constricted.
Reproduction: Probably oviparous.
Danger to man: Unknown.
Venom: Thought to have virtually no effect on man. There is even debate as to whether the snake is venomous or whether the fangs are not just enlarged teeth adapted for holding onto smooth-scaled lizards.

A nocturnal snake that is found in rocky desert areas.

LOOK OUT FOR
- Small irregular head shields.
- Very flat head that is distinct from the neck.
- Has large eyes with vertical pupils.
- Active at night and terrestrial.

Many-spotted Snake
Amplorhinus multimaculatus

OTHER NAMES
Reed Snake (E)
Rietslang (A)

MILDLY VENOMOUS

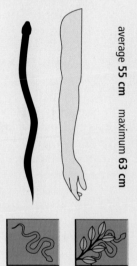

average 55 cm   maximum 63 cm

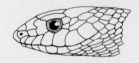

Length: Adults average 40–55 cm with a maximum length of just over 63 cm.

Scale count: Midbody scales are in 17 rows, with 133–154 ventrals and 56–91 subcaudals, which are usually paired but may be single. The anal shield is entire. There are 8 (sometimes 7) upper labials, the 4th and 5th (sometimes the 3rd and 4th) entering the eye, and 9 or 10 lower labials, as well as 1 preocular and 2 postoculars. Temporals are 2 + 2 or 1 + 2.

Colour: Above, uniform green or olive to olive brown, or with dark brown to black spots or blotches. A pale dorsolateral stripe may extend down either side of the body. Scattered scales are often edged in white or yellowish white, creating a somewhat flecked effect. The belly is dull green to olive or bluish green.

Preferred habitat: Reed beds and riverside vegetation in fynbos, grassland and montane forest.

Habits: A slow-moving, secretive but common snake that forages for food in the day, usually in damp or marshy areas. Preferred habitats include waterside vegetation and reed beds, especially in the Cape, where it may be referred to as the Cape Reed Snake. If disturbed, it may coil into a tight spring, like the Common Slug-eater (*Duberria lutrix*), and will strike readily.

Similar species: May be confused with the Spotted Skaapsteker (*Psammophylax rhombeatus*) or some of the grass, whip or sand snakes.

Bill Branch

An olive brown phase of the Many-spotted Snake.

The venom of this snake is not considered dangerous to man.

- Small head not very distinct from rest of body.
- Medium-sized eyes with round pupils.
- May coil in a tight spring.
- Bites readily.

Enemies: Other snakes.

Food and feeding: Frogs, lizards and small rodents.

Reproduction: Viviparous, giving birth to between 4 and 8 (but as many as 13) young in late summer. The young are 12–20 cm long.

Danger to man: None.

Venom: The venom, which is not considered dangerous to man, may cause some local pain, inflammation, swelling and free bleeding. Antivenom is neither effective nor required.

A slow-moving, diurnal snake that is found in marshy areas.

A green phase of the Many-spotted Snake from KwaZulu-Natal.

If disturbed, the Many-spotted Snake may coil into a tight spring, as does the Common Slug-eater.

Telescopus s. semiannulatus

Common Tiger Snake
Telescopus semiannulatus

OTHER NAMES
Gewone tierslang (A)

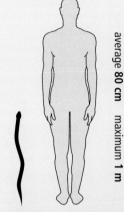

average 80 cm   maximum 1 m

MILDLY VENOMOUS

Length: The adults average 50–80 cm, but may exceed 1 m.

Scale count: Midbody scales are in 19 rows (sometimes 17 or 21) with 190–244 ventrals and 51–83 paired subcaudals. The anal shield is usually divided, but may be entire. There are 8–9 upper labials, the 3rd, 4th and 5th entering the eye, but this is variable, and 11–12 (sometimes 10 or 13) lower labials, as well as 1 preocular and 2 postoculars. Temporals are variable, usually 2 + 2 or 2 + 3.

Colour: Above, orange-pink to dull salmon pink with 22–75 dark brown to black crossbars or blotches on the body and tail. The underside is yellowish to orange-pink.

Preferred habitat: Varied. Rocky regions in the Namib Desert, karoo scrub, arid and moist savanna and lowland forest, where it shelters under bark, loose flakes of rock and in rock crevices.

Habits: A nocturnal snake that spends most of the day concealed in rock crevices or under the bark of trees. Though largely a ground-dweller, it often ventures into trees, shrubs and old buildings, where it hunts for food. During summer, after rains, tiger snakes often cross tarred roads and as a result passing vehicles kill many individuals. Like the Red-lipped Herald Snake (*Crotaphopeltis hotamboeia*), this snake puts on an impressive display when threatened or cornered, raising its head off the ground and striking viciously.

Similar species: May be confused with the Coral Snake (*Aspidelaps lubricus*), the Zebra Cobra (*Naja nigricollis nigricincta*) and Beetz's Tiger Snake (*Telescopus beetzii*).

The Common Tiger Snake feeds largely on lizards, especially geckos.

Enemies: Other snakes.
Food and feeding: Mainly lizards, especially geckos. Fledgling birds, bats and small rodents are also taken.
Reproduction: Oviparous, laying 3–20 eggs (24–55 x 10–17 mm) during the summer. The hatchlings measure 17–23 cm.
Danger to man: No danger to man.
Subspecies: There are 2 subspecies in southern Africa.

The Eastern Tiger Snake (*Telescopus semi-annulatus semiannulatus*), discussed above, is more widespread, occurring over the eastern two thirds of the range. It has between 20 and 50 dark blotches on the back.

The Damara Tiger Snake (*Telescopus semiannulatus polystictus)* occurs in the highveld areas of Namibia, extending into the Richtersveld. It has 52–75 dark blotches on the body and tail. It is possible that these 2 sub-species are, in fact, different species.
Venom: None.

LOOK OUT FOR

- A nocturnal snake with head distinct from the body.
- Has large eyes with vertical pupils.
- Has 20–75 dark brown to black crossbars or blotches on the body and tail.
- May lift its head and strike viciously when threatened.
- Often found on tarred roads after heavy rains.

An Eastern Tiger Snake from Polokwane.

Wulf Haacke

A Damara Tiger Snake from Keetmanshoop.

The Common Tiger Snake is nocturnal and spends most of the day concealed in rock crevices or under bark.

Beetz's Tiger Snake
Telescopus beetzii

OTHER NAMES
Namib Tiger Snake (E)
Beetz se tierslang (A)

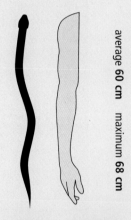

MILDLY VENOMOUS

average 60 cm   maximum 68 cm

Length: Adults average 40–60 cm with a maximum length of nearly 68 cm.

Scale count: Midbody scales are in 21 rows (sometimes 19), with 190–220 ventrals and 40–59 pairs of subcaudals. The anal shield is usually entire but may be divided. There are 9–10 upper labials, the 3rd, 4th and 5th entering the eye (sometimes the 4th, 5th and 6th), and 11–12 lower labials, as well as 1 preocular and 2 postoculars. Temporals are 2 + 3, 2 + 2 or 3 + 2.

Colour: Above, sandy buff to chestnut with a series of dark brown to black blotches on the back and tail (30–39 on the back and 12–20 on the tail). Usually has a dark spot on the crown of the head. The belly is uniform pinkish tan to sandy buff.

Preferred habitat: Rocky, arid regions in the Karoo, but is excluded from desert proper.

Habits: A nocturnal snake that inhabits arid rocky regions, preferring narrow rock crevices for shelter but also known to utilize deserted termite mounds. It emerges at night and forages for lizards. Many individuals are killed by vehicles while crossing roads at night. Beetz's Tiger Snake is often found in close proximity to the Coral Snake (*Aspidelaps lubricus*) and may well compete with the latter for food and shelter. Though seldom seen, this snake is quite abundant in some areas. It is endemic to southern Africa.

This endemic snake is common in some areas and can often be seen crossing roads at night.

This snake inhabits rocky, arid parts of the Karoo.

Similar species: May be confused with the Coral Snake, the Zebra Cobra (*Naja nigricollis nigricincta*) and the Common Tiger Snake (*Telescopus semiannulatus*).
Enemies: Other snakes.

Beetz's Tiger Snake has 30–39 dark blotches on its back.

LOOK OUT FOR

- A nocturnal snake with head distinct from the body.
- Has large eyes with vertical pupils.
- Has 30–39 dark brown to black blotches on the body and 12–20 on the tail.
- Often found at night crossing roads.

Food and feeding: Mainly lizards, especially geckos.
Reproduction: Oviparous, laying 3–5 elongate eggs (33–55 mm x 10–14 mm) in summer. The young measure 17–19 cm.
Danger to man: None.
Venom: Not thought to have any harmful effect on man.

Beetz's Tiger Snake is often found in close proximity to the Coral Snake.

Marbled Tree Snake
Dipsadoboa aulica

OTHER NAMES
Marmerslang (A)

MILDLY VENOMOUS

average 60 cm   maximum 85 cm

Length: Adults average 40–60 cm with a maximum length of 85 cm.
Scale count: Midbody scales are in 17 rows, with 172–197 ventrals and 75–100 subcaudals, either paired or single. There are 8 (sometimes 7) upper labials, the 3rd, 4th and 5th entering the eye, though this may vary, and 10 (sometimes 9) lower labials, as well as 1 preocular and 2 postoculars. Temporals are 1 + 1 + 2.
Colour: Above, red-brown to light brown with 38–50 faint whitish crossbars. The head is finely spotted or marbled with white and the tongue is white. The belly is creamy white with reddish brown lateral speckling. The iris of the eye is lime green.
Preferred habitat: Lowland forest and moist savanna.
Habits: An attractive nocturnal snake that shelters in hollow trees, under loose bark, in thatched roofs and in shaded plant debris in the day and emerges at dusk to hunt. It is often encountered near human dwellings, while hunting for geckos. When threatened, it coils loosely into a striking position with its head flattened and raised off the ground. It strikes viciously with its mouth agape but does not have a dangerous bite.
Similar species: Because of the 38–50 faint white crossbars and the white spots or mottling on the head, this snake is not easily confused with other snakes.
Enemies: Other snakes.
Food and feeding: Lizards, especially geckos, frogs, toads and small rodents.
Reproduction: Oviparous, laying 7–9 smallish eggs (23–29 x 10–13 mm) in summer. The young measure 18 cm.
Danger to man: None.
Venom: Of no consequence to man.

A nocturnal snake that shelters under bark and in hollow trees.

LOOK OUT FOR

- Head distinct from the rest of the body.
- Large eye with vertical pupil.
- White tongue.
- The head is finely spotted or marbled with white.
- Active from dusk onward.

Cross-barred Tree Snake

Dispadoboa flavida

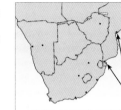

average **45 cm**   maximum **63 cm**

OTHER NAMES
Gebande slang (A)
Dwarsgestreepte slang (A)

Length: Adults average 30–45 cm with a maximum length of 63 cm.
Scale count: Midbody scales are in 17 rows, with 170–197 ventrals and 79–106 subcaudals, either paired or unpaired. The anal shield is entire. There are 8 upper labials, the 3rd, 4th and 5th entering the eye, and 10 lower labials, as well as 1 preocular and 2 postoculars. Temporals are 1 + 1 + 2.
Colour: Above, red-brown with 58–82 faint whitish crossbars. The head is finely spotted or marbled with white above and has a distinct brown stripe on either side from the nose through the eye to the angle of the jaw. The belly is creamy white.
Preferred habitat: Lowland forest.
Habits: A nocturnal snake that shelters under loose bark or in crevices. When threatened, it coils loosely into a striking position with its head flattened and raised off the ground. It strikes viciously with its mouth agape but is quite harmless.
Similar species: Because of its red-brown coloration, whitish crossbars and the brown stripes on either side of the head, it is not easily confused with other snakes.
Enemies: Other snakes.
Food and feeding: Lizards, especially geckos, and tree frogs.
Reproduction: Oviparous.
Danger to man: None.
Subspecies: Only one of the subspecies of the Cross-barred Tree Snake (*Dipsadoboa flavida broadleyi*) is found within our range.
Venom: Of no consequence to man.

When threatened, this snake strikes viciously.

LOOK OUT FOR

■ Head distinct from the rest of the body.
■ Large eyes with vertical pupils.
■ Brown stripe on either side of the head from nose through the eye to the angle of the jaw.
■ The head is finely spotted or marbled with white.
■ Active at night.

Bill Branch

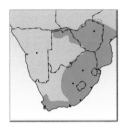

Herald Snake

Crotaphopeltis hotamboeia

OTHER NAMES
Red-lipped Snake (E)
Rooilipslang (A)

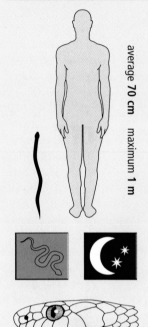

MILDLY VENOMOUS

average 70 cm maximum 1 m

Length: Adults average 45–70 cm, but have been known to reach a length of 1 m.

Scale count: Midbody scales are in 19 rows (sometimes 21), with 139–174 ventrals and 24–47 pairs of subcaudals. The anal shield is entire. There are 8 (sometimes 7 or 9) upper labials, the 3rd, 4th and 5th entering the eye, but this may vary, and 9–10 (sometimes 11) lower labials, as well as 1 preocular (sometimes 2) and 2 (sometimes 3) postoculars. Temporals are 1 + 2 or 1 + 1.

Colour: Above, olive green or grey with white speckles that occasionally form transverse bars, especially in juveniles. The head is usually darker than the body and the upper lip is red, white, orange-red, yellow or blackish. The temporal region is glossy iridescent black to purplish black and more diagnostic of the species than the lip colour. The underside is white to mother-of-pearl cream. Hatchlings have distinctive black heads.

Preferred habitat: Very common in marshy areas, in fynbos, lowland forest, moist savanna and grassland.

Habits: Common and widespread, it is often found in gardens where it seeks shelter in rockeries, under building rubble and in compost heaps. Because of its nocturnal habits, people often incorrectly refer to it as a Night Adder.

Marius Burger

The white speckles on the back of the Herald Snake, as well as its reddish lip are distinctive features.

It preys predominantly on toads and prefers damp localities. When threatened, the Herald Snake will raise its flattened head horizontally, while hissing and striking with its mouth agape. It bites readily. This species and the Brown House Snake (*Lamprophis capensis*) are without doubt the 2 most common garden snakes in southern Africa.

Similar species: Even though there is no resemblance, this snake is often incorrectly identified as a Night Adder.

Enemies: Other snakes and spiders of the genus *Latrodectus*.

Food and feeding: Feeds on amphibians, including rain frogs (*Breviceps* spp.), as well as the occasional lizard. Once this snake grabs its prey in its jaws, it hangs onto it while its mild venom takes effect. Also known to eat snakes in captivity.

Reproduction: Oviparous, laying 6–19 eggs (25–32 x 10–13 mm) in early summer. The young measure 8–18 cm.

Danger to man: No danger to man.

Venom: Not thought to have any harmful effect on man.

LOOK OUT FOR

- Iridescent blue-black on top of head.
- Upper lip may be red, orange-red, yellow, white or blackish.
- Active at night and common in suburban gardens.
- Dark body often has white specks or dots.
- Found in damp locations.

This specimen lacks the red lip.

When threatened, the head is flattened horizontally and the snake may strike out viciously.

Barotse Water Snake

Crotaphopeltis barotseensis

OTHER NAMES
Barotsewaterslang (A)

MILDLY VENOMOUS

aaverage 50 cm   maximum 70 cm

Length: Adults average 40–50 cm with a maximum length of nearly 70 cm.

Scale count: Midbody scales are in 17 rows, with 151–158 ventrals and 35–39 pairs of subcaudals. The anal shield is entire. There are 8 upper labials, the 3rd, 4th and 5th entering the eye, but this may vary, and 9–11 lower labials, as well as 1 preocular and 2 postoculars. Temporals are 1 + 2.

Colour: Above, uniform iridescent grey-brown to grey with dark-edged scales. The belly is off-white to pale brown.

Preferred habitat: Papyrus swamp in the Okavango Swamps, Chobe River and upper Zambezi River.

Habits: Very little is known about the Barotse Water Snake. It is largely aquatic and closely associated with permanent water where it inhabits papyrus swamps. It is docile and seldom attempts to bite.

Similar species: Could be confused with a variety of other grey-brown snakes.

Enemies: Unknown.

Food and feeding: Feeds on frogs.

Reproduction: Oviparous, laying 6–8 eggs in summer.

Danger to man: None.

Venom: Very little is known about the venom of this snake but it is thought to have virtually no effect on man.

LOOK OUT FOR

- Head not very distinct from rest of body.
- Has smooth glossy scales.

Steve Spawls

Very little is known about this secretive snake.

Black-headed Centipede-eater

Aparallactus capensis

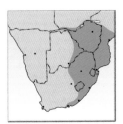

OTHER NAMES
Cape Centipede-eater (E)
Swartkop-honderdpootvreter (A)

Length: Adults average 20–30 cm in length, but can exceed 40 cm.
Scale count: Midbody scales are in 15 rows, with 126–186 ventrals and 29–63 single subcaudals. The anal shield is entire. There are 5 or 6 upper labials, the 3rd and 4th (sometimes 2nd and 3rd) entering the eye, and 5 (sometimes 4 or 6) lower labials, as well as 1 preocular and 1 postocular. Temporals are 0 + 1 + 1 or 1 + 1.
Colour: Above, yellowish or reddish brown to grey-brown with a black head backed by a black collar that narrows on the sides of the neck. The underside is usually white to dirty white.
Preferred habitat: Commonly found in old termite mounds in lowland forest, moist savanna and grassland.
Habits: This slender snake is common throughout its range and is usually found in disused termite mounds and under logs and stones. It is nocturnal and is very active after rains. Many individuals may inhabit a single termite mound to which they are attracted by warmth, suitable shelter and food. The Centipede-eater bites readily when handled but its teeth are minute and seldom pierce skin. It is often caught by inexperienced snake collectors but does not do well in captivity and soon starves to death.

maximum 40 cm

average 30 cm

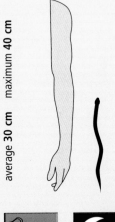

The Black-headed Centipede-eater feeds exclusively on centipedes.

Similar species: This snake has very distinct, dark markings on the head and neck and cannot easily be confused with other snake species, apart from the closely related Mozambique Centipede-eater (*Aparallactus nigriceps*) to which it is closely related. However, the Mozambique Centipede-eater is rare and limited in its distribution.

Enemies: Other snakes such as garter snakes (*Elapsoidea* spp.) and the stiletto snakes (*Atractaspis* spp.), spiders and scorpions.

Food and feeding: Feeds on centipedes, which it seizes and then chews along the length of the body until its venom takes effect. If the centipede bites the snake, it will release its prey and start the chewing process again. The centipede is swallowed headfirst.

LOOK OUT FOR

- Has a black head with a black collar that narrows on the sides of the neck.
- A small slender snake with head not distinct from the rest of the body.

Occasionally, centipedes manage to kill and eat the snake instead.

Reproduction: Oviparous, laying 2–4 elongate eggs (32 x 4–5 mm) during summer. The young measure 9–12 cm and are replicas of the adults, complete with the dark head.

Danger to man: No danger to man.

Venom: Thought to have virtually no effect on man.

Note the markings on the head that give it its common name.

This snake is often dug out of deserted termite mounds by snake enthusiasts, but seldom survives in captivity because of its specialized diet.

MILDLY VENOMOUS

Reticulated Centipede-eater
Aparallactus lunulatus

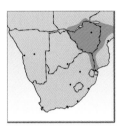

OTHER NAMES
Gebande honderdpootvreter (A)

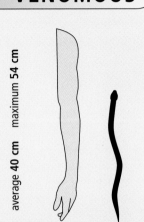

average 40 cm   maximum 54 cm

Length: Adults average 30–40 cm with a maximum length of nearly 54 cm.

Scale count: Midbody scales are in 15 rows, with 144–176 ventrals and 48–65 single subcaudals. The anal shield is entire. There are 6 (sometimes 7) upper labials, the 3rd and 4th entering the eye, and 6 (sometimes 5) lower labials, as well as 1 preocular and 1 postocular. Temporals are 0 + 1 + 1 or 0 + 1 + 2.

Colour: Above, grey to olive or brown, often with dark-edged scales that give a reticulated effect. Juveniles have a black collar on the nape, followed by up to 12 blotches. These markings fade in adults. The belly is greenish white.

Preferred habitat: Moist savanna.

Habits: An inoffensive snake that inhabits sandy soil in moist savanna, where it may be found under loose boulders, stones, logs and other debris. It is partially a burrowing species and may also be found just below the soil surface in the loose sand under grass tussocks. This snake is back-fanged and mildly venomous, but is not inclined to bite. Because of its limited gape and the fact that the fangs are situated far back in the mouth, it finds it rather difficult to inflict a bite on a human.

Similar species: Juveniles cannot be mistaken as they have a black collar on the nape and up to 12 dark blotches on the body, although these fade with age.

Enemies: Other snakes.

Food and feeding: Feeds on centipedes and scorpions.

Reproduction: Oviparous, laying 3–4 elongate eggs (30 x 7 mm) in summer.

Danger to man: None.

Subspecies: Only the typical race of Reticulated Centipede-eater (*Aparallactus lunulatus lunulatus*) occurs within our range.

Venom: Has virtually no effect on man.

The Reticulated Centipede-eater has 12 blotches on the body that fade with age.

LOOK OUT FOR

■ Black collar and up to 12 black blotches on the body.
■ A small slender snake with head not distinct from the body.

Black Centipede-eater

Aparallactus guentheri

OTHER NAMES
Swarthonderdpootvreter (A)

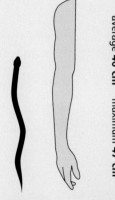

MILDLY VENOMOUS

average 40 cm   maximum 47 cm

Length: Adults average 40 cm with a maximum length of 47 cm.
Scale count: Midbody scales are in 15 rows, with 150–173 ventrals and 49–60 single subcaudals. The anal shield is entire. There are 6 (sometimes 5) upper labials, the 3rd and 4th (sometimes the 2nd and 3rd) entering the eye, and 5 (sometimes 6) lower labials, as well as 1 preocular and 1 postocular. Temporals are 0 + 1 + 1 or 1 + 2.
Colour: Above, bluish grey to shiny black with 2 narrow yellow collars on the nape. The chin and belly are off-white to greyish.
Preferred habitat: Found in high-rainfall areas in moist savanna and montane forest.
Habits: This distinctive species is mostly associated with evergreen forests in areas of high rainfall. It may be found under any form of shelter, including rocks and logs. Otherwise it is very similar to the Reticulated Centipede-eater (*Aparallactus lunulatus*) in habits.
Similar species: Cannot be misidentified as it has 2 narrow yellow collars on the neck, which are unique to this species.
Enemies: Other snakes.
Food and feeding: Apparently feeds exclusively on centipedes.
Reproduction: Oviparous, the number of eggs laid is not known.
Danger to man: None.
Venom: Has virtually no effect on man.

LOOK OUT FOR

■ A small slender snake with head not distinct from the body.
■ Has 2 narrow yellow collars on the neck.

This snake is easy to identify as it has two narrow yellow collars on the neck.

Bill Branch

MILDLY VENOMOUS

average 25 cm   maximum 30 cm

Mozambique Centipede-eater
Aparallactus nigriceps

OTHER NAMES
Mosambiekse honderdpootvreter (A)

Length: Adults average 25 cm, reaching a maximum length of 30 cm.
Scale count: Midbody scales are in 15 rows, with 108–123 ventrals and 20–35 subcaudals. The anal shield is entire. There are 5 upper labials, the 2nd and 3rd entering the eye, and 5 lower labials, as well as 1 preocular and 1 postocular. Temporals are 0 + 1 + 1.
Colour: Above, reddish to light or olive brown with a broad black collar on the nape. The head and neck are also black and the belly cream to yellowish white.
Preferred habitat: Restricted to coastal bush in lowland forest.
Habits: This rare and localized snake is probably similar to the Black-headed Centipede-eater (*Aparallactus capensis*) in habits and it appears to be restricted to the area around Inhambane on the southern Mozambique plain. This snake has not been found in well over 100 years.
Similar species: Museum specimens indicate that it is very similar to the Black-headed Centipede-eater, but the collar on the neck is much broader.
Enemies: Other snakes.
Food and feeding: Probably feeds exclusively on centipedes.
Reproduction: Unknown.
Danger to man: None.
Venom: Nothing is known of the venom of this snake but it is thought to have virtually no effect on man.

LOOK OUT FOR

- A small, slender snake with head not distinct from the body.
- The head and neck are black with a broad black collar in the neck region.

This rare snake has not been seen in over 100 years! No photographs or illustrations are, therefore, available. It inhabits coastal bush and lowland forest.

Natal Purple-glossed Snake

Amblyodipsas concolor

MILDLY VENOMOUS

OTHER NAMES
Natalse persglansslang (A)
Natalse purpergrondslang (A)

Length: Adults average 35–50 cm and may reach a length of 85 cm.
Scale count: Midbody scales are in 17 rows, with 133–157 ventrals and 28–39 paired subcaudals. The anal shield is divided. There are 7 upper labials, the 3rd and 4th entering the eye, and 7 (sometimes 6) lower labials, with no preoculars and 1 postocular. Temporals are 0 + 1 + 1.
Colour: Above, uniform glossy dark brown to black with a purplish sheen. The belly is slightly paler.
Preferred habitat: Moist forested areas, moist savanna, montane grassland and lowland forest.
Habits: A burrowing species that may be found in humic soil in moist well-wooded and forest areas. Also occurs in sandy soils on the Bluff in Durban. Generally, it is a rare snake and is seldom encountered, but may be common in certain localities. It is a docile species that seldom attempts to bite, even when handled. This snake is endemic to southern Africa.
Similar species: Easily confused with other purple-glossed snakes (*Amblyodipsas* spp.), the Natal Black Snake (*Macrelaps microlepidotus*) and the stiletto snakes (*Atractaspis* spp.).
Enemies: Other snakes.

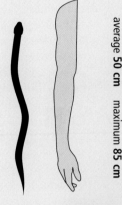

average 50 cm   maximum 85 cm

A rare burrowing snake that is seldom encountered.

Food and feeding: Adults eat other snakes while juveniles are known to feed on lizards, especially skinks.

Reproduction: Somewhat confusing as records indicate that this species lays eggs *and* produces live young. In one instance, 10 hatchlings averaging 18,5 cm, and 2 unhatched eggs (30 x 18 mm) were found under 10 cm of moist soil at the edge of a closed coastal forest in Hluhluwe Game Reserve in KwaZulu-Natal in February. Another female from Gauteng reportedly laid 11 eggs (26–32 x 15–17 mm) in December while another Gauteng female produced 12 live young in March.

Danger to man: Not considered dangerous.

Venom: The venom of this snake has not been studied but is not considered dangerous to man.

The Natal Purple-glossed Snake is a docile species that seldom attempts to bite.

This snake is dark brown to black with a purplish sheen.

The Natal Purple-glossed Snake is easily confused with other purple-glossed snakes and the Natal Black Snake.

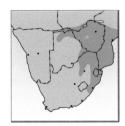

Common Purple-glossed Snake

Amblyodipsas polylepis

MILDLY VENOMOUS

OTHER NAMES
Gewone persglansslang (A)
Gewone purpergrondslang (A)

Length: Adults average 50–75 cm with a maximum length of 1,12 m. Females grow much larger than males.

Scale count: Midbody scales are in 19–21 rows (rarely 23), with 154–215 ventrals and 15–31 paired subcaudals. The anal shield is divided. There are 6 (sometimes 5) upper labials, the 3rd and 4th (sometimes 2nd and 3rd) entering the eye, and 7 (sometimes 6 or 8) lower labials, with no preocular and 1 postocular (sometimes none). Temporals are 0 + 1.

Colour: Uniform glossy black to dark brown above and below with a purplish sheen. This colour changes to an opaque bluish shade prior to shedding.

Preferred habitat: From lowland forest to moist savanna.

Habits: A rare burrowing species that is seldom encountered except perhaps at night after heavy rain, or in the day once the soil becomes waterlogged. Odd individuals have also been found under large stones. It is docile, seldom attempting to bite. If threatened, it may hide its head under a body coil and move the tip of its tail in an attempt to distract its aggressor and protect the vulnerable head.

Similar species: Easily confused with other purple-glossed snakes (*Amblyodipsas* spp.), the Natal Black Snake (*Macrelaps microlepidotus*) and the stiletto snakes (*Atractaspis* spp.).

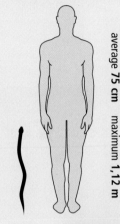

average 75 cm   maximum 1,12 m

A rare burrowing snake that may be seen on the ground surface at night after heavy rains.

The Common Purple-glossed snake is docile and seldom attempts to bite.

LOOK OUT FOR

- A thick-bodied snake with a blunt head.
- The body has a purplish sheen.
- Very small eyes.

Enemies: Other snakes.

Food and feeding: Burrowing reptiles including blind snakes, legless skinks and amphisbaenids. Large meals may be constricted prior to swallowing.

Reproduction: Probably oviparous but the number of eggs laid is not known.

Danger to man: Not considered dangerous to man.

Subspecies: Only the typical race of Common Purple-glossed Snake (*Amblyodipsas polylepis polylepis*) occurs within our range.

Venom: The venom of this snake has not been studied but is not considered dangerous to man.

This snake is easily confused with other purple-glossed snakes and the Natal Black Snake.

When threatened, it may hide its head under a body coil and move its tail to distract the aggressor.

Amblyodipsas m. microphthalma

Eastern Purple-glossed Snake

Amblyodipsas microphthalma

OTHER NAMES
Oostelike persglansslang (A)
Oostelike purpergrondslang (A)

Length: Adults average 25–30 cm, seldom exceeding 33 cm.
Scale count: Midbody scales are in 15 rows, with 120–168 ventrals and 18–26 paired subcaudals. The anal shield is divided. There are 5 upper labials, the 2nd and 3rd entering the eye, and 6 (sometimes 5) lower labials, with no preocular and 1 postocular. Temporals are 0 + 1.
Colour: Above, uniform dark brown to black with a purplish sheen. The upper lip, throat and 2 scale rows on the lower flanks are white to yellow. The belly usually has a dark line down the centre bordered by white or yellow, which extends onto the flanks, but may be black.
Preferred habitat: Deep alluvial soil to rocky thornveld in lowland forest and moist savanna.
Habits: A small burrowing snake that may be found burrowing in deep sandy soil or under stones and logs. It is sometimes exposed during bulldozing operations as it burrows quite deep. This snake is endemic to southern Africa.
Similar species: Easily confused with other purple-glossed snakes (*Amblyodipsas* spp.), the Natal Black Snake (*Macrelaps microlepidotus*) and the stiletto snakes (*Atractaspis* spp.).
Enemies: Other snakes.
Food and feeding: Legless skinks and amphisbaenids.
Reproduction: Unknown but probably oviparous.

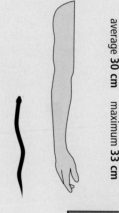

average 30 cm   maximum 33 cm

Wulf Haacke

This small burrowing snake inhabits deep alluvial soil, where it may be exposed during bulldozing operations.

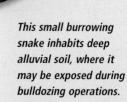

Danger to man: Not considered dangerous.
Subspecies: There are 2 subspecies in southern Africa.

The Eastern Purple-glossed Snake (*Amblyodipsas microphthalma microphthalma*), discussed above, has a white-yellow belly and 120–153 ventrals and is found in KwaZulu-Natal.

The Black White-lipped Snake (*Amblyodipsas microphthalma nigra*) usually has a black belly and is found in moist savanna in Limpopo Province. It has 146–168 ventral scales.

Venom: The venom of this snake has not been studied but is not considered dangerous.

Found in lowland forest and moist savanna habitat.

The Black White-lipped Snake is found in the Limpopo Province.

The venom of this snake has not been studied, but is not considered to be dangerous to man.

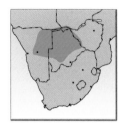

Kalahari Purple-glossed Snake

Amblyodipsas ventrimaculata

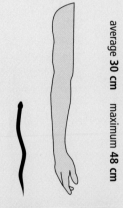
OTHER NAMES
Kalahari purpergrondslang (A)
Kalahari persglansslang (A)

Length: Adults average 30 cm but may reach a length of 48 cm.

Scale count: Midbody scales are in 15 rows, with 172–205 ventrals and 18–29 paired subcaudals. The anal shield is divided. There are 5 upper labials, the 2nd and 3rd entering the eye, and 5 lower labials, with no preocular and 1 postocular. Temporals are 0 + 1.

Colour: Above, yellow with a broad purplish black stripe down the centre of the back. The sides, upper lip and underside of the tail are yellow while the belly is uniform white, and may occasionally have black blotches.

Preferred habitat: Sandy soil in arid savanna.

Habits: A small snake that inhabits sandy soil in moist regions of the Kalahari where it may seek refuge under logs. It is nocturnal and may be found on the surface at night, especially during rain.

Similar species: May be confused with other purple-glossed snakes (*Amblyodipsas* spp.) and the stiletto snakes (*Atractaspis* spp.), but it has yellow sides.

Enemies: Other snakes.

Food and feeding: Burrowing reptiles including legless skinks (*Typhlacontias* spp.), amphisbaenids and garter snakes (*Elapsoidea* spp.).

Reproduction: Oviparous. A female has been found carrying 3 eggs.

Danger to man: Not considered dangerous to man.

Venom: The venom of this snake has not been studied but is not considered dangerous to man.

average 30 cm   maximum 48 cm

LOOK OUT FOR

- A small snake with blunt snout and small eyes.
- Sides, upper lip and underside of tail are yellow.

Wulf Haacke

The Kalahari Purple-glossed Snake feeds on burrowing reptiles.

Gerard's Black & Yellow Burrowing Snake

Chilorhinophis gerardi

OTHER NAMES
Gerard se swart-en-geel-grondslangetjie (A)

average 40 cm   maximum 50 cm

Length: Averages 40 cm, but may reach 50 cm.

Scale count: Midbody scales are in 15 rows, with 244–294 ventrals and 19–31 paired subcaudals. The anal shield is divided. There are 4 upper labials, the 3rd entering the eye, and 5 lower labials, as well as 1 preocular and 1 postocular. Temporals are 0 + 1.

Colour: Above, yellow to greenish yellow with 3 distinct black stripes. Both the head and tail tip are black above, the head having yellow spots or blotches. The tail is bluish white laterally. The throat and chin are white and the belly bright orange.

Preferred habitat: Moist savanna.

Habits: A small, distinctly marked snake that inhabits moist savanna where it burrows in loose sand. It is a secretive nocturnal species and is seldom seen, unless ploughed up, or after heavy rain when it may be found on the surface. If threatened, it curls itself into loose coils, hides the head and raises the tail, curling it to create a decoy. It may even attempt mock strikes with its tail.

Similar species: It is very difficult to misidentify this snake, especially with the three clear black stripes down its back on a yellow to greenish yellow background.

Enemies: Unknown.

Food and feeding: Small snakes, including its own type, amphisbaenids and other burrowing reptiles.

Reproduction: Oviparous, laying up to 6 elongate eggs (30–32 mm x 6–8 mm) in summer.

Danger to man: None.

Subspecies: Only the typical race of Gerard's Black and Yellow Burrowing Snake (*Chilorhinophis gerardi gerardi*) occurs within our range.

Venom: The venom of this snake has not been studied but is not considered dangerous to man.

This secretive nocturnal snake is seldom encountered unless ploughed up.

John Visser

LOOK OUT FOR

- A very small slender snake with rounded snout.
- The eyes have round pupils.
- Has 3 black stripes down the back on a yellow to greenish yellow background.

Save Quill-snouted Snake

Xenocalamus sabiensis

OTHER NAMES
Previously known as Sabi Quill-snouted Snake (E)
Saveskerpneusslang (A)
Savespitsneusslang (A)

average 40 cm   maximum 51 cm

MILDLY VENOMOUS

Length: Adults average 30–40 cm with a maximum length of nearly 51 cm.

Scale count: Midbody scales are in 17 rows, with 187–218 ventrals and 22–33 paired subcaudals. The anal shield is divided. There are 5–6 upper labials, the 2nd and 3rd (sometimes 3rd and 4th or only the 3rd) entering the eye, and 6 lower labials, with no preocular and 1 postocular. Temporals are 0 + 1.

Colour: Above, uniform black with yellow on the lower flanks. The belly is white and may have a few brown blotches.

Preferred habitat: Alluvial sand in moist savanna.

Habits: This burrowing species inhabits alluvial sand on the Mozambique plain and in south-eastern Zimbabwe, where it is rare. Specimens are sometimes driven to the surface by excessive rain, or are uncovered during excavation operations. This snake is endemic to southern Africa.

Similar species: May be confused with other quill-snouted snakes (*Xenocalamus* spp.). These snakes have a unique snout, which makes them easy to distinguish from other snakes.

Enemies: Other snakes.

Food and feeding: Mainly amphisbaenids.

Reproduction: Oviparous, laying 3–4 elongate eggs.

Danger to man: None.

Venom: The venom of this snake has not been studied but is not considered dangerous to man.

This rare burrowing snake inhabits alluvial sand.

LOOK OUT FOR

- Has a small elongate quill-shaped head.
- Minute eyes with round pupils.
- Is uniformly black above with yellow on the lower flanks.
- Belly may have a few brown blotches.

John Visser

MILDLY VENOMOUS

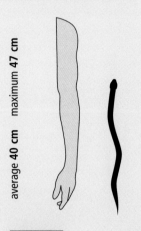

average 40 cm   maximum 47 cm

Transvaal Quill-snouted Snake

Xenocalamus transvaalensis

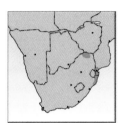

OTHER NAMES

Transvaalse spitsneusslang (A)

Transvaalse skerpneusslang (A)

Length: Adults average 30–40 cm with a maximum length of nearly 47 cm.

Scale count: Midbody scales are in 17 rows, with 183–192 ventrals and 23–32 paired subcaudals. The anal shield is divided. There are 5 upper labials, the 2nd and 3rd entering the eye, and 5 or 6 lower labials, with no preocular and 1 postocular. Temporals are 0 + 1.

Colour: Black above, sometimes with pale-centred or yellow-edged scales, giving it a chequered appearance. The belly and lower flanks are white to yellow and may have dark blotches.

Preferred habitat: Alluvial sand in lowland forest and moist savanna.

Habits: An inoffensive slender burrower that is harmless to man. It inhabits alluvial sand where it may be threatened by agricultural activities. This snake is listed as rare in the latest *South African Red Data Book – Reptiles and Amphibians* (Branch, 1988) and is endemic to southern Africa.

Similar species: May be confused with other quill-snouted snakes (*Xenocalamus* spp.), but has yellow-edged scales on a black background that often give it a chequered appearance. These snakes have a unique snout, which makes them easy to distinguish from other snakes.

Enemies: Other snakes.

Food and feeding: Burrowing skinks and worm lizards.

Reproduction: Oviparous, laying 2 elongate eggs (28 x 6 mm) in early summer.

Danger to man: None.

Venom: The venom of this snake has not been studied but is not considered dangerous to man.

The Transvaal Quill-snouted Snake is threatened by agricultural activities and is considered rare.

LOOK OUT FOR

- Has a small elongate quill-shaped head.
- Minute eyes with round pupils.
- Is black above with yellow scales that may give it a chequered appearance.
- Small slender snake.

Wulf Haacke

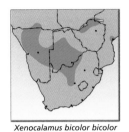

Xenocalamus bicolor bicolor

Bicoloured Quill-snouted Snake

Xenocalamus bicolor

OTHER NAMES
Tweekleurspitsneusslang (A)
Tweekleurskerpneusslang (A)

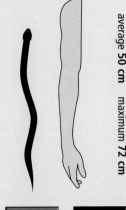

average 50 cm   maximum 72 cm

Length: Adults average about 50 cm with a maximum length of nearly 72 cm.

Scale count: Midbody scales are in 17 rows, with 186–256 ventrals and 20–37 paired subcaudals. The anal shield is divided. There are 5–6 upper labials, the 3rd and 4th entering the eye, and 5 (sometimes 4) lower labials, with no preocular and 1 postocular. Temporals are 0 + 1.

Colour: Variable, but the following colour phases are the most common: (a) the typical bicoloured phase with the back purple-brown to black and the lower flanks off-white to yellowish. The belly is white, sometimes with dark blotches. (b) The spotted phase; yellow above with 2 rows of irregular purple-brown spots. The belly is uniform white. (c) The reticulated phase; the back is brown to grey with pale-edged scales. The lower flanks and belly are white. (d) The melanistic phase; the overall colour is uniform black above and below. Various intermediate colour phases have been observed.

Preferred habitat: Alluvial sand in moist savanna, arid savanna and karoo scrub. The Striped Quill-snouted Snake (*Xenocalamus bicolor lineatus*) is found in lowland forest and moist savanna while the Waterberg Quill-snouted Snake (*Xenocalamus bicolor australis*) is found in moist savanna in the Waterberg range in the Limpopo Province.

Habits: An inoffensive nocturnal burrower that lives deep down in alluvial sand. It is seldom seen but may be found under rotting logs or exposed during bulldozing operations. A specimen has been found near Bloemfontein in a deserted termite mound. Individuals are occasionally flushed to the surface during heavy rain.

Similar species: May be confused with other quill-snouted snakes but can be distinguished by the coloration. These snakes have a unique snout, which makes them easy to distinguish from other snakes.

Enemies: Other snakes.

Food and feeding: Burrowing skinks and worm lizards.

Reproduction: Oviparous, laying 3–4 elongate eggs (40–47 x 15 mm) in midsummer. The young measure 20 cm.

A nocturnal burrower that may be flushed to the surface by heavy rains.

Wulf Haacke

Danger to man: None.

Subspecies: There are 3 subspecies in southern Africa.

The Bicoloured Quill-snouted Snake (*Xenocalamus bicolor bicolor*), discussed above, is the most widespread of the subspecies. It occurs in all of the colour phases and has 6 upper labials and high ventral counts.

The Striped Quill-snouted Snake (*Xenocalamus bicolor lineatus*) has a brown to black dorsal stripe with chrome yellow sides and a pale yellow belly. It is a small snake with a maximum length close to 60 cm. It has 6 upper labials, 15 midbody scale rows and a strongly compressed head.

The Waterberg Quill-snouted Snake (*Xenocalamus bicolor australis*) is dark slate to purplish brown above with creamy to yellowish lower flanks and undersides. It has 5 (sometimes 6) upper labials and 186–216 ventrals.

LOOK OUT FOR
- Has a small elongate quill-shaped head.
- Minute eyes with round pupils.
- Slender snake.

The Bicoloured Quill-snouted Snake is the most widespread of the subspecies.

Venom: The venom of this snake has not been studied, but is not considered dangerous to man.

The Striped Quill-snouted Snake has a brown to black dorsal stripe and a pale belly.

The quill-snouted snakes are easily distinguished from other snakes by their unique snout.

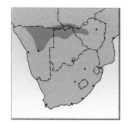

Elongate Quill-snouted Snake

Xenocalamus mechowii

MILDLY VENOMOUS

OTHER NAMES
Westelike spitsneusslang (A)
Westelike skerpneusslang (A)

Length: Adults average 50 cm with a maximum length of nearly 85 cm.

Scale count: Midbody scales are in 17 rows, with 247–296 ventrals and 22–32 paired subcaudals. The anal shield is divided. There are 6 (sometimes 5) upper labials, the 3rd and 4th entering the eye, and 5 lower labials, with no preocular and 2 postoculars. Temporals are 0 + 1.

Colour: Above, lemon yellow to light purple-brown with a double row of brownish blotches. The belly is white to yellowish brown, sometimes with darker brown blotches. Uniform black specimens are also found, albeit rarely.

Preferred habitat: Kalahari sand in arid savanna.

Habits: A secretive burrower that lives in Kalahari sand. It may be found on the surface at night and is rather docile, seldom attempting to bite.

Similar species: May be confused with other quill-snouted snakes (*Xenocalamus* spp.), but has unique coloration. These snakes have a unique snout, which makes them easy to distinguish from other snakes.

Enemies: Other snakes.

Food and feeding: Amphisbaenids.

Reproduction: Oviparous, laying up to 4 elongate eggs.

Danger to man: None.

Subspecies: Only 1 subspecies of Elongate Quill-snouted Snake (*Xenocalamus merchowii inornatus*) is found within our range.

Venom: The venom of this snake has not been studied, but is not considered dangerous to man.

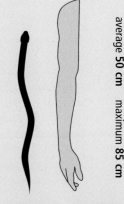

average 50 cm   maximum 85 cm

The Elongate Quill-snouted Snake has a double row of brownish blotches down the back.

LOOK OUT FOR

- Has a small elongate quill-shaped head with a prominent depressed snout.
- Minute eyes with round pupils.
- Slender snake.
- Has 2 irregular rows of dark blotches on the back.

Wulf Haacke

Cream-spotted Mountain Snake

Montaspis gilvomaculata

OTHER NAMES
Roomgevlekte bergslang (A)

Length: A smallish snake, averaging 30 cm and probably not exceeding 50 cm.

Scale count: Midbody scales are in 21 rows, with 145–151 ventrals and 53–59 paired subcaudals. The anal shield is entire. There are 7 upper labials, the 3rd and 4th entering the eye, and 9 lower labials, with 1 preocular and 2 postoculars. Temporals are 1 + 2.

Colour: Above, shiny blackish brown. The dorsal head shields and upper lip have creamy spots while the chin and throat are largely cream, but are edged in brown. The belly is dark brown with pale-edged scales and small cream spots that fade towards the tail.

Preferred habitat: Mountain streams and vleis at high altitude in grassland.

Habits: The first known specimen was collected in the Cathedral Peak Forest Reserve in 1980. Since then only a few more individuals have been collected. This snake does not attempt to bite when handled, but may flatten its body and move with jerky movements. It may also, if stressed, emit a foul-smelling substance from its cloaca in self-defence.

average 30 cm   maximum 50 cm

An unusual snake that was described quite recently and is known from only a few specimens.

The Cream-spotted Mountain Snake is a terrestrial diurnal snake that lives in wetlands in the high treeless Drakensberg. It is probably a good swimmer and appears to be well adapted to survival in a cold environment where mean daytime temperatures seldom exceed 14 °C in summer. It is endemic to southern Africa.

Similar species: May be confused with the Herald Snake (*Crotaphopeltis hotamboeia*) but has distinct creamy spots on the upper lip, while the chin and throat are largely cream with brown edging.

Enemies: Unknown.

Food and feeding: It actively hunts frogs along waterside vegetation and in reed beds. It may throw a few coils around its prey while subduing it.

Reproduction: A female has been found carrying 6 eggs during March.

Danger to man: No real threat to humans.

Venom: Nothing is known of the veom of this snake, but it is not considered dangerous.

LOOK OUT FOR
■ Only found at high altitude in the Drakensberg.
■ Has distinct cream spots on the upper lip while the chin and throat have brown-edged cream markings.
■ Medium-sized eyes with round pupils.

This snake inhabits wetlands at high altitudes.

This snake actively hunts for frogs along waterside vegetation.

A diurnal snake that occurs high up in the Drakensberg where it copes well in a cold environment.

Wulf Haacke

FANGLESS AND NON-VENOMOUS SNAKES

None of the fangless snakes possesses venom, but they do have teeth in both upper and lower jaws and some, in particular the Southern African Python (*Python natalensis*) and large Mole Snakes (*Pseudaspis cana*), are capable of inflicting painful bites.

Most of the fangless snakes are oviparous or egg-laying, with the exception of the slug-eaters (*Duberria* spp.) and the Mole Snake.

With very few exceptions, these snakes are not well studied. Some are so secretive and so seldom encountered that we know little or nothing of their habits and behaviour.

Many non-venomous snakes, such as house snakes, use constriction to kill their prey, while others, such as egg-eaters, specialize on particular prey types.

Though they lack fangs, these snakes usually have many teeth.

Bill Branch

Many of these snakes, like this East African Shovel-snout, are specialized feeders.

Southern African Python

Python natalensis

OTHER NAMES
Previously known as the Rock Python (E)
Suider-Afrikaanse luislang (A)
Inhlwathi (Z)
Intlwathi (X)

DANGEROUS

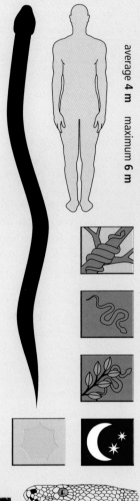

average 4 m　maximum 6 m

Length: The largest snake in southern Africa, it averages 3–4 m and may reach 6 m elsewhere in Africa. Large specimens (over 5 m) are rare nowadays.

Scale count: Midbody scales are in 78–95 rows, with 261–291 ventrals and 63–84 paired subcaudals. The anal shield is entire. There are 12–15 upper labials, none entering the eye, and 17–20 lower labials. There are 8–13 scales around the eye. Temporals are numerous and variable.

Colour: Above, dark brown with grey-brown blotches and dark speckling, and widely spaced dark blotches on the sides. There is a dark arrowhead marking on the crown of the head. The underside is white to dirty white with dark blotches.

Preferred habitat: Fairly widespread, preferring rocky outcrops in arid and moist savanna as well as in lowland forest.

Habits: Most active at night, though very fond of basking – especially after a large meal. It often ambushes its prey, latches on with its powerful recurved teeth, and constricts it. Contrary to popular belief, it does not crush its prey to death and never breaks any bones in the process. Death is thought to result from cardiac failure. It is also incorrect to say that a python has to anchor its tail around a tree before it can constrict its prey. This snake is fond of water and may dive into deep pools where it can remain submerged for very long periods.

This is by far the largest snake in southern Africa, and may exceed 5 m in length.

Pythons are extremely valuable as they help to control rodent populations, especially dassies (*Procavia capensis*) and cane rats (*Thryonomys swinderianus*). Unfortunately, they have been killed indiscriminately in the past and this persists today. The Southern African Python is listed as vulnerable in the latest *South African Red Data Book – Reptiles and Amphibians* (Branch, 1988) and may not be killed or captured. Both its skin and fat are still used in traditional medicine.

Similar species: This large, bulky snake cannot easily be confused with other snakes.

Enemies: Mongooses, meerkats, crocodiles, wild dogs, hyenas, honey badgers and other snakes. Many are killed while crossing roads. Some are also killed for their skin and fat.

Food and feeding: Diet includes dassies, cane rats, hares, monkeys, small antelopes and game birds. Fishes, monitor lizards (*Varanus* spp.) and crocodiles (*Crocodylus niloticus*) are also taken. Juveniles feed largely on ground-living birds and rodents.

Reproduction: Oviparous, laying 30–60 eggs (in exceptional cases more than 100), depending on the size of the female. The eggs are about 10 cm in diameter (a little smaller than a tennis ball) and weigh 130–160 g. Once the female has deposited her eggs in a suitable site, such as a hollowed-out termite mound or ant bear hole, she will coil around her eggs and remain there until they hatch. During this period she will not feed, but may leave the eggs to bask and drink. The female basks to generate extra body heat, which she then

> ### LOOK OUT FOR
> - A large, bulky snake.
> - Has several heat-sensitive pits on the upper and lower lip.
> - Likes to bask in the sun, especially after a meal.
> - Partial to water and often dives into deep pools where it can remain submerged for long periods.
> - Most active at dusk and at night.

transfers to the eggs by coiling around them. The eggs hatch after 2–3 months and the young measure 50–70 cm. If undisturbed, the babies and the mother remain at the nest site for more than 2 weeks and move off on their own only after the first shed is complete. Thus the mother may afford some protection to the young during this time. They may take up to 10 years to reach sexual maturity.

Danger to man: Pythons have been known to kill people in the past but today large individuals are very rare. Because of the python's size and the fact that it has numerous strong, recurved teeth, a bite may cause considerable tissue damage and the victim may even need stitches. Pythons do lunge and bite readily and cause painful wounds that often require medical attention.

First-aid procedures: A bite from a python must be treated as a dirty wound: washed, disinfected and monitored for signs of sepsis. Medical advice should be sought.

A versatile snake that may be found in water, among rocks, or even in trees.

Anchieta's Dwarf Python

Python anchietae

OTHER NAMES
Angola Dwarf Python (E)
Anchieta se dwergluislang (A)
Angoladwergluislang (A)

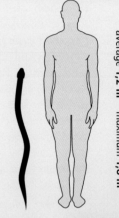

average 1,2 m   maximum 1,8 m

Length: Adults average 1–1,2 m with a maximum length of 1,8 m.

Scale count: Midbody scales are in 57–61 rows, with 253–267 ventrals and 46–57 paired subcaudals. The anal shield is entire. There are 14 upper labials, none entering the eye, and 15–16 lower labials. There are 15–18 scales around the eye. Temporals are numerous and variable.

Colour: Most of the head is covered by a large reddish brown triangular marking bordered on the sides by creamy white black-edged bands. The top and sides of the body are reddish brown with black-edged creamy white blotches and bands. The belly is creamy white to yellowish with brown spots on the sides.

Preferred habitat: Riverine bush and rugged rocky habitat in Namib Desert and karoo scrub.

Habits: This small, placid python is one of the rarest snakes in southern Africa and is known from relatively few individuals. It inhabits dry, rocky sandveld regions and riverine bush, where it is seldom encountered. In captivity it is primarily active at night. Captive individuals are known to roll up into a defensive ball with the head concealed, very much like the Ball Python or Royal Python (*Python regius*) of West Africa. Anchieta's Dwarf Python is fully protected in Namibia.

Richard Boycott

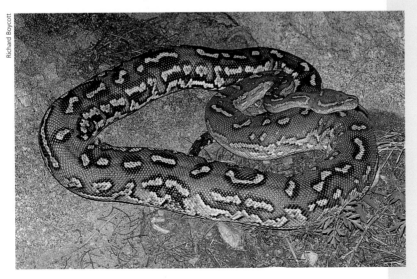

This small python is extremely rare and is fully protected in Namibia.

Similar species: May be confused with a small Southern African Python (*Python natalensis*), but they do not occur in the same areas, and the Southern African Python is much larger and bulkier.

Enemies: Unknown. Very popular in private collections and can be seen for sale at some overseas snake shows.

Food and feeding: Rodents, such as gerbils and rats, and birds. Captive specimens feed on laboratory mice and sparrows. The prey is constricted prior to being swallowed.

Reproduction: A gravid, wild-caught female laid 5 eggs (62 x 37 mm) in November / December (early summer). Incubation took 75 days and the young were 44–50 cm long. Another captive female produced 4 eggs on 20 November, measuring 90–95 x 40-42 mm. These young measured 49–51 cm.

Danger to man: None.

LOOK OUT FOR

■ A small, gentle python.
■ Has 5 heat-sensitive pits on the upper lip.
■ The body scales are very small and smooth.

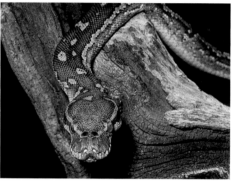

Anchieta's Dwarf Python feeds on rodents and birds.

This rare snake is often collected illegally for the pet trade.

Like the Ball Python of West Africa, Anchieta's Dwarf Python may also roll into a ball with its head concealed in its coils.

Brown House Snake
Lamprophis capensis

OTHER NAMES
Bruinhuisslang (A)
Umzingandlu (Z)
Inkwakhwa (X)

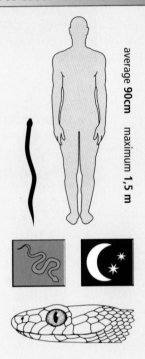

average 90cm maximum 1,5 m

Length: The average length of adults is 60–90 cm, but those from KwaZulu-Natal are known to reach lengths of 1,5 m.
Scale count: Midbody scales are in 25–35 rows, with 186–228 ventrals and 45–71 paired subcaudals. The anal shield is entire. There are 8 (sometimes 9) upper labials, the 4th and 5th entering the eye, but this is variable, and 9 (sometimes 8 or 10) lower labials, as well as 1 or 2 preoculars and 2 postoculars. Temporals are 1 + 2 but this varies.
Colour: Above, uniform light to reddish brown (often with reddish blotches on the anterior half of the body) or dark olive to black, especially in old specimens. There are 2 light stripes on either side of the head, 1 running from the tip of the snout across the upper half of the eye and sometimes continuing along the anterior third of the body, while the other runs from the lower half of the eye to the angle of the mouth. This characteristic distinguishes the Brown House Snake from all other South African snakes. The underside is yellowish to mother-of-pearl white. Juveniles may have indistinct spots or mottling dorsally.
Preferred habitat: Found almost everywhere. Common around human dwellings, hence the common name.
Habits: A common nocturnal constrictor that forages for rodents. It is often found around houses but, because of its nocturnal habits,

The Brown House Snake can usually be identified by the light markings on the sides of the head.

Rodents form the bulk of this snake's diet.

Note the bulging eyes – this specimen is from Namaqualand.

LOOK OUT FOR

- A terrestrial nocturnal snake.
- Usually has a distinct light stripe that runs from the tip of the snout to the upper half of the eye and continues to the back of the head, as well as another light stripe from the lower half of the eye to the angle of the jaw.
- Common around human dwellings.

is not seen often, except during cleaning-up operations when it may be found beneath building rubble, in compost heaps or even in tool sheds and outbuildings. It preys on rodents, which it secures with its sharp teeth and then constricts. This snake has the ability to devour an entire rodent family in a single session. The Brown House Snake may bite

readily if threatened. One individual in Namibia was observed shamming death, like the Rinkhals (*Hemachatus haemachatus*).

Similar species: Large individuals resemble small pythons; however, the light markings on the head are distinct.

Enemies: Other snakes, including the File Snake (*Mehelya capensis*), cobras (*Naja* spp.), whip snakes (*Psammophis* spp.), monitors (*Varanus* spp.) and spiders of the genus *Latrodectus*. It is also preyed upon by birds of prey, particularly owls, and carnivorous mammals. It is often killed by humans when encountered in residential gardens.

Food and feeding: Mainly rodents and other small vertebrates, including bats and birds. Lizards, especially skinks, are also taken. Frogs are occasionally eaten.

Reproduction: Oviparous, laying 8–18 eggs (25–56,2 x 12–24 mm) in summer. The young measure 19–26 cm. Captive females may produce several batches of eggs in a season.

Subspecies: A large-eyed thin form that occurs in Namibia may well be a separate species.

Danger to man: None.

Note: Southern African specimens have rece-ntly undergone a name change – from *Lamprophis fuliginosus* to *Lamprophis capensis*.

This snake tends to frequent human dwellings, hence the common name.

Olive House Snake
Lamprophis inornatus

OTHER NAMES
Black House Snake (E)
Nagslang (A)
Olyfhuisslang (A)

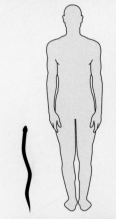

HARMLESS

average 75 cm   maximum 1,3 m

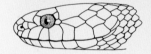

Length: Adults average 45–75 cm and may reach 1,3 m.
Scale count: Midbody scales are in 21–25 rows, with 170–196 ventrals and 45–70 paired subcaudals. The anal shield is entire. There are 8 upper labials, the 3rd, 4th and 5th (sometimes the 4th and 5th) entering the eye, but this is variable, and 8 (sometimes 7) lower labials, as well as 1 preocular (sometimes 2) and 2 postoculars (sometimes 1). Temporals are 1 + 2.
Colour: Above, uniform olive green, olive grey, light brown, or brownish black to black, with underparts uniformly dark as above or slightly lighter, especially in the vicinity of the chin, throat and forepart of the body.
Preferred habitat: Moist savanna, lowland forest and fynbos.
Habits: Very similar in habits to the Brown House Snake (*Lamprophis capensis*) but prefers moister habitats. This snake is not nearly as common as the Brown House Snake. It is partial to rubble and debris, and is also found near human dwellings. This snake is endemic to southern Africa.
Similar species: Could be mistaken for a number of other uniformly coloured snakes, including the Black Mamba (*Dendroaspis polylepis*).
Enemies: Other snakes and predatory birds.
Food and feeding: This snake feeds on lizards, rodents and other snakes.
Reproduction: Oviparous, laying 5–15 eggs (32–45 x 20–25 mm) in summer. The young measure 19–24 cm.
Danger to man: None.

LOOK OUT FOR

- A nocturnal terrestrial snake.
- Has small eyes.
- Plain olive green to grey or black above with no markings.
- Strictly terrestrial, seldom venturing into trees or bushes.

An endemic snake that is active at night. It is partial to rubble and debris, and is also found near human dwellings.

Aurora House Snake

Lamprophis aurora

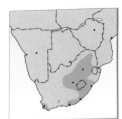

OTHER NAMES
Auroraslang (A)

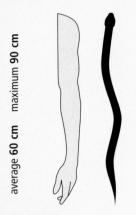

maximum 90 cm   average 60 cm

Length: Adults average 45–60 cm but may reach a length of 90 cm.
Scale count: Midbody scales are in 21–23 rows, with 165–185 ventrals and 35–58 paired subcaudals. The anal shield is entire. There are 8 upper labials, the 4th and 5th (sometimes the 3rd, 4th and 5th) entering the eye, and 8 (sometimes 7 or 9) lower labials, as well as 1 preocular (sometimes 2) and 2 postoculars. Temporals are 2 + 3.
Colour: Above, shiny olive green with a bright yellow to orange vertebral stripe from the top of the head to the tip of the tail. Below, yellowish to light greenish white. Juveniles are darker in colour and may have a speckled appearance, including black speckles on the head.
Preferred habitat: Favours damp localities in grasslands, moist savanna, lowland forest and fynbos.
Habits: A colourful, nocturnal snake that may bask in the early mornings or late afternoons. It may also emerge on overcast days. The Aurora House Snake is very secretive and is seldom seen. It is a harmless constrictor and seldom attempts to bite. It is endemic to southern Africa.
Similar species: Juveniles may be confused with the striped phase of the Harlequin Snake (*Homoroselaps lacteus*).
Enemies: Snakes and predatory birds. Habitat destruction around Johannesburg has had an effect on local populations.
Food and feeding: Nestling rodents, lizards and frogs.
Reproduction: Oviparous, laying 8–12 eggs (35–50,5 x 12,2–20 mm) in summer. The young measure 20–22,5 cm.
Danger to man: None.

LOOK OUT FOR

- Uniform olive green above with distinct yellow to orange stripe down back.
- Strictly terrestrial, seldom venturing into trees or bushes.
- Nocturnal, but may bask in the early morning or late afternoon.
- Often active on overcast days.

The Aurora House Snake has a distinct yellow to orange stripe down the centre of its back.

HARMLESS

Spotted Rock Snake
Lamprophis guttatus

HARMLESS

OTHER NAMES
Spotted House Snake (E)
Gevlekte rotsslang (A)

Length: Adults average 30–50 cm, seldom exceeding 62 cm.
Scale count: Midbody scales are in 21–25 rows, with 186–230 ventrals and 46–72 paired subcaudals. The anal shield is entire. There are 7 (sometimes 9) upper labials, the 3rd, 4th and 5th (sometimes the 4th and 5th) entering the eye, and 8 lower labials, as well as 1 preocular and 2 or 3 postoculars. Temporals are 1 + 2.
Colour: Above, yellowish brown to pinkish grey with reddish brown to dark brown blotches or spots that are arranged in adjacent or alternate pairs, sometimes forming a zigzag pattern down the back. The underside is white to yellowish white. The colour of this snake varies regionally. Specimens from Calvinia in the Northern Cape are usually light to medium brown with very dark brown spots that decrease in size towards the tail.
Preferred habitat: Found in fynbos, karoo scrub, grassland, moist savanna and lowland forest.
Habits: A secretive snake that is found in narrow rock cracks and under exfoliating rock flakes. It is very common in some areas in the western half of its distribution, but is rare in others. The Spotted Rock Snake inhabits mountainous and rocky areas, seeks shelter during the day, and hunts at night. It is endemic to southern Africa.
Similar species: Because of the markings on its back, this snake is not easily confused with other species.
Enemies: Other snakes.
Food and feeding: Lizards, mainly geckos of the genera *Pachydactylus* and *Afroedura*, which also inhabit rocky areas, lacertids and skinks. Rodents are also taken.
Reproduction: Oviparous, laying 3–6 eggs (38 x 20 mm) in summer.
Danger to man: None.

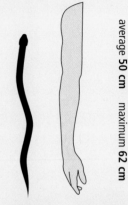

average 50 cm   maximum 62 cm

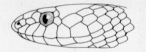

A secretive snake that inhabits narrow rock cracks.

LOOK OUT FOR

- Dark blotches or spots down the back arranged in alternate pairs that may form a zigzag pattern.
- Active at night.
- Prefers rocky areas where it lives in narrow rock cracks.

Marius Burger

HARMLESS

Fisk's House Snake
Lamprophis fiskii

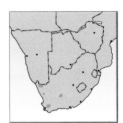

OTHER NAMES
Fisk se huisslang (A)

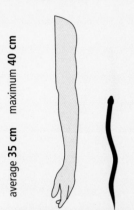

maximum 40 cm

average 35 cm

Restricted largely to karoo scrub.

An extremely rare snake that is known from fewer than 20 individuals.

Length: A diminutive species averaging 25–35 cm, but not exceeding 40 cm.
Scale count: Midbody scales are in 21–23 rows, with 178–183 ventrals and 28–34 paired subcaudals. The anal shield is entire. There are 7 or 8 upper labials, the 4th and 5th entering the eye, and 7 or 8 lower labials, as well as 1 preocular and 2 postoculars. Temporals are 1 + 2.
Colour: Lemon yellow above with dark brown spots in a double alternating series, or sometimes in a single series anteriorly, which often fuse to form short, irregular crossbars on the sides of the body. The scales are dark-centred with yellowish white borders. The head is lemon yellow with a dark brown bar between the eyes and a horseshoe-shaped bar across the snout, which passes backward on either side, across the eyes and to the angle of the jaw. The lips and underside are a uniform creamy white colour.
Preferred habitat: Restricted largely to karoo scrub.
Habits: A little known, rare and elusive snake. The few recorded specimens have mostly been found on the roads at night, 1 while it was raining. It is undoubtedly nocturnal and spends most of its life underground. When threatened, it will coil and uncoil the front and rear parts of its body while hissing – behaviour typical of shovel-snout snakes of the genus *Prosymna*. It is listed as rare in the current *South African Red Data Book – Reptiles and Amphibians* (Branch, 1988) and is known from fewer than 20 specimens.
Similar species: The markings of this snake are unique and it cannot easily be confused with other snakes.
Enemies: Unknown, probably other snakes.
Food and feeding: The stomach contents of a wild-caught specimen revealed a Burchell's sand lizard (*Pedioplanis burchelli*). Captive specimens have taken geckos and are known to constrict their prey.
Reproduction: A captive female laid 8 eggs in summer.
Danger to man: None.

Bruce Taubert

LOOK OUT FOR

■ Lemon yellow with dark spots down the back.
■ Active at night.

Yellow-bellied House Snake

Lamprophis fuscus

OTHER NAMES
Geelpenshuisslang (A)

Length: A small snake that averages 40–50 cm, with a maximum length of 76 cm.

Scale count: Midbody scales are in 19 rows, with 165–202 ventrals and 51–74 paired subcaudals. The anal shield is entire. There are 7 or 8 upper labials, the 3rd and 4th (sometimes 5th and 6th) entering the eye, and 7 or 8 lower labials, as well as 1 preocular (sometimes 2) and 2 postoculars. Temporals are 1 + 2.

Colour: Plain olive brown to light olive green above with yellow upper lip, sides and belly. The sides are usually brighter than the belly.

Preferred habitat: From fynbos scrub to arid savanna and grassland.

Habits: This secretive, rare snake is nocturnal and is found in termite mounds and under stones. Specimens have been found near Grahamstown on rocky, grassy hillsides with semi-closed tree canopy. These snakes were found under rocks close to streams and were gentle and docile, making no attempt to bite. This snake is endemic to South Africa and is listed as rare in the current *South African Red Data Book – Reptiles and Amphibians* (Branch, 1988).

Similar species: Easily confused with the Olive House Snake (*Lamprophis inornatus*) and some of the water snakes of the genus *Lycodonomorphus*, as well as a number of other harmless snakes.

Enemies: Other snakes.

Food and feeding: Mainly lizards. A common Mountain Lizard (*Tropidosaura montana*) was found in the stomach of a specimen caught in the southern Cape. Dwarf shrews and other nestling rodents are also taken.

Reproduction: Oviparous, laying a small clutch of eggs.

Danger to man: None.

average 50 cm   maximum 76 cm

A specimen from Grahamstown.

LOOK OUT FOR

- A plain olive brown to olive green snake.
- Active at night.
- Upper lip, sides and belly usually yellow in colour.

A rare nocturnal snake that may be found in termite mounds.

Richard Boycott

Swazi Rock Snake

Lamprophis swazicus

HARMLESS

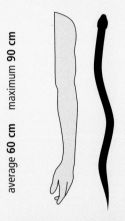

OTHER NAMES
Swazirotsslang (A)

Length: Adults average 50–60 cm, reaching nearly 90 cm.
Scale count: Midbody scales are in 17 rows, with 199–208 ventrals and 75–91 paired subcaudals. The anal shield is entire. There are 8 upper labials, the 3rd, 4th and 5th entering the eye, and 9–11 lower labials, as well as 1 preocular and 2 postoculars. Temporals are 1 + 2.
Colour: Dark red to beige or light brown above. The belly is cream to creamy white.
Preferred habitat: Restricted to moist savanna.
Habits: A slender-bodied snake with prominent eyes. It inhabits narrow rock crevices and exfoliating rock flakes on rocky outcrops. This snake is nocturnal and climbs well, like the Tiger Snake (*Telescopus semiannulatus*). It is endemic to southern Africa and is listed as rare in the current *South African Red Data Book – Reptiles and Amphibians* (Branch, 1988).
Similar species: A rather plain, nondescript snake that could be confused with a variety of other harmless snakes.
Enemies: Unknown, probably other snakes.
Food and feeding: Small lizards, especially geckos and skinks. Small birds are probably also taken.
Reproduction: A large female collected in October was carrying 7 elongate eggs (29–36 x 10–13 mm).
Danger to man: None.

Richard Boycott

LOOK OUT FOR

- A nocturnal inhabitant of rocky areas.
- Climbs well.
- Is slender-bodied with prominent eyes.

The Swazi Rock Snake is nocturnal, feeding on lizards and birds.

average 60 cm   maximum 90 cm

Dusky-bellied Water Snake

Lycodonomorphus laevissimus

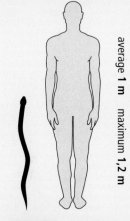

average 1 m   maximum 1,2 m

OTHER NAMES

Swartwaterslang (A)
Ivuzamanzi limnyama (Z)
Inyushu emdaka (X)

Length: Adults average 70–100 cm and may reach a length of nearly 1,2 m.

Scale count: Midbody scales are in 19 rows, with 154–179 ventrals and 53–89 paired subcaudals. The anal shield is entire. There are 8 (sometimes 7) upper labials, the 4th and 5th (sometimes 3rd and 4th) entering the eye, and 8 (sometimes 7) lower labials, as well as 1 preocular and 2 postoculars. Temporals are 1 + 2.

Colour: Above, plain dark olive grey to brownish black or black. The lower flanks may be pale with elongate dark spots that form an irregular longitudinal line. The upper lip has dark spots. The underside is cream to yellow or orange-yellow with dark blotches that form a jagged broad band down the centre of the belly.

Preferred habitat: Streams and rivers in lowland forest, moist savanna and grassland.

Habits: A common aquatic snake that favours pools and well-wooded streams. It is active during the day and often swims while completely submerged. It is bad-tempered and, in addition to biting readily, may also give off a foul smell in self-defence. It is, however, harmless and does not possess venom.

Similar species: Could be confused with a variety of other harmless snakes, especially the Common Brown Water Snake (*Lycodonomorphus rufulus*), but can be distinguished on the basis of the dark blotches on the belly.

An aquatic snake that favours well-wooded streams.

Marius Burger

Marius Burger

- Active during the day.
- Usually has dark spots on the upper lip.
- Has dark blotches down the belly that form a broad band.
- An aquatic snake that frequents pools and streams.
- The eyes are situated on top of the head.

The markings on this snake's belly give it its common name.

Enemies: Other snakes, water mongooses (*Atilax paludinosus*), monitors (*Varanus* spp.) and birds of prey.

Food and feeding: Feeds on frogs, tadpoles and fish. Smaller prey is swallowed while under water; larger food items are constricted and, if swallowing is prolonged, carried to the edge of the water and then swallowed above the surface.

Reproduction: Oviparous, laying 4–17 eggs.

Danger to man: None.

A harmless snake that does not possess any venom.

A diurnal snake that lives in streams and rivers, where it often swims completely submerged.

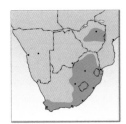

Common Brown Water Snake

Lycodonomorphus rufulus

OTHER NAMES
Bruinwaterslang (A)
Ivuzamanzi elimdubu (Z)
Izilenzi (X)

HARMLESS

average 60 cm maximum 85 cm

Length: Adults average 45–60 cm, seldom exceeding 85 cm. Females are generally longer than males.

Scale count: Midbody scales are in 19 rows, with 158–179 ventrals and 53–86 paired subcaudals. The anal shield is entire. There are 7 or 8 upper labials, the 3rd and 4th, or 4th and 5th (sometimes 4th, 5th and 6th) entering the eye, and 8 (sometimes 7 or 9) lower labials, as well as 1 preocular (sometimes 2) and 2 postoculars. Temporals are 1 + 2, and sometimes 1 + 3.

Colour: Above, uniform dark blackish to olive or light brown. The underparts are beautiful mother-of-pearl, pink or yellowish.

Preferred habitat: The well-watered, eastern half of southern Africa. Prefers rivers, streams, vleis and damp areas in grasslands, moist savanna, lowland forest and fynbos.

Habits: A nocturnal, aquatic snake that swims very well. Usually confined to very damp localities near streams and rivers. It is mainly active at night, but may hunt along shaded streams during the day.

This snake is common throughout much of its range and can be found beneath rocks, logs and other debris. Zulu people traditionally believe it to be very dangerous. It is, in fact, a shy, harmless snake.

The Common Brown Water Snake is nocturnal, but may hunt along shaded streams during the day.

Marius Burger

As the name indicates, this snake favours water and swims well.

Similar species: May be confused with other harmless snakes such as the Brown House Snake (*Lamprophis capensis*). Distinguished by its plain colour and plain pink or yellowish belly.

Enemies: Monitors (*Varanus* spp.), predatory birds, other snakes and even hunting spiders.

Food and feeding: A powerful constrictor that feeds on frogs, tadpoles, small fish and occasionally nestlings and rodents.

Reproduction: Oviparous, laying 6–23 eggs (20–41,9 x 12–21,8 mm) in midsummer. The young measure 15–22 cm.

Danger to man: None.

LOOK OUT FOR

- Plain dark blackish brown above with a beautiful mother-of-pearl, pink or yellow underside.
- Excellent swimmer.
- Largely active at night.
- The pupils are vertical.

Atherton de Villiers

The Common Brown Water Snake may be confused with a variety of other harmless snakes.

Floodplain Water Snake

Lycodonomorphus obscuriventris

OTHER NAMES
Vloedvlaktewaterslang (A)

HARMLESS

average 55 cm   maximum 66 cm

Length: Adults average 45–55 cm, the longest recorded specimen being a female from Beira in Mozambique that measured 66 cm.

Scale count: Midbody scales are in 19 rows, with 164–175 ventrals and 37–52 paired subcaudals. The anal shield is entire. There are 8 (sometimes 9) upper labials, the 4th and 5th (sometimes 5th and 6th) entering the eye, and 8 lower labials, as well as 1 preocular and 2 postoculars. Temporals are 1 + 2.

Colour: Shiny dark grey-brown to blackish above with a distinct light stripe on the upper lip. The underside is yellow to yellow-orange, sometimes with dusky markings. The tail darkens towards the tip.

Preferred habitat: Pans, small streams and vleis in moist savanna.

Habits: A crepuscular nocturnal constrictor that hunts for food in the late afternoon or early evenings and is most likely to be found foraging in vegetation along pans, streams and vleis.

Similar species: Could be confused with a variety of harmless snakes including the Herald Snake (*Crotaphopeltis hotamboeia*) and the other water snakes (*Lycodonomorphus* spp.). It has a distinct light stripe on the upper lip and is limited in the extent of its distribution in southern Africa.

Enemies: Predatory birds and snakes.

Food and feeding: Frogs, including the Bubbling Kassina (*Kassina senegalensis*), puddle frogs (*Phrynobatrachus* spp.) and young Bullfrogs (*Pyxicephalus edulis*).

Reproduction: Unknown, but probably oviparous, laying small clutches of eggs like other water snakes in the genus.

Danger to man: None.

LOOK OUT FOR

- Crepuscular and nocturnal.
- Has a distinct light stripe along the upper lip.
- Found in or near water.
- The eye has a small elliptical pupil.

Bill Branch

Lives in pans, small streams and vleis, where it hunts at night.

HARMLESS

Mulanje Water Snake
Lycodonomorphus leleupi

OTHER NAMES
Mulanjewaterslang (A)

average 85 cm   maximum 93 cm

Length: Adults average 70–85 cm with a maximum length of 93 cm.
Scale count: Midbody scales are in 21 rows, with 164–171 ventrals and 51–76 paired subcaudals. The anal shield is entire. There are 8 upper labials, the 4th and 5th entering the eye, and 8 (sometimes 7 or 9) lower labials, as well as 1 preocular (sometimes 2) and 2 postoculars. Temporals are 1 + 2, and sometimes 1 + 3.
Colour: Glossy olive black above with a yellowish white to dull orange belly, usually with dark infusions. There is a dark stripe beneath the tail.
Preferred habitat: Small streams, pans and vleis in moist savanna.
Habits: Very similar in habits to the Common Brown Water Snake (*Lycodonomorphus rufulus*), often sharing the same habitat. It differs from the Common Brown Water Snake in that is diurnal. This snake is aquatic and is found in streams, dams and irrigation furrows, where it actively hunts its prey.
Similar species: Easily confused with a variety of other harmless snakes, especially water snakes (*Lycodonmorphus* spp.).
Enemies: Other snakes, predatory birds and monitors (*Varanus* spp.).
Food and feeding: Small fish and frogs. A specimen was captured while swallowing a small catfish (*Clarias gariepinus*). Captive individuals are known to take fish and frogs, including the African Clawed Frog or Platanna (*Xenopus laevis*).
Reproduction: Oviparous, laying up to 9 eggs (25 x 13 mm).
Subspecies: Only 1 subspecies of Mulanje Water Snake (*Lycodonomorphus leleupi mulanjensis*) occurs within our range.
Danger to man: None.

Colin Tilbury

LOOK OUT FOR
■ Active during the day.
■ Found in or near water.

This snake is very similar to the Common Brown Water Snake in habits, but is active during the day.

Mole Snake
Pseudaspis cana

OTHER NAMES
Molslang (A)

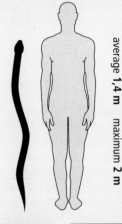

average 1,4 m maximum 2 m

Length: Adults average 1–1,4 m, but are known to exceed 2 m, especially in the Cape.

Scale count: Midbody scales are in 25–31 rows, with 175–218 ventrals and 43–70 paired subcaudals. The anal shield is divided. There are 7 (sometimes 6 or 8) upper labials, the 4th entering the eye, and 10–13 lower labials, as well as 1 preocular (sometimes 2) and 3 (sometimes 2 or 4) postoculars. Temporals are 3 + 4 or 2 + 4 but this varies.

Colour: Adults are usually uniform light grey to light brown, dark brown, brick red or black above and yellowish, sometimes with darker infusions, below. Juveniles are marked very differently and are usually light reddish brown to greyish brown with dark, usually zigzag markings, light spots and mottling above. Below, white to yellowish, sometimes with darker infusions.

Preferred habitat: A variety of habitats including mountainous regions and even desert. Particularly common in sandy scrub-covered and grassveld regions.

Habits: A large, powerful constrictor with a pointed snout and a small head very well adapted for its burrowing existence. It spends most of its time underground in search of food. Here is pushes its way through soft sand in search of moles and other rodents. Its prey is usually seized by the head and constricted.

Graham Alexander

The Mole Snake is well adapted for its burrowing existence.

Individual Mole Snakes may grow to lengths in excess of 2 m.

The Mole Snake feeds on a variety of small rodents and birds.

LOOK OUT FOR

- Varies tremendously in colour from nearly black to light brown. Juveniles often have rhombic markings.
- Pointed snout and small head.
- Spends much of its time underground in animal burrows.
- The eyes have a round pupil.

Adult males are known to engage in combat during the mating season, biting one another and inflicting nasty wounds, which often result in permanent scars. The Mole Snake, although not venomous, can be quite vicious when threatened and will hiss and lunge forward with its mouth agape. Unfortunately, this useful snake is often mistaken for a cobra or mamba and is usually killed on sight.

Similar species: May be confused with the Black Mamba (*Dendroaspis polylepis*) or a cobra, especially the Cape Cobra (*Naja nivea*). Young Mole Snakes may also be confused with the Dwarf Beaked Snake (*Dipsina multimaculata*) or the Spotted Skaapsteker (*Psammophylax rhombeatus*).
Enemies: Predatory birds and snakes. Many individuals are killed by vehicles while basking on tarred roads.
Food and feeding: Adults feed on rats, moles, gerbils and other small land mammals. Birds and nestlings are taken, as are eggs, which are swallowed whole. Juveniles feed largely on lizards.
Reproduction: Viviparous, giving birth to an average of 25–50 young or as many as 95 in late summer. The newborn snakes measure 20–31 cm.
Danger to man: Not considered harmful, but large adults may inflict a painful bite.

A juvenile Mole Snake with distinct markings.

A Black Mole Snake from Limpopo.

Olive Marsh Snake
Natriciteres olivacea

OTHER NAMES
Olyfkleurige vleislang (A)

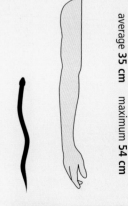

HARMLESS

average 35 cm   maximum 54 cm

Bill Branch

This snake has distinctive black labial sutures.

Length: Adults average 25–35 cm with a maximum length of 54 cm.

Scale count: Midbody scales are in 19 rows, with 17 scale rows at the rear, 130–153 ventrals and 57–87 paired subcaudals. The anal shield is divided. There are 8 (sometimes 7 or 9) upper labials, the 4th and 5th entering the eye (but variable), and 9–11 (sometimes 8) lower labials, as well as 1 preocular (sometimes 2) and 3 (sometimes 1 or 2) post-oculars. Temporals are 1 + 2 but variable.

Colour: Above, pale brown to dark olive or blackish with a darker (often maroon) band down the back, frequently edged with minute white spots. The lips are white with black labial sutures. The under-side is yellow to orange-yellow with dark olive to slate grey edges. The eye is golden brown.

Preferred habitat: Moist savanna.

Habits: An inoffensive, slow-moving diurnal snake that seldom ventures far from water, inhabiting vleis, pans and other marshy, damp areas. It seeks refuge under stones, logs and crevices in the clay banks of streams and is most active in the mornings. Like some of the sand snakes of the genus *Psammophis*, it spins its body when captured by the tail, often snapping off the tip. Many adults have truncated tails, suggesting previous close encounters with predators. The Olive Marsh Snake adjusts well to captivity and seldom attempts to bite.

Similar species: Easily confused with a variety of other harmless snakes.

Enemies: Predatory birds (including hamerkops) and snakes.

Food and feeding: Small fish, frogs, tadpoles and flying termites.

Reproduction: Oviparous, laying 3–11 (usually 6) eggs, measuring 21–23 x 7–15 mm, in summer.

Danger to man: None.

LOOK OUT FOR

- Active during the day.
- Found in or near water.
- The eye is golden brown, the pupil round.
- Has black-edged lip scales.

A slow-moving diurnal snake that favours water.

Steve Spawls

HARMLESS

average 35 cm   maximum 46 cm

Southern Forest Marsh Snake

Natriciteres sylvatica

OTHER NAMES
Suidelike woudvleislang (A)

Length: A slightly smaller snake than the Olive Marsh Snake (*Natriciteres olivacea*), measuring 30–35 cm with a maximum length of 46 cm.

Scale count: Midbody scales are in 17 rows, 15 towards the rear, with 125–143 ventrals and 60–84 paired subcaudals. The anal shield is divided. There are 8 (sometimes 7) upper labials, the 4th and 5th entering the eye (but variable), and 8 (sometimes 9) lower labials, as well as 1 preocular (sometimes 2) and 3 (sometimes 4) postoculars. Temporals are 1 + 2.

Colour: Above, dark olive brown to blackish, occasionally with a faint yellow collar. There is a broad, darker vertebral band that is usually bordered by minute white dots. The belly is yellow to orange with dark grey borders. The scales on the upper lip are yellow, bordered in black.

Preferred habitat: Lowland and montane evergreen forest.

Habits: A poorly known snake that inhabits swamps, lakes and streams adjacent to montane and lowland evergreen forest. It is secretive and may be found under stones, logs or other suitable hiding places at the edge of forest paths. Like some of the sand snakes of the genus *Psammophis*, it spins its body when captured by the tail, often snapping off the tip.

Similar species: Easily confused with a number of other harmless snakes, especially some of the whip or sand snakes of the genus *Psammophis*.

Enemies: Unknown.

Food and feeding: Small fish, frogs and fish-eating spiders.

Reproduction: Oviparous, laying 5–6 eggs.

Danger to man: None.

Note: This snake was formerly regarded as the subspecies *Natriciteres variegata sylvatica*, but research indicates that it is a full species.

A secretive snake that favours lakes, streams and swamps.

Bill Branch

LOOK OUT FOR

- Found in or near water.
- Very secretive.
- The belly is yellow to orange with dark grey borders.

Bangweulu Swamp Snake

Limnophis bangweolicus

OTHER NAMES
Eastern Striped Swamp Snake (E)
Bangweulu-moerasslang (A)

Length: Adults average 45–50 cm with a maximum length of 63 cm.

Scale count: Midbody scales are in 19 rows, with 132–147 ventrals and 45–68 paired subcaudals. The anal shield is divided. There are 8 upper labials, the 3rd and 4th entering the eye (but variable), and 8–10 lower labials, as well as 1 preocular and 2 or 3 postoculars. Temporals are 1 + 2.

Colour: Above, dark olive brown with a pale stripe on either side that extends along most of the body length. The sides are paler with the 3–4 outer scale rows black-edged, forming long, thin lines down the body. The belly is yellow to brick red.

Preferred habitat: Marshy areas in moist savanna.

Habits: A poorly known species that resembles a robust Olive Marsh Snake (*Natriciteres olivacea*). It occurs in swampy areas and is invariably found in or near water. It is an inoffensive species that is not inclined to bite, even when first handled. Closely associated with water and appears to dehydrate easily.

Similar species: Easily confused with a number of other harmless snakes, but is limited in range.

Enemies: Unknown. Probably other snakes, large fish, monitors (*Varanus* spp.) and crocodiles (*Crocodylus niloticus*).

Food and feeding: Small fish and frogs.

Reproduction: Oviparous. The number of eggs laid is unknown.

Danger to man: None.

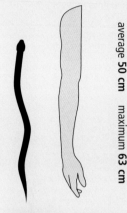

average 50 cm   maximum 63 cm

LOOK OUT FOR

- Usually found in or near water.
- Has a yellow to brick red belly.
- The eyes have round pupils.

A poorly known snake that inhabits swampy areas.

Bill Branch

Jan's Shovel-snout
Prosymna janii

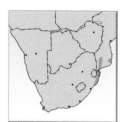

OTHER NAMES
Mozambique Shovel-snout (E)
Jan se graafneusslang (A)

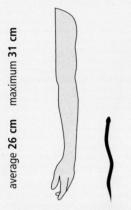

average 26 cm   maximum 31 cm

Length: A small snake, averaging 20–26 cm with a maximum length of just over 31 cm.

Scale count: Midbody scales are in 15 or 17 rows, with 107–129 ventrals and 24–36 paired subcaudals. The anal shield is entire. There are 6 (sometimes 5 or 7) upper labials, the 3rd and 4th entering the eye, and 8 (sometimes 7 or 9) lower labials, as well as 1 preocular (sometimes 2) and 2 (sometimes 0, 1 or 3) postoculars. Temporals are 1 + 2.

Colour: Above, orange-yellow to pale red-brown with a series of large dark brown to blackish blotches that become smaller as they extend down the back. The belly is uniform creamy white.

Preferred habitat: Lowland forest and moist savanna.

Habits: A nocturnal burrower that remains just below the surface in loose sandy soil. Males come to the surface in spring in search of females, but even then this secretive species is seldom encountered. In self-defence it inflates itself and, after raising the forepart of the body off the ground, will slowly sway to and fro with mouth agape.

Similar species: Because the snout is depressed forming a shovel shape, this snake may be confused with other species of shovel-snouts. Otherwise this snake is not easily confused with other species as it has large dark brown to blackish blotches on the back that become smaller as they extend towards the tail.

Enemies: Other snakes.

Food and feeding: This snake's diet is restricted to small reptile eggs, especially hard-shelled gecko eggs.

Reproduction: Oviparous, laying up to 5 eggs in summer.

Danger to man: None.

A nocturnal burrower that feeds on reptile eggs.

Bill Branch

LOOK OUT FOR

- Active at night.
- Spends most of its time just under the surface in sandy soil.
- A small snake, averaging 20–26 cm.
- The eyes have round pupils.
- The snout is depressed, forming a shovel shape.
- Has large, dark blotches on the back becoming smaller towards the tail.

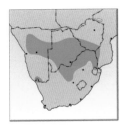

Two-striped Shovel-snout

Prosymna bivittata

OTHER NAMES
Tweestreepgraafneusslang (A)

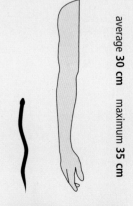

HARMLESS

Length: Adults average 25–30 cm with a maximum length of just over 35 cm.

Scale count: Midbody scales are in 15 rows, with 154–180 ventrals and 22–32 paired subcaudals. The anal shield is entire. There are 6 (sometimes 5) upper labials, the 3rd and 4th entering the eye, and 8 (sometimes 7) lower labials, as well as 1 preocular and 2 post-oculars (sometimes 1). Temporals are 1 + 2, 2 + 2 or 2 + 3.

Colour: Above, greyish brown to purple-brown or reddish brown with a broken orange to yellowish stripe down the vertebrae. The belly is uniform cream to white.

Preferred habitat: Moist savanna to dry savanna entering karoo scrub in the west.

Habits: A burrowing species that favours sandy areas and may be found under stones or logs or on the surface after heavy rains. Captured individuals are known to coil and uncoil quickly.

Similar species: May be confused with other shovel-snout snakes (*Prosymna* spp.) but has an orange to yellow stripe down the back that may or may not be broken.

Enemies: Other snakes.

Food and feeding: Mainly reptile eggs. A captive specimen ate both snake and lizard eggs, by cutting open the soft-shelled eggs with its long rear maxillary teeth, then swallowing them as far as the neck region. The snake first swallowed the contents of the eggs, and then the caved-in eggshells.

Reproduction: Oviparous, laying 3–4 eggs (27–28 x 7–9 mm).

Danger to man: None.

The Two-striped Shovel-snout may be found under stones or logs.

LOOK OUT FOR

- Active at night.
- Spends most of its time just under the surface in sandy soil but may be found sheltering under stones or logs.
- The eyes have round pupils.
- The snout is depressed forming a shovel shape.
- Has a broken orange or yellow stripe down the back.

average 30 cm   maximum 35 cm

Bill Branch

Angola Shovel-snout
Prosymna angolensis

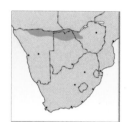

OTHER NAMES
Angolagraafneusslang (A)

maximum 36 cm

average 28 cm

Length: Adults average 24–28 cm, but grow to a length of 36 cm.
Scale count: Midbody scales are in 15 rows, with 121–163 ventrals and 16–26 paired subcaudals. The anal shield is entire. There are 6 (sometimes 5 or 7) upper labials, the 3rd and 4th entering the eye, and 7 or 8 lower labials, as well as 1 preocular and 1 postocular (sometimes 2). Temporals are 1 + 2 (sometimes 2 + 2 or 2 + 3).
Colour: Above, light yellowish brown, with or without a paired series of dark blackish spots. The back may, however, be uniform or with dark-edged and pale-centred scales. The flanks and belly are creamy yellow to yellowish white.
Preferred habitat: Moist savanna.
Habits: Very little is known of the habits of this burrowing snake.
Similar species: It is the only shovel-snout snake through most of its range and has the characteristic depressed snout that resembles a shovel.
Enemies: Other snakes.
Food and feeding: Unknown but probably reptile eggs.
Reproduction: Oviparous, the number of eggs laid is unknown.
Danger to man: None.

D Steele / Getaway / Photo Access

LOOK OUT FOR

- Active at night.
- The eyes have round pupils.
- A small snake, averaging 24–28 cm.
- The snout is depressed, forming a shovel shape.

This snake prefers moist savanna habitat in northern Namibia and the Caprivi Strip, and also occurs eastwards into northern Botswana and western Zimbabwe. Few specimens have been collected and no photographs are available.

South-western Shovel-snout

Prosymna frontalis

OTHER NAMES
Suidwestelike graafneusslang (A)

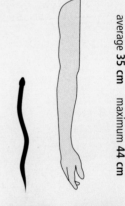

average 35 cm   maximum 44 cm

Length: Adults average 30–35 cm with a maximum length of 44 cm. This is southern Africa's largest shovel-snout snake.

Scale count: Midbody scales are in 15 rows, with 153–199 ventrals and 32–54 paired subcaudals. The anal shield is entire. There are 6 (sometimes 7) upper labials, the 3rd and 4th (sometimes the 4th and 5th) entering the eye, and 8 or 9 (sometimes 10) lower labials, as well as 1 preocular and 2 (sometimes 1) postoculars. Temporals are 1 + 2 (sometimes 2 + 3).

Colour: Above, light brown to chestnut with darker-edged scales, producing a mosaic or striped pattern. There is a broad dark brown to black collar or band behind the head, followed by smaller dark bands and blotches. These become paler down the anterior third of the body. The belly is usually uniform white or creamy yellow to pale brown.

Preferred habitat: Rocky areas in the Namib Desert and karoo scrub.

Habits: Very little is known of the habits of this snake. It favours rocky areas in an arid environment and may be found foraging at night, especially after rains.

Similar species: Because it has the characteristic depressed snout, may be confused with other shovel-snouts. Otherwise, it is not easily confused with other species, since it has a dark brown to black collar behind the head followed by smaller dark bands and blotches that become paler down the anterior third of the body.

Enemies: Other snakes.

Food and feeding: Reptile eggs.

Reproduction: Oviparous. A gravid female from Windhoek laid 3 eggs in January, measuring 37–39 x 10–12 mm. The hatchlings measured 14–14,5 cm.

Danger to man: None.

The South-western Shovel-snout forages for reptile eggs at night, favouring rocky areas.

LOOK OUT FOR

- Active at night.
- The eyes have round pupils.
- Depressed snout forms a shovel shape.
- Has a dark brown to black collar behind the head followed by smaller dark bands and blotches that become progressively paler down the anterior third of the body.

Marius Burger

HARMLESS

East African Shovel-snout

Prosymna stuhlmannii

OTHER NAMES
Gespikkelde graafneusslang (A)

maximum 35 cm

average 26 cm

Length: Adults average 22–26 cm with a maximum length of about 35 cm.

Scale count: Midbody scales are in 15 rows, with 124–164 ventrals and 17–39 paired subcaudals. The anal shield is entire. There are 6 (sometimes 5 or 7) upper labials, the 3rd and 4th (but variable) entering the eye, and 8 (sometimes 7 or 9) lower labials, with 1 preocular (sometimes 0 or 2) and 2 postoculars (sometimes 1). Temporals are 1 + 2, but this varies.

Colour: Above, dark brown to metallic black, either uniform or with each scale pale-centred; alternatively with a paired series of irregularly placed small whitish spots flanking the vertebrae, forming indistinct rows. The belly is white to yellowish or brownish white or (rarely) brown-black.

Preferred habitat: Lowland forest and moist savanna.

Habits: Often found under stones and logs, in decaying vegetable matter and in termite mounds. It is a docile snake that seldom attempts to bite. It appears to be less fossorial than other members of this genus. This species differs from many of the other shovel-snouts in that it does not appear to coil and uncoil in defence.

Similar species: May be confused with other shovel-snouts because of its characteristic depressed snout. However, it usually has small whitish spots flanking the vertebrae that may form indistinct rows.

Enemies: Other snakes.

Food and feeding: Reptile eggs, especially gecko eggs. Young lizards may also form part of this snake's diet. Captive individuals have reportedly taken mealworms.

Reproduction: Oviparous, laying 3–4 eggs (19–30 x 6–8 mm).

Danger to man: None.

The East African Shovel-snout may be found under stones or logs or in termite mounds.

LOOK OUT FOR

- Active at night.
- The eyes have round pupils.
- The snout is depressed, resembling a shovel.
- Usually has small whitish spots flanking the vertebrae that may form indistinct rows.

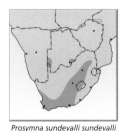

Prosymna sundevalli sundevalli

Sundevall's Shovel-snout

Prosymna sundevalli

OTHER NAMES
Sundevall se graafneusslang (A)

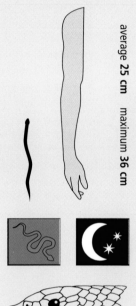

average 25 cm maximum 36 cm

Length: Adults average 25 cm with a maximum length of 36 cm.

Scale count: Midbody scales are in 15 rows, with 131–170 ventrals and 17–34 paired subcaudals. The anal shield is entire. There are 6 (sometimes 5 or 7) upper labials, the 3rd and 4th (but variable) entering the eye, and 7 or 8 lower labials, as well as 1 preocular (sometimes 2) and 2 (sometimes 1 or 3) postoculars. Temporals are 1 + 2 or 2 + 2, but this may vary.

Colour: Above, pale brown, yellowish to reddish brown or dark brown with light and dark mottling that may form 2 (rarely 4) rows or lines over the back and tail. The head is dark brown with a pale yellowish patch on the crown. The belly is white to creamy or yellowish white, sometimes with dusky blotches.

Preferred habitat: Its range includes fynbos, moist savanna and grassland areas and extends into arid savanna.

Habits: Commonly found in old termite mounds and under rocks. When disturbed, it may coil and uncoil quickly, possibly as a means of defence.

Similar species: May be confused with other shovel-snout snakes (*Prosymna* spp.). It has the characteristic depressed snout that resembles a shovel.

Bill Branch

Sundevall's Shovel-snout is commonly found in old termite mounds.

Enemies: Other snakes.

Food and feeding: Reptile eggs and small lizards. May also feed on invertebrates.

Reproduction: Oviparous, laying 2–5 elongate eggs (28 x 9 mm). The young measure 10–11 cm.

Subspecies: There are 2 subspecies in southern Africa. The nominate form (*Prosymna sundevalli sundevalli*), described above, occurs in the southern parts of the range, and has a longer tail.

The Lined Shovel-snout (*Prosymna sundevalli lineata*) occurs in Mpumalanga, the Limpopo Province, eastern Botswana, Mozambique and Zimbabwe, with an isolated record from northern KwaZulu-Natal. It has 17–27 subcaudals.

Danger to man: None.

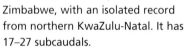

The Lined Shovel-snout occurs in the northern parts of the range.

> **LOOK OUT FOR**
> ■ Active at night.
> ■ The eyes have round pupils.
> ■ The snout is depressed, forming a shovel shape.

Bill Branch

Richard Boycott

Sundevall's Shovel-snout occurs in the southern parts of the range, and has a longer tail.

When disturbed, Sundevall's Shovel-snout may coil and uncoil quickly.

Visser's Shovel-snout
Prosymna visseri

OTHER NAMES
Visser se graafneusslang (A)

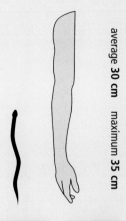

average 30 cm   maximum 35 cm

Length: Adults average 30 cm with a maximum length of nearly 35 cm.

Scale count: Midbody scales are in 15 rows, with 189–210 ventrals and 37–57 paired subcaudals. The anal shield is entire. There are 6 upper labials, the 3rd and 4th entering the eye, and 7 lower labials, as well as 1 preocular and 2 postoculars. Temporals are 1 + 2.

Colour: Above, dark brown with a yellow vertebral stripe from the neck to the tip of the tail. This stripe may be broken. The belly is white.

Preferred habitat: Karoo scrub in northern Namibia.

Habits: This elusive snake has been found at Kamanyab in Namibia but is generally found further northwards into Angola. Unlike the other shovel-snouts, which are mainly fossorial, it favours deep granite fissures where it probably preys on gecko eggs.

Similar species: May be confused with other shovel-snout snakes (*Prosymna* spp.). It has the characteristic depressed snout that resembles a shovel. This snake has a yellow vertebral stripe that may be broken.

Enemies: Other snakes.

Food and feeding: Reptile eggs, especially gecko eggs.

Reproduction: Unknown but probably egg-laying like other members of the genus.

Danger to man: None.

LOOK OUT FOR

- Active at night.
- The eyes have round pupils.
- The snout is depressed, forming a shovel shape.
- Has a yellow vertebral stripe from the neck to the tip of the tail. The stripe may be broken.

Bill Branch

Visser's Shovel-snout is found in deep granite fissures.

HARMLESS

Semiornate Snake
Meizodon semiornatus

OTHER NAMES
Suidelike bosslang (A)
Halfgevlekte slang (A)

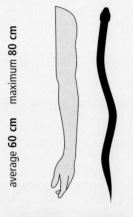

average 60 cm   maximum 80 cm

Length: Adults average 40–60 cm and may reach 80 cm.
Scale count: Midbody scales are in 21 rows, with 167–196 ventrals and 66–91 paired subcaudals. The anal shield is divided. There are 8 (sometimes 9) upper labials, the 4th and 5th (sometimes the 5th and 6th) entering the eye, and 7 lower labials, as well as 1 preocular (sometimes 2) and 2 postoculars (sometimes 1). Temporals are 2 + 2 or 2 + 3, but this varies.
Colour: Above, olive to olive brown with dark crossbars on the front half of the body. These markings are very pronounced in juveniles. The head is black and the eyes partly ringed in white. The belly is white to yellowish white or grey, often darkening towards the sides.
Preferred habitat: Lowland forest and moist savanna.
Habits: A diurnal and terrestrial fast-moving species that inhabits well-wooded areas where it forages for food in thick vegetation along rivers. It is a shy, docile snake that seldom attempts to bite. May also be active at dusk. The Semiornate Snake is usually associated with rotting vegetation and leaf litter but has been found under the bark of trees as high as 2 m off the ground. Several individuals have been found together and it is probable that this harmless species is gregarious to an extent.
Similar species: Juveniles have very distinct dark crossbars on the front half of the body. In adults, the markings are often faded, making identification difficult. Could be confused with some other harmless snakes.

Bill Branch

The dark crossbars on the front of the body fade with age.

This snake is associated with rotting vegetation, but has been found as high as 2 m off the ground.

Enemies: Other snakes.
Food and feeding: Mainly lizards, especially skinks and day geckos (*Lygodactylus* spp.).

This shy, diurnal snake prefers to forage in thick vegetation for its food.

LOOK OUT FOR

■ A small, slender snake with a flat head.
■ The eyes have round pupils.
■ The head is black and the front half of the body has irregular black bars.
■ Juveniles are more conspicuously barred.

Frogs, including the Tremelo Sand Frog (*Tomopterna cryptotis*), and small rodents are also taken.
Reproduction: Oviparous, laying 2–3 elongate eggs (29–40 x 8–10 mm). The young measure 18–20 cm.
Subspecies: Only the typical race of Semiornate Snake (*Meizodon semiornatus semiornatus*) occurs within our range.
Danger to man: None.

The Semiornate Snake may be found under the bark of trees or in rotting vegetation.

Spotted Bush Snake

Philothamnus semivariegatus

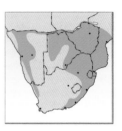

HARMLESS

average 90 cm   maximum 1,3 m

OTHER NAMES
Previously known as the Variegated Bush Snake (E)
Gespikkelde bosslang (A)
Inambezulu (X)

Length: Adults average 60–90 cm and seldom, if ever, exceed 1,3 m.
Scale count: Midbody scales are in 15 rows, with 175–204 ventrals
and 122–166 paired subcaudals. The anal shield is divided. There are
8–12 upper labials, the 4th, 5th and 6th (but this varies) entering the
eye, and 9–12 lower labials, as well as 1 preocular and 2 postoculars.
Temporals are 2 + 2, but this is also variable.
Colour: Variable, but usually bright green to olive green above
with black spots or crossbars on the anterior half or two-thirds
of the body. The head is usually green or blue-green in colour.
The underside is greenish white to yellowish, with distinctly keeled
ventral scales. The dorsal coloration of specimens from Zimbabwe
is usually blue-green on the anterior parts, passing to bronze towards
the tip, and lemon yellow below, also turning to bronze on the
posterior parts.
Preferred habitat: River banks, shrubs and bushes or rocky regions
in karoo scrub, moist savanna and lowland forest.
Habits: A beautifully marked diurnal snake that moves gracefully,
or in short bursts if disturbed. It is an excellent climber and, with
its keeled belly scales, can easily climb up the rough bark of a tree
or even up face-brick walls. It often enters houses and outbuildings,
especially those that have shrubs planted against the windows. When
threatened, it may inflate its neck to expose the vivid blue skin
between the scales. Like the Boomslang (*Dispholidus typus*), it will

Lizards, especially geckos, are actively hunted during the day.

Richard Boycott

Sets of crossbars are usually limited to the anterior half of the snake.

raise its head off the ground and undulate the neck. The Spotted Bush Snake is very common throughout most if its range, often inhabiting the space between walls and corrugated roofs where it feeds on geckos. It soon moves off when disturbed and bites readily if handled. At night it sleeps loosely coiled on the outer branches of vegetation. This snake is well camouflaged and is very difficult to see in its natural environment.

Similar species: Because of its colour it is often mistaken for the Green Mamba (*Dendroaspis angusticeps*) or the Boomslang .

Enemies: Other snakes, especially vine snakes (*Thelotornis* spp.), and predatory birds.

Food and feeding: Mainly lizards, especially geckos, chameleons (*Chamaeleo* and *Bradypodion*) and frogs (not toads).

LOOK OUT FOR

- Usually has black speckles on the front half of the body.
- An expert climber.
- Often inhabits space between walls and corrugated roofing, especially in KwaZulu-Natal.
- Active during the day.
- Eye has a round pupil with a golden or orange iris.
- The tongue is bright blue with a black tip.

Reproduction: Oviparous, laying 3–12 eggs (28–41 x 8–15 mm) in midsummer. The young measure 23–30 cm.

Danger to man: None.

This active and alert snake is diurnal and an excellent climber. It is common in suburban gardens.

HARMLESS

Ornate Green Snake
Philothamnus ornatus

OTHER NAMES
Rooistreepgroenslang (A)

average 70 cm   maximum 80 cm

Length: Adults average 50–70 cm with a maximum length of 80 cm.
Scale count: Midbody scales are in 15 rows, with 147–174 ventrals and 85–106 paired subcaudals. The anal shield is divided. There are 8 (sometimes 9 or 10) upper labials, the 3rd, 4th and 5th (but variable) entering the eye, and 9–11 lower labials, as well as 1 preocular and 2 (sometimes 3) postoculars. Temporals are 1 + 1, 1 + 2 or 2 + 1, but this varies.
Colour: Above, emerald green with a yellow-edged reddish to red-brown vertebral stripe that extends from the head to the tip of the tail. The belly is white with a creamy bronze tint.
Preferred habitat: Moist savanna.
Habits: A shy, diurnal snake that inhabits vleis, the fringes of permanent water, reeds along small streams and open grassland, sometimes far from permanent water. When confronted, it may inflate the neck region exposing the vividly marked skin and will strike out fiercely and bite. The Ornate Green Snake is often found in close proximity to the Green Water Snake (*Philothamnus hoplogaster*) and occasionally the Angola Green Snake (*P. angolensis*).
Similar species: The stripe down the centre of the back distinguishes this snake from other members of the genus.
Enemies: Other snakes.
Food and feeding: Frogs.
Reproduction: Oviparous, the number of eggs laid is unknown.
Danger to man: None.

Wulf Haacke

LOOK OUT FOR

- A slender snake with a rounded head.
- It is emerald green with a yellow-edged reddish to red-brown vertebral stripe that extends from the head to the tip of the tail.
- The iris is yellow or orange.

Like the Boomslang, this snake inflates its neck when threatened.

Angola Green Snake
Philothamnus angolensis

OTHER NAMES
Previously known as the Western Green Snake (E)
Angolagroenslang (A)

HARMLESS

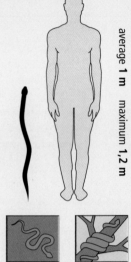

average 1 m   maximum 1,2 m

Length: Adults average 1 m with a maximum length of nearly 1,2 m.
Scale count: Midbody scales are in 15 rows, with 149–170 ventrals
and 87–120 paired subcaudals. The anal shield is divided. There are
8–10 upper labials, the 4th, 5th and 6th (but this is variable) entering
the eye, and 9 or 10 (sometimes 8 or 11) lower labials, as well as
1 preocular (sometimes 2) and 2 postoculars (sometimes 1 or 3).
Temporals are 1 + 1, but this varies.
Colour: Above, bright emerald green, usually with scattered scales
bearing bluish white spots. The skin beneath the scales is black and
the belly uniform pale green to yellow-green.
Preferred habitat: Lowland forest, moist savanna and the margins
of arid savanna regions.
Habits: A diurnal arboreal snake that is associated with reed beds,
trees, bushes and other vegetation along vleis and rivers. It is fast
and a skilful climber, sometimes found up to 10 m above the ground.
It is known to drop into water when disturbed, swimming gracefully
with its head and neck elevated above the surface. It actively hunts its
prey, climbing into vegetation, and may be seen basking. Individuals
are preyed upon by snake-eating birds and the vine snakes (*Thelotornis* spp.). If threatened, it may inflate the neck region, exposing
the black skin between the scales. It strikes out fiercely, hissing and
holding its mouth agape, but is not venomous.
Similar species: May be confused with other members of the genus
and the Green Mamba (*Dendroaspis angusticeps*).

*This diurnal snake is
an excellent climber,
utilizing trees, shrubs,
and reed beds.*

Enemies: Predatory birds and snakes, especially the vine snakes.

Food and feeding: Nestlings and birds in the nest, lizards (especially chameleons) and frogs. Captive specimens are known to take laboratory mice.

Reproduction: Oviparous, laying 4–8 but as many as 16 eggs (25–43 x 9–18 mm) in summer. Communal breeding may take place and up to 85 eggs have been found in a hollow beneath rotting vegetation. The young measure 22–26 cm.

Danger to man: None.

A Spotted Bush Snake, like this one, could well be mistaken for an Angola Green Snake.

LOOK OUT FOR

- ■ A slender snake with a long tail.
- ■ The skin between the scales is black.
- ■ Active during the day.
- ■ An excellent climber.
- ■ The eye has a round pupil.

Peter Steyn / Photo Access

This diurnal, arboreal snake is associated with reed beds, trees, bushes and other vegetation along vleis and rivers.

If threatened, this snake will inflate the neck region and bite fiercely, but is not venomous.

Green Water Snake
Philothamus hoplogaster

OTHER NAMES
South-eastern Green Snake (E)
Groenwaterslang (A)
Suidoostelike groenslang (A)
Umhlwazi (X)

HARMLESS

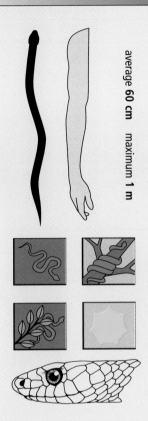

average 60 cm maximum 1 m

Length: Full-grown adults average 60 cm and reach a maximum length of nearly 1 m.

Scale count: Midbody scales are in 15 rows, with 140–165 ventrals and 73–106 paired subcaudals. The anal shield is divided. There are 8 (sometimes 7 or 9) upper labials, the 4th and 5th (but variable) entering the eye, and 9–11 lower labials, as well as 1 preocular (sometimes 2) and 2 (sometimes 3) postoculars. Temporals are 1 + 1, but this is variable.

Colour: Bright emerald green above, occasionally with black bars on the anterior third of the back, and white to bluish white or yellow below.

Preferred habitat: Quite varied but common in moist savanna and lowland forest.

Habits: An active and alert diurnal snake that favours damp localities such as reed swamps, riverine thickets and the flood plains of lakes and rivers. The Green Water Snake sleeps on the outer edge of vegetation, loosely coiled. It is an excellent swimmer, but is also at home in shrubs and trees, where it climbs well.

Similar species: Because of its colour it is often mistaken for the Green Mamba (*Dendroaspis angusticeps*). This snake is also easily confused with other harmless green snakes of the genus *Philothamnus*.

Enemies: Predatory birds and other snakes.

Food and feeding: Mainly frogs, which may be captured in water

Bill Branch

Specimens occasionally have black bars or spots in the neck region.

The Green Water Snake swims well and favours shrubs and bushes.

and then carried back to land before they are swallowed. Fish and small lizards are also taken, while juveniles reportedly eat grasshoppers.

Reproduction: Oviparous, laying 3–8 elongate eggs (25–34 x 8–12 mm) in early summer. The young snakes measure 15–20 cm.

Danger to man: None.

LOOK OUT FOR

- Usually bright emerald green above with a white or yellow belly.
- Very good swimmer.
- Active during the day.
- Eye has a round pupil.

The Green Water Snake favours damp localities such as flood plains and reed swamps.

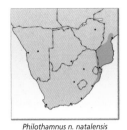

Philothamnus n. natalensis

Natal Green Snake
Philothamnus natalensis

OTHER NAMES
Eastern Green Snake (E)
Natalse groenslang (A)
Ivusamanzi eliluhlaza (Z)

HARMLESS

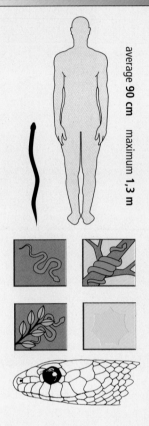

average 90 cm   maximum 1,3 m

Length: Adults average 75–90 cm but may reach a length of 1,3 m.
Scale count: Midbody scales are in 15 rows, with 156–182 ventrals
and 108–135 paired subcaudals, which are keeled. The anal shield is
divided. There are 8 or 9 upper labials, the 4th and 5th or 5th and
6th (but variable) entering the eye, and 10–11 (sometimes 9 or 12)
lower labials, as well as 1 preocular and 2 (sometimes 3) postoculars.
Temporals are 2 + 2, but this varies.
Colour: Above, uniform bright green to turquoise green, with a
paler greenish white or light yellowish belly. Juveniles may have dark
crossbars on the forebody.
Preferred habitat: Lowland forest to moist savanna, arid savanna
and grassland.
Habits: An alert, diurnal snake that is quite similar to the Green
Water Snake (*Philothamnus hoplogaster*) in habits, but is more arboreal. With the help of its keeled ventral and subcaudal scales, it climbs
well and, if disturbed basking on the ground, is quick to ascend into
the safety of its leafy environment. This snake inhabits a wide range
of habitats and is common near rivers and other water bodies.
It favours dense vegetation, where it is well camouflaged. When
captured it may inflate its neck and will bite viciously. Captive individuals soon calm down. Like most of the other members of this genus
it is preyed upon by the vine snakes (*Thelotornis* spp.).
Similar species: Because of its colour it is often mistaken for a
Green Mamba (*Dendroaspis angusticeps*). This snake is also easily

*The Eastern Natal
Green Snake is very
similar to the Green
Water Snake in habits,
but is more arboreal.*

The Western Natal Green Snake is usually turquoise green, especially on the head and tail.

confused with other harmless green snakes of the genus *Philothamnus*.

Enemies: Predatory birds and other snakes.

Food and feeding: Frogs and geckos.

Reproduction: Oviparous, laying 4–6 (but as many as 14) eggs (20–33,3 x 8–15,6 mm) in summer. The young are about 15 cm long.

Subspecies: There are 2 subspecies.

The Eastern Natal Green Snake (*Philothamnus natalensis natalensis*), described above, has keeled subcaudals and usually has 9 upper labials. Its dorsal coloration is bright green to yellow-green.

The Western Natal Green Snake (*Philothamnus natalensis occidentalis*) is usually a turquoise green, especially on the head and tail. The subcaudals are not keeled. It has 111–135 subcaudal scales and 8 or 9 upper labials.

Danger to man: None.

LOOK OUT FOR

- Usually uniform bright green above with a white or light yellow belly.
- Very good climber.
- Active during the day.
- Eye has a round pupil.

Because of its colour, the Eastern Natal Green Snake is often mistaken for the Green Mamba.

Duberria lutrix lutrix

Common Slug-eater
Duberria lutrix

OTHER NAMES
Gewone slakvreter (A)
Tabakrolletjie (A)

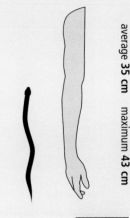

HARMLESS

average 35 cm   maximum 43 cm

Length: Adults average 30–35 cm, but reach a maximum length of 43 cm.

Scale count: Midbody scales are in 15 rows, with 116–142 ventrals and 24–51 paired subcaudals. The anal shield is entire. There are 6 (sometimes 5, 7 or 8) upper labials, the 3rd and 4th (but variable) entering the eye, and 6 (sometimes 5, 7 or 8) lower labials, as well as 1 preocular and 1 or 2 postoculars. Temporals are 1 + 2, but this varies.

Colour: Above, a distinct, broad reddish brown band runs along the centre of the back, flanked by a greyish band on either side of the body. There may also be broken black dorsolateral lines. These markings are unclear in specimens that are about to shed. The underside is usually cream to yellowish white, edged with black or dark grey dotted lines, so there is a light band down the centre of the belly.

Preferred habitat: Largely a grassland inhabitant, but also found in moist savanna, lowland forest and fynbos.

Habits: A common, harmless species that favours damp localities where it preys on snails and slugs. This snake is terrestrial and diurnal. It can be found beneath virtually any form of cover, including rocks, logs, grass tufts and vegetation. It is a useful snake as it keeps down the snail population in gardens.

The slug-eater seldom attempts to bite, usually choosing to roll up tightly into a spiral with its head concealed, very much like a roll of tobacco, hence the Afrikaans name, *tabakrolletjie*. It also has powerful scent glands, which may be used in self-defence.

Similar species: May be confused with other small harmless snakes, especially small Mole Snakes (*Pseudaspis cana*).

This snake feeds exclusively on slugs and snails, hence its common name.

The Common Slug-eater has powerful scent glands that may be used in self-defence.

Enemies: Predatory birds and other snakes.
Food and feeding: Preys only on slugs and snails, which it locates by following the slime trail. When consuming a snail, it will grasp the forepart of its prey and slowly pull the rest out of the shell.
Reproduction: Viviparous, giving birth in late summer to 6–22 young, depending largely on the size of the female. The young measure 8–11 cm.
Subspecies: There are 2 subspecies in southern Africa.
The Common Slug-eater (*Duberria lutrix lutrix*), discussed above, occurs in the southern parts of the range and usually has black dorsolateral lines. This subspecies also has 2 postoculars.
The Zimbabwean Slug-eater (*Duberria lutrix rhodesiana*) is dark olive to brown above, with a thin, only faintly marked, bro- ken vertebral line. The ventrum is blue with paired, triangular dark spots on each ventral shield. It inhabits moist savanna and has 20–39 subcaudals and only 1 postocular.
Danger to man: None.

LOOK OUT FOR

- Has a small head, hardly distinct from the rest of the body.
- Has powerful scent glands, which may be used in self-defence, especially when handled.
- May roll up into a tight spiral.
- Favours damp localities.

When threatened, it usually chooses to roll up tightly into a spiral with its head concealed.

This harmless snake is very useful as it keeps down snail populations in gardens.

Variegated Slug-eater
Duberria variegata

OTHER NAMES
Spotted Slug-eater (E)
Gevlekte slakvreter (A)

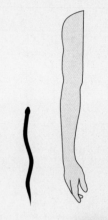

Length: Adults average 25–30 cm with a maximum length of 40 cm.
Scale count: Midbody scales are in 15 rows, with 91–110 ventrals and 20–40 paired subcaudals. The anal shield is entire. There are 6 (sometimes 7) upper labials, the 3rd and 4th or 4th and 5th entering the eye, and 6 (sometimes 4, 5 or 7) lower labials, as well as 1 pre-ocular and 1–2 postoculars. Temporals are 1 + 2 or 1 + 1.
Colour: Above, olive brown to dark chocolate brown with 3 rows of dark spots or blotches that may form crossbars. Pale speckling may, however, obscure the dark ground colour. The belly is yellow to dirty white, reticulated with darker markings, which predominate towards the rear.
Preferred habitat: Lowland forest.
Habits: A secretive, slow-moving snake that is similar to the Common Slug-eater (*Duberria lutrix*) in habits. It may be encountered during the day or at night, usually burrowing just below the surface in loose sand or decaying vegetation. This snake has not been observed rolling up in a defensive spiral like the Common Slug-eater. It is endemic to southern Africa and may be locally common where it occurs.
Similar species: May be confused with other small harmless snakes.
Enemies: Predatory birds and other snakes.
Food and feeding: Mainly soft-shelled snails and slugs.
Reproduction: Viviparous, giving birth to between 7 and 20 young, depending on the size of the female. The young are about 9–10 cm long.
Danger to man: None.

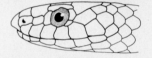

LOOK OUT FOR

- Has a small head hardly distinct from the rest of the body.
- Favours damp localities.

A secretive snake that burrows just below the soil surface.

Common Wolf Snake
Lycophidion capense

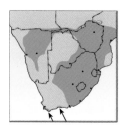

HARMLESS

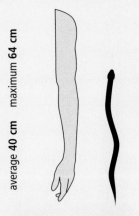

maximum 64 cm

average 40 cm

OTHER NAMES
Cape Wolf Snake (E)
Gewone wolfslang (A)
Kaapse wolfslang (A)

Length: Adults average 30–40 cm but may reach a maximum length of 64 cm. Females grow substantially larger than males.

Scale count: Midbody scales are in 17 rows, with 159–205 ventrals and 24–52 paired subcaudals. The anal shield is entire. There are 8 upper labials, the 3rd, 4th and 5th (but variable) entering the eye, and 8 (sometimes 7) lower labials, as well as 1 preocular and 2 post-oculars (sometimes 1). Temporals are 1 + 2 or 2 + 2.

Colour: Above, light brown to dark brown, purplish brown or black, sometimes with the dorsal scales white-edged, giving a speckled effect. The underside is usually white, sometimes with darker mottling and occasionally with an irregular dark band down the middle.

Preferred habitat: Lowland forest and fynbos to moist savanna, grassland and karoo scrub.

Habits: A terrestrial, slow-moving constrictor that seldom attempts to bite. It is active at night when it hunts for lizards, especially skinks and geckos. It is fond of damp localities and is often found under stones, logs, piles of thatch grass, rubbish heaps or in deserted termite mounds. It has long, recurved teeth on both upper and lower jaws, which account for its common name. The teeth enable it to hold onto slippery prey. It flattens its entire body when under threat.

Similar species: May be confused with a variety of other insignifi-cant-looking snakes, including the venomous Southern Stiletto Snake (*Atractaspis bibronii*).

A Common Wolf Snake from Gauteng.

Richard Boycott

A slow-moving, terrestrial constrictor that hunts at night.

Enemies: Other snakes.

Food and feeding: Mainly lizards, including skinks and geckos. Snakes are also eaten.

Reproduction: Oviparous, laying 3–9 eggs (22–31,6 x 10–14,9 mm) in early summer. The young measure 12–19,6 cm.

Subspecies: Only the typical race of Common Wolf Snake (*Lycophidion capense capense*) is found within our range.

Danger to man: None.

Marius Burger

The Common Wolf Snake is easily confused with the Southern Stiletto Snake.

The Common Wolf Snake feeds mainly on lizards.

This snake has long, recurved teeth in the upper and lower jaws, hence its common name.

Variegated Wolf Snake
Lycophidion variegatum

HARMLESS

OTHER NAMES
Bont wolfslang (A)

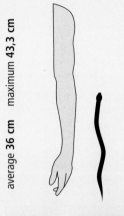

average 36 cm   maximum 43,3 cm

Length: Adults average 30–36 cm with a maximum length of 43,3 cm.
Scale count: Midbody scales are in 17 rows, with 185–204 ventrals and 30–40 paired subcaudals. The anal shield is entire. There are 8 upper labials, the 3rd, 4th and 5th (but variable) entering the eye, and 8 (sometimes 7) lower labials, as well as 1 preocular and 2 postoculars (sometimes 1). Temporals are 1 + 2 or 2 + 2.
Colour: Usually black above and below but with white markings on the scale margins. In some specimens, especially from Zimbabwe, the white is very pronounced. The belly occasionally has pale markings.
Preferred habitat: Rocky outcrops in moist savanna.
Habits: This inoffensive nocturnal snake inhabits rocky outcrops in moist savanna where it may be found under stones, dead aloes and logs. It is a solitary, slow-moving snake that actively seeks its prey in narrow crevices.
Similar species: May be confused with a variety of other innocuous-looking snakes, as well as the venomous Southern Stiletto Snake (*Atractaspis bibronii*).
Enemies: Other snakes.
Food and feeding: Lizards, especially skinks that are captured while they are at rest. Geckos are also taken.
Reproduction: Oviparous, laying 2–3 eggs.
Danger to man: None.

Niels Jacobsen

LOOK OUT FOR

- Has a speckled pattern.
- A flattened head, barely distinct from the rest of the body.
- Active at night.
- A small, slender snake.

A slow-moving nocturnal snake that feeds on lizards.

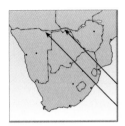

Spotted Wolf Snake

Lycophidion multimaculatum

HARMLESS

OTHER NAMES
Gespikkelde wolfslang (A)

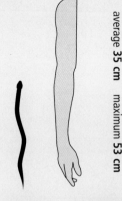

average 35 cm   maximum 53 cm

Length: Adults average 30–35 cm with a maximum length of approximately 53 cm.

Scale count: Midbody scales are in 17 rows, with 153–188 ventrals and 22–38 paired subcaudals. The anal shield is entire. There are 8 upper labials, the 3rd, 4th and 5th entering the eye, and 8 lower labials, as well as 1 preocular and 2 postoculars. Temporals are 1 + 2.

Colour: Colour variable. Within southern Africa the body is reddish brown to grey with white flecks and finer white flecks on the head. A paired series of irregular dark blotches down the back may form crossbars. The belly is white but the chin may be darker.

Preferred habitat: Moist savanna in the Caprivi Strip and elsewhere to the north.

Habits: This nocturnal snake actively hunts its prey and will take lizards while they are sleeping in their burrows.

Similar species: May be confused with a variety of other insignificant-looking snakes, including the venomous Southern Stiletto Snake (*Atractaspis bibronii*).

Enemies: Other snakes.

Food and feeding: Lizards, especially skinks, which are captured while at rest.

Reproduction: Oviparous.

Danger to man: None.

LOOK OUT FOR

- A flattened head, barely distinct from the rest of the body.
- Active at night.
- A small, slender snake.

The range of the Spotted Wolf Snake extends from the southern DRC, Angola, the nothern border of Namibia and western Zambia, entering the southern African region in the Caprivi Strip.

John Visser

Namibian Wolf Snake
Lycophidion namibianum

HARMLESS

OTHER NAMES
Namibwolfslang (A)

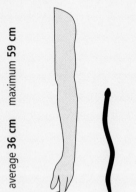

average 36 cm　maximum 59 cm

Length: Adults average 30–36 cm with a maximum length of about 59 cm.

Scale count: Midbody scales are in 17 rows, with 193–213 ventrals and 30–42 paired subcaudals. The anal shield is entire. There are 8 upper labials, the 3rd, 4th and 5th entering the eye, and 9 lower labials, as well as 1 preocular and 2 postoculars. Temporals are 1 + 2.

Colour: The body is reddish brown to dark brown with light speckling. The belly and lower flanks are white with dark brown markings down the centre of the belly.

Preferred habitat: Karoo scrub and rocky habitat in the Namib Desert.

Habits: A nocturnal snake that actively hunts its prey. It is restricted to northern Namibia and is endemic to southern Africa. It has long, recurved teeth that enable it to hang onto its slippery prey.

Similar species: May be confused with a variety of other insignificant-looking snakes, as well as the venomous Southern Stiletto Snake (*Atractaspis bibronii*).

Enemies: Other snakes.

Food and feeding: Lizards.

Reproduction: Oviparous.

Danger to man: None.

Bill Branch

LOOK OUT FOR

■ A flattened head, barely distinct from the rest of the body.
■ Active at night.
■ A small, slender snake.

Like the other wolf snakes, the Namibian Wolf Snake feeds on lizards.

Hellmich's Wolf Snake
Lycophidion hellmichi

OTHER NAMES
Hellmich se wolfslang (A)

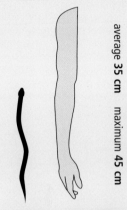

average 35 cm   maximum 45 cm

Length: Adults average 30–35 cm with a maximum length of close to 45 cm. Females grow much larger than males.

Scale count: Midbody scales are in 17 rows, with 196–214 ventrals and 33–45 paired subcaudals. The anal shield is entire. There are 8 upper labials, the 3rd, 4th and 5th (but this varies) entering the eye, and 8 (sometimes 7) lower labials, as well as 1 preocular and 2 post-oculars (sometimes 1). Temporals are 1 + 2 or 2 + 2.

Colour: Variable, with a broad, pale brown band right down the back from the nose to the tip of the tail. On either side of the verte-brae are dark brown spots, usually in pairs but sometimes forming a zigzag pattern down the back. The flanks are usually pale brown with pale-edged ventrals while the rest of the belly is dark.

Preferred habitat: Rocky areas in the Namib Desert.

Habits: Very little is known of this snake.

Similar species: Could be confused with a number of other harmless snakes.

Enemies: Other snakes.

Food and feeding: Unknown, probably lizards.

Reproduction: Unknown. Probably oviparous.

Danger to man: None.

LOOK OUT FOR

- A flattened head, barely distinct from the rest of the body.
- Active at night.
- A small, slender snake.

Wulf Haacke

Very little is known of this rare snake.

HARMLESS

Eastern Wolf Snake
Lycophidion semiannule

OTHER NAMES
Oostelike wolfslang (A)

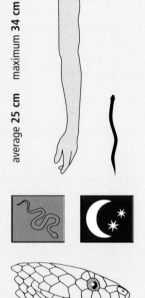

average 25 cm   maximum 34 cm

Length: A small snake averaging 20–25 cm with a maximum length of 34 cm.

Scale count: Midbody scales are in 17 rows, with 139–157 ventrals and 19–30 paired subcaudals. The anal shield is entire. There are 8 upper labials, the 3rd, 4th and 5th (but variable) entering the eye, and 8 (sometimes 7) lower labials, as well as 1 preocular and 2 (sometimes 1) postoculars. Temporals are 1 + 2 or 2 + 2.

Colour: Variable; the dorsal colour may be greyish blue to shiny purplish brown. Some specimens may have crossbars. The scales are faintly edged with a silvery grey colour. The head is also pale-edged with a conspicuous dark arrowhead marking. The belly is purplish brown with pale-edged ventral scales.

Preferred habitat: Lowland forest in Mozambique.

Habits: A rare and secretive snake that is similar to the Common Wolf Snake (*Lycophidion capense*) in habits. It is terrestrial and has been found in grass tussocks, under plant debris and in exotic pine plantations. This snake is endemic to southern Africa.

Similar species: May be confused with a variety of other insignificant-looking snakes, including the venomous Southern Stiletto Snake (*Atractaspis bibronii*).

Enemies: Other snakes.

Food and feeding: Unknown, but probably lizards.

Reproduction: Unknown, probably oviparous.

Danger to man: None.

Ian Michler / SIL

LOOK OUT FOR

■ A flattened head, barely distinct from the rest of the body.
■ Active at night.
■ A small, slender snake.

The Eastern Wolf Snake is rare and secretive and occurs in lowland forests in Mozambique.

Pygmy Wolf Snake
Lycophidion pygmaeum

OTHER NAMES
Pigmeewolfslang (A)

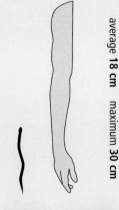

Length: A small snake, averaging 15–18 cm with a maximum length of about 30 cm.

Scale count: Midbody scales are in 17 rows, with 140–155 ventrals and 21–28 paired subcaudals. The anal shield is entire. There are 8 upper labials, the 3rd, 4th and 5th entering the eye, and 9 or 10 lower labials, as well as 1 preocular and 2 postoculars. Temporals are 1 + 2.

Colour: Uniform black with a white band around the snout. The scales on the back are stippled in white, but not towards the rear. The edges of the belly as well as the throat region have white stippling, otherwise the underside is black.

Preferred habitat: Lowland forest in northern Zululand.

Habits: A very small wolf snake that is secretive and strictly terrestrial. It seeks shelter beneath logs and in grass tussocks and is also found in pine plantations. This snake is endemic to southern Africa.

Similar species: Could be confused with a number of harmless snakes as well as the Southern Stiletto Snake (*Atractaspis bibronii*). The broad white band around the snout distinguishes this snake from other species. It also has a limited distribution.

Enemies: Other snakes.

Food and feeding: Diet consists largely of burrowing skinks of the genus *Scelotes*.

Reproduction: Oviparous. A large female contained 3 eggs.

Danger to man: None.

LOOK OUT FOR

- A small, slender snake.
- A flattened head, barely distinct from the rest of the body.
- Active at night and found on the ground.
- The snout has a broad white band.

This small, secretive snake is endemic to southern Africa.

Bill Branch

HARMLESS

Dwarf Wolf Snake
Lycophidion nanum

OTHER NAMES
Dwergwolfslang (A)

maximum 30 cm

average 23 cm

Length: A small snake, averaging 20–23 cm but may reach, or even exceed, 30 cm.

Scale count: Midbody scales are in 17 rows, with 151-164 ventrals and 21–28 paired subcaudals. The anal shield is entire. There are 6–7 upper labials, the 3rd and 4th (but variable) entering the eye, and 6 lower labials, as well as 1 preocular and 2 postoculars (sometimes 1). Temporals are 1 + 2 but variable.

Colour: Uniform blue-black to black above with a stippled white band around the snout. The chin and throat are brownish and the belly blackish.

Preferred habitat: Flood plains in moist savanna.

Habits: A secretive snake. Most specimens have been collected in *miombo* woodland.

Similar species: Could be confused with a variety of harmless snakes as well as the Southern Stiletto Snake (*Atractaspis bibronii*). The stippled white band around the snout is distinctive.

Enemies: Other snakes.

Food and feeding: Amphisbaenids of the genus *Chirindia*, and possibly skinks.

Reproduction: Oviparous, laying 2 elongate eggs (26 x 6 mm).

Danger to man: None.

Ian Michler / SIL

LOOK OUT FOR

■ A small, slender snake.
■ A flattened blunt head, barely distinct from the rest of the body.
■ Active at night and found on the ground.
■ The snout has a stippled white band.
■ Has small eyes with vertical pupils.

Flood plain areas in moist savanna are the preferred habitat of this secretive snake.

Southern File Snake
Mehelya capensis

OTHER NAMES
Cape File Snake (E)
Suidelike vylslang (A)
Inhlangwana (Z)
Intlangu (X)

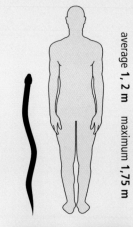

average 1,2 m   maximum 1,75 m

Length: Adults average between 70 cm and 1,2 m but may reach a length of just over 1,75 m. The females grow much larger than the males.

Scale count: Midbody scales are in 15 rows (sometimes 17), with 193–244 ventrals and 44–61 paired subcaudals. The anal shield is entire. There are 7 (sometimes 6 or 8) upper labials, the 3rd and 4th entering the eye, and 8 (sometimes 7) lower labials, as well as 1 pre-ocular (sometimes 2) and 1 or 2 postoculars. Temporals are 1 + 2.

Colour: Above, grey to grey-brown or purplish brown with a distinctive white to creamy vertebral stripe from the neck to the tip of the tail. The mauve to light pink skin between the scales is very conspicuous. The belly is an ivory to yellowish colour.

Preferred habitat: Lowland forest and moist savanna.

Habits: The Southern File Snake is a docile, inoffensive snake that rarely attempts to bite, even when first captured. It has a robust, triangular body with rough, strongly keeled scales, hence the common name. This nocturnal species spends most of the day hiding in holes in the ground, cavities in walls, in hollow logs, deserted termite mounds or other suitable shelters. It emerges at dusk to hunt and is especially active after rain. Though largely terrestrial, it will climb into

The Southern File Snake feeds on other snakes, including venomous species.

This snake is uniquely triangular, with a distinctive light vertebral stripe.

shrubs and trees in search of food. Captured individuals exude a foul-smelling substance from glands in the anal region. Many African communities regard this snake as a harbinger of death.

Similar species: Is unique with its triangular body, rough scales, lumpy head and distinctive vertebral stripe. Can only be confused with other file snakes (*Mehelya* spp.).

Enemies: Other snakes.

Food and feeding: Mainly snakes, including venomous species like the Black Mamba (*Dendroaspis polylepis*) and Puff Adder (*Bitis arietans*). The Southern File Snake appears to have some immunity to snake venoms. Terrestrial lizards, toads and small mammals are also taken. The prey is often swallowed while still alive. Captive specimens readily

LOOK OUT FOR

- Triangular shape with rough scales and distinctive cream to white vertebral stripe.
- Light pink skin between the scales.
- Active at night.

take laboratory mice. Individuals are often killed while crossing tarred roads.

Reproduction: Oviparous, laying 5–13 eggs (47–55 x 20–31 mm) in summer. More than 1 clutch may be laid in a season. The young measure 29–45 cm.

Subspecies: Only the typical race of Southern File Snake (*Mehelya capensis capensis*) is found within our range.

Danger to man: None.

The Southern File Snake is feared by many African communities and is said to be a harbinger of death.

Angola File Snake

Mehelya vernayi

OTHER NAMES
Angola-vylslang (A)

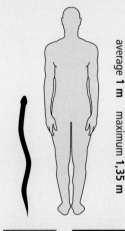

average 1 m   maximum 1,35 m

Length: Similar in size to the Southern File Snake (*Mehelya capensis*) with adults averaging 1 m, and reaching a maximum of 1,35 m.
Scale count: Midbody scales are in 19 rows, with 256–268 ventrals and 60–68 paired subcaudals. The anal shield is entire. There are 7 upper labials, the 3rd, 4th and 5th entering the eye, and 8 lower labials, as well as 1 preocular (sometimes 2) and 1 postocular (sometimes 2). Temporals are 1 + 2.
Colour: Dark reddish brown above but lacking the white vertebral stripe of the Southern File Snake. The scales have pale tips that become paler down the sides, giving the snake a speckled appearance. The belly is usually a plain creamy white but may have some dark lateral markings.
Preferred habitat: Rocky mountain regions in the Namib Desert and karoo scrub.
Habits: This snake resembles the Southern File Snake and is similar in habits and behaviour.
Similar species: Very similar to the Southern File Snake, but lacks the light vertebral line.
Enemies: Other snakes.
Food and feeding: Lizards and toads have been found in the gut of captured specimens.
Reproduction: Oviparous, laying a few eggs measuring 30 x 15 mm.
Danger to man: None.

LOOK OUT FOR

- Has a triangular body with strongly keeled scales.
- The head is broad and flat and distinct from the rest of the body.
- Active at night.

The Angola File Snake resembles the Southern File Snake but lacks a vertebral line.

Wulf Haacke

Black File Snake

Mehelya nyassae

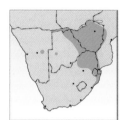

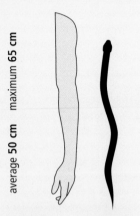

HARMLESS

maximum 65 cm

average 50 cm

OTHER NAMES
Swartvylslang (A)

Length: Adults average 35–50 cm with a maximum length of 65 cm. The females grow much larger than the males.

Scale count: Midbody scales are in 15 rows, with 165–184 ventrals and 51–79 paired subcaudals. The anal shield is entire. There are 7 (sometimes 6) upper labials, the 3rd and 4th entering the eye, and 8 (sometimes 7) lower labials, as well as 1 (sometimes 2) preocular and 1 postocular. Temporals are 1 + 2 or 1 + 3.

Colour: Above, uniform purple-brown to blackish with mauvish pink skin between the scales. The underside is dark olive brown to black or yellowish white to white.

Preferred habitat: Lowland forest and moist savanna.

Habits: A rare nocturnal snake that is similar to the Southern File Snake (*Mehelya capensis*) in habits and behaviour, but is probably more terrestrial. Specimens have been found in holes, under rocks and in deserted termite mounds as well as under plant debris. Captive individuals are known to move with jerky movements, hiding the head under coils of the body. Individuals may excrete a foul-smelling transparent liquid from the cloaca when handled. This fluid may cause a tingling or burning sensation and is very sticky and extremely diffi-cult to wash off.

Colin Tilbury

The Black File Snake is nocturnal and actively hunts for food.

This snake feeds largely on lizards and may also take frogs.

Similar species: The Black File Snake is similar to the Southern File Snake but lacks the light vertebral stripe and has a smaller head. The head is smooth.

Enemies: Other snakes.

Food and feeding: Mainly terrestrial lizards, especially skinks and lacertids. Frogs are also taken.

Reproduction: Oviparous, laying 2–6 eggs. The young measure 20–22 cm.

Danger to man: None.

LOOK OUT FOR

- Has a triangular body with strongly keeled scales.
- The head is broad and flat and distinct from the rest of the body.
- Active at night.
- Uniformly purple-brown to blackish.
- The skin between the scales is pink.
- The tongue is pink and white.

Like the other file snakes, the body is triangular and the head broad and flat.

Common Egg-eater

Dasypeltis scabra

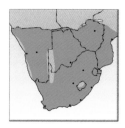

HARMLESS

maximum 1,16 m

average 75 cm

OTHER NAMES
Rhombic Egg-eater (E)
Gewone eiervreter (A)

Length: Adults average 45–75 cm with a maximum length of 1,16 m.
Scale count: Midbody scales are in 21–27 rows, with 180–243
ventrals and 38–78 paired subcaudals. The anal shield is entire.
There are 7 (sometimes 6 or 8) upper labials, the 3rd and 4th (sometimes the 2nd and 3rd) entering the eye, and 7–9 lower labials, as
well as 1 preocular (sometimes 2) and 2 (sometimes 3) postoculars.
Temporals are 2 + 3, but this varies.
Colour: Light brown to grey-brown or dark brown above, with a
series of dark squarish blotches down the back and narrow dark bars
down either side of the body. A V-shaped marking on the nape is
usually preceded by 2 similar but narrower markings on the head.
The underside is white, sometimes with dark spots and flecks.
The inside of the mouth is black. Uniform brown specimens with
virtually no markings have been recorded.
Preferred habitat: A common snake throughout most of southern
Africa, except the true desert and closed-canopy forest areas.
Habits: This snake is most abundant in dry thornveld and grassland,
where it may be found in virtually any situation. It is nocturnal,
spending most of the day hiding beneath rocks or under loose bark.
It frequents disused termite mounds, especially in winter when
it hibernates.

The harmless Common Egg-eater feeds exclusively on birds' eggs.

Marius Burger

The Common Egg-eater (above) resembles the venomous Rhombic Night Adder, but lacks the distinct V-marking on the head.

When agitated, it will coil and uncoil, allowing the roughly keeled scales on its sides to rub against each other, causing a hissing or rasping sound that is similar to the hiss of some adders. It will also strike out viciously with its mouth agape, exposing the dark lining of the mouth. As its diet consists largely of eggs, its teeth serve no purpose and are greatly reduced.

Similar species: The rhombic marking of this snake may cause confusion with the Rhombic Night Adder (*Causus rhombeatus*) in south-eastern Africa and with the Horned Adder (*Bitis caudalis*) in south-western Africa.

Enemies: Predatory birds and other snakes.

LOOK OUT FOR

- Rhombic markings.
- 1 or more dark V-markings on the neck behind the head (the Rhombic Night Adder, page 90, has a V-marking on the head).
- The inside of the mouth is black.
- Active at night.
- The tongue is black.

Food and feeding: Feeds on birds' eggs. An egg is taken into the virtually toothless mouth and passed on to the neck region.

When threatened, this snake may coil and uncoil in one spot, its roughly keeled scales rubbing together and emitting a hissing sound similar to the hiss of some adders.

There it is cracked lengthwise by a series of bony projections that are part of the vertebrae. Muscular contractions then crush the egg and the contents are swallowed. The crushed shell is regurgitated in a neat boat-shaped package. The pieces of shell are held together by the underlying membrane.

Reproduction: Oviparous, laying 6–25 eggs (27–46 x 15–20 mm) in summer. The young measure 21–26 cm. Captive specimens may produce more than 1 clutch in a season.

Danger to man: None.

The Common Egg-eater climbs well, easily reaching birds' nests in search of food.

As this snake's diet consists largely of eggs, its teeth serve no purpose and are greatly reduced.

N Greaves / Phc

Egg-eaters regurgitate crushed eggshells in neat boat-shaped packages that are held together by the underlying membranes.

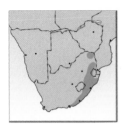

Southern Brown Egg-eater

Dasypeltis inornata

OTHER NAMES
Suidelike bruin eiervreter (A)

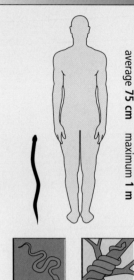

average 75 cm   maximum 1 m

Length: Adults average 60–75 cm but may reach, or exceed, 1 m.
Scale count: Midbody scales are in 23–27 rows, with 208–237 ventrals and 69–92 paired subcaudals. The anal shield is entire. There are 7 (sometimes 6 or 8) upper labials, the 3rd and 4th (sometimes the 2nd and 3rd) entering the eye, and 7–9 lower labials, as well as 1 preocular (sometimes 2) and 2 (sometimes 3) postoculars. Temporals are 2 + 3, but this varies.
Colour: Above, uniform yellowish red to reddish brown, olive or dark brown and somewhat lighter on the lower flanks. The skin between the scales is darker and the belly uniform white to pale yellowish brown.
Preferred habitat: Lowland forest and moist savanna.
Habits: A nocturnal inhabitant of grassland and open coastal woodland where it seeks refuge under rocks or in any other suitable hiding place. At night it seeks birds' eggs and is amazingly skilled at locating them. The keepers of a small aviary near Durban removed 7 adults in 1 month. As the diet of this snake consists solely of birds' eggs its teeth serve no purpose and are greatly reduced. This snake is endemic to southern Africa.
Similar species: May be confused with several harmless snakes including the Brown House Snake (*Lamprophis capensis*), but lacks the characteristic pale stripes on either side of the head and has rough, dull scales.

This snake is attracted to aviaries, where it seeks birds' eggs.

Marius Burger

The Southern Brown Egg-eater may exceed 1 m in length.

LOOK OUT FOR

- Active at night.
- Uniform yellowish red to reddish brown above.
- The head is small, barely discernable from the neck, and the eye has a vertical pupil.

Enemies: Other snakes and predatory birds.

Food and feeding: Birds' eggs. An egg is taken into the virtually toothless mouth and passed onto the neck region. There it is cracked lengthwise by a series of bony projections that are part of the vertebrae. Muscular contractions then crush the egg and the contents are swallowed. The crushed shell is regurgitated in a neat, boat-shaped package. The pieces of shell are held together by the underlying membrane.

Reproduction: Oviparous, laying 7–17 eggs (21–35 x 14–21 mm) in summer. The young are 20–28 cm long.

Danger to man: None.

The hatchling Southern Brown Egg-eater is a perfect replica of the adult.

East African Egg-eater
Dasypeltis medici

OTHER NAMES
Oos-Afrika-eiervreter (A)

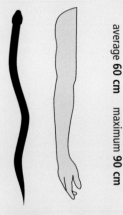

Length: Adults average 50–60 cm with a maximum length of nearly 90 cm.

Scale count: Midbody scales are in 23–27 rows, with 215–259 ventrals and 71–109 paired subcaudals. The anal shield is entire. There are 7 upper labials, the 3rd and 4th entering the eye, and 7–9 lower labials, as well as 1 preocular and 2 postoculars. Temporals are 2 + 3.

Colour: Above, pinkish brown with about 5 darker V-markings from the head onto the neck. These are followed by a distinct dark brownish vertebral stripe interrupted by regular white patches. Fine dark dorsal stippling is also characteristic. The sides have narrow dark vertical bars and the belly is cream to pink with grey to brown stippling.

Preferred habitat: Lowland forest to moist savanna.

Habits: Little is known about the habits and behaviour of this snake. The southern African population seems to be associated with lowland evergreen forest and several individuals have been found in gardens adjacent to coastal dune forest. Like the Common Egg-eater (*Dasypeltis scabra*), this snake will coil and uncoil when agitated, rubbing its strongly keeled dorsal scales against each other, causing a hissing or rasping sound, similar to the hiss of some adders. It will also strike aggressively, but is completely harmless.

Wulf Haacke

This specialized snake feeds exclusively on birds' eggs, which are swallowed whole and crushed in the neck region. The contents are swallowed and the crushed egg shell regurgitated.

average 60 cm   maximum 90 cm

This snake is often found in suburban gardens.

Similar species: Quite similar to the Common Egg-eater and may also be confused with the Common or Rhombic Night Adder (*Causus rhombeatus*).
Enemies: Predatory birds and other snakes.

LOOK OUT FOR

- Rhombic markings.
- 1 or more light V-markings on the neck behind the head (the Rhombic Night Adder has a dark V-shaped marking on the head).
- The inside of the mouth is pink.
- Active at night.

Food and feeding: Birds' eggs. An egg is taken into the virtually toothless mouth and passed onto the neck region. There it is cracked lengthwise by a series of bony projections that are part of the vertebrae. Muscular contractions then crush the egg and the contents are swallowed. The crushed shell is regurgitated in a neat, boat-shaped package. The pieces of shell are held together by the underlying membrane.
Reproduction: Oviparous, laying 6–28 eggs (24 x 8 mm). The young are just over 20 cm in length.
Subspecies: Only the typical race of East African Egg-eater (*Dasypeltis medici medici*) is found within our range.
Danger to man: None.

The Common Egg-eater (above) may be confused with the East African Egg-eater.

Kunene Racer
Coluber zebrinus

OTHER NAMES
Kuneneslang (A)

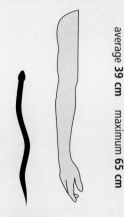

HARMLESS

Length: Average 30–39 cm, while one specimen of 65 cm has been collected.

Scale count: There are 23 rows at midbody, approximately 195 ventrals and 90 paired subcaudals. The anal shield is divided. There are 9 upper labials, the 5th and 6th entering the eye.

Colour: Grey above, becoming pale to white on the sides. There are several irregular crossbars on the back that fade towards the tail, as well as dark vertical bars on the sides. The top of the head is uniform grey to brown and both the lips and snout are a yellowish colour. The underside is white.

Preferred habitat: Scrub among stones in northern Namibia.

Habits: A recent discovery in the Kunene Valley. It is terrestrial and active during the day. It may mimic the venomous Zebra Cobra (*Naja nigricollis nigricincta*) because of its coloration and patterning.

Similar species: May be confused with the Zebra Cobra.

Enemies: Unknown.

Food and feeding: Unknown.

Reproduction: Unknown.

Danger to man: None.

average 39 cm   maximum 65 cm

LOOK OUT FOR

- Active during the day.
- Has large eyes with round pupils.
- Largely terrestrial.
- Has crossbars not unlike those of the Zebra Cobra.
- Extremely limited in distribution.

The Kunene Racer is a recent discovery in southern Africa that is easily confused with the Zebra Cobra.

Bill Branch

BLIND & WORM SNAKES

Typhlopidae/Leptotyphlopidae

Blind snakes are primitive snakes with cylindrical bodies, highly polished, close-fitting scales and small heads. They have no teeth on the lower jaw and have internal vestiges of a pelvic girdle. All are well adapted for a burrowing existence, with reduced eyes, a cylindrical body and a head that is not distinct from the rest of the body, together with a very short tail that terminates in a spine. All of the blind snakes are similar in appearance and colour and shed their skins in compact rings. They feed largely on termites and other small invertebrates.

Worm snakes, also known as thread snakes, are small and thin. Like the blind snakes, they are primitive burrowers and feed on termites and ants. They also feed on fleas. Their bodies are cylindrical and they have blunt heads and short tails. Worm snakes have no teeth in the upper jaw and have only one lung and one oviduct (the tube that carries eggs from the ovary). There are internal vestiges of a pelvic girdle. They have reduced eyes that may be visible as dark spots beneath the skin; however they are blind. The forked tongue is usually small and white.

Both Blind and Worm snakes have reduced eyes.

Blind Snakes have no teeth on the lower jaw and their tails end in a sharp spine.

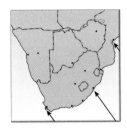

Flowerpot Snake
Ramphotyphlops braminus

OTHER NAMES
Blompotslang (A)

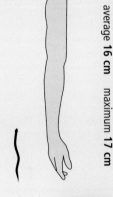

average 16 cm   maximum 17 cm

Length: Adults average 16 cm with a maximum length of 17 cm.
Scale count: There are 20 scale rows around the body with 300–350 dorsal scales.
Colour: Above, uniform dark grey to pale brown with the belly somewhat paler. The snout, cloacal region and tail tip are a creamy colour.
Preferred habitat: Humic soil in and around cities. It has been introduced from Australasia.
Habits: A successful snake that inhabits humic soil and is probably southern Africa's only introduced snake species. It is often transported in pot plants, hence the common name. This is an all-female (parthenogenetic) species in which unfertilized ova develop directly into new individuals, permitting the females to produce viable eggs without having to mate. This has enabled snakes of this genus to establish themselves on oceanic islands and on most continents. In the past, individuals were also accidentally trapped in the sand used by ships as ballast. Easily found beneath rocks and other forms of shelter within cities such as Durban, Cape Town and Beira.
Similar species: Easily confused with other blind or worm snakes.
Enemies: Other snakes.
Food and feeding: Termites, ants and their larvae as well as other small invertebrates.
Reproduction: Oviparous, laying 2–6 minute eggs (6 x 2 mm). The hatchlings are just over 4 cm long – possibly the smallest snake in the world at that stage.
Danger to man: None.

LOOK OUT FOR

■ Very small and slender with a cylindrical body.
■ Usually found under some form of cover in humic soil.

Bill Branch

Often transported in pot plants, hence the common name.

HARMLESS

Boyle's Beaked Blind Snake

Rhinotyphlops boylei

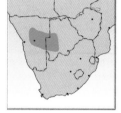

maximum 22 cm

average 18 cm

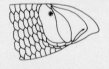

OTHER NAMES
Boyle se haakneusblindeslang (A)

Length: Adults average 15–18 cm with a maximum length of about 22 cm.

Scale count: There are 26–28 scale rows around the body with 351–377 dorsal scales.

Colour: Above, olive brown with yellow-edged scales over the centre of the back. The scales on either side of the body are pale with the dark coloration reduced to a spot on each scale. The belly is uniform cream to pale yellowish, as are the sides of the head and lower body.

Preferred habitat: Dry savanna in western Botswana and eastern Namibia.

Habits: A species endemic to southern Africa that inhabits sandveld regions. As the common name indicates, this snake has a beaked snout (see illustration), the function of which has not been investigated. However, the hard edge that the 'beak' forms on the snout is likely to be used for burrowing.

Similar species: Easily confused with other blind or worm snakes. The scales on the back are yellow-edged.

Enemies: Other snakes.

Food and feeding: Unknown.

Reproduction: Unknown.

Danger to man: None.

Vanessa Burger / Photo Access

LOOK OUT FOR

- A small and slender snake with a cylindrical body.
- Has a beaked snout.
- The scales on the back are yellow-edged.

Sandveld regions in dry savanna are the preferred habitat of this secretive species, which is not often observed due to its fossorial habits.

Delalande's Beaked Blind Snake

Rhinotyphlops lalandei

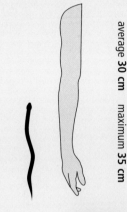

HARMLESS

OTHER NAMES
Delalande se haakneusblindeslang (A)

Length: Adults average 25–30 cm but may reach, or even exceed, a length of 35 cm.

Scale count: There are 26–30 scale rows around the body with 337–441 dorsal scales.

Colour: Above, uniform pale to dark slate or grey-brown. Each scale is pale-edged, producing a chequered effect. The belly is pink-grey to straw yellow or sometimes paler with only patches of straw yellow to pink-grey. The young are flesh coloured.

Preferred habitat: A wide range of habitats including fynbos, grassland and moist savanna.

Habits: A burrowing snake with a wide distribution. It is endemic to southern Africa. Individuals may be found in soil under rocks or logs, in deserted termite mounds or on the surface at night, especially after rain.

Similar species: Easily confused with other blind or worm snakes. The back, however, has a chequered effect.

Enemies: Other snakes, especially the Spotted Harlequin Snake (*Homoroselaps lacteus*).

Food and feeding: Invertebrates, including termites.

Reproduction: Oviparous, laying 2–8 eggs.

Danger to man: None.

average 30 cm   maximum 35 cm

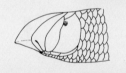

LOOK OUT FOR

- A slender snake with a cylindrical body.
- Has a chequered pattern on its back.
- Has a beaked snout.
- The scales on the back are yellow-edged.

This snake is preyed upon by a variety of other snakes.

Marius Burger

HARMLESS

Schinz's Beaked Blind Snake
Rhinotyphlops schinzi

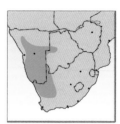

maximum 28 cm

average 20 cm

OTHER NAMES
Schinz se haakneusblindeslang (A)

Length: Adults average 15–20 cm, with a maximum length of about 28 cm.
Scale count: There are 22–26 scale rows around the body with 413–469 dorsal scales.
Colour: Above, pink to yellowish with bluish black to reddish brown spots or blotches, the latter often forming irregular crossbars across the back. The belly is uniform pink to yellowish. The dark eyes are very prominent.
Preferred habitat: Dry savanna, karoo scrub and the Namib Desert.
Habits: A fossorial snake that inhabits semidesert to arid savanna. It is endemic to southern Africa and probably burrows into hard ground. It may be found at night and may be killed by vehicles while crossing roads at night, especially after rain. This snake has a beaked snout (see illustration).
Similar species: The bluish black to reddish brown markings on the back are unique and this snake cannot, therefore, easily be misidentified.
Enemies: Other snakes.
Food and feeding: Invertebrates.
Reproduction: Probably oviparous.
Danger to man: None.

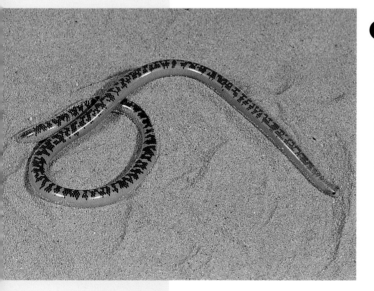

LOOK OUT FOR

- A small, slender snake with a cylindrical body.
- Has a beaked snout.
- Has bluish black to reddish brown spots on the back.
- The small dark eyes are very prominent.

This snake can be identified by the darker spots or blotches on its back.

Rhinotyphlops s. schlegelii

Schlegel's Beaked Blind Snake

Rhinotyphlops schlegelii

OTHER NAMES
Schlegel se haakneusblindeslang (A)

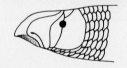

average 60 cm   maximum 1 m

Length: Adults average 60 cm with a maximum length of nearly 1 m.

Scale count: There are 36–44 scale rows around the body with 332–623 dorsal scales.

Colour: Variable, with adults sometimes a uniform brown to dark olive or black above. However, the dorsal colour is usually yellow to yellow-green or brownish yellow, with irregular, more or less transverse, dark brown to black blotches. The belly is uniform straw yellow.

Preferred habitat: From coastal forest to moist savanna.

Habits: This snake burrows into soil but may come to the surface after heavy rain. Otherwise it may be found in soil under rocks and logs. Individuals are also exposed during ploughing operations. Large individuals are seldom seen, as they appear to live deep underground. This is southern Africa's largest blind snake by far. In large specimens, the back half of the body is often distended by fat, which it stores in order to overwinter. This snake has the habit of digging its sharply-pointed tail into one's hand when handled.

Similar species: May be confused with other blind snakes and various harmless snakes, as well as the Southern Stiletto Snake (*Atractaspis bibronii*), but often has dark brown to black blotches on the body.

Enemies: Other snakes.

Food and feeding: Mainly termites and their larvae. Other burrowing invertebrates are also taken.

Bill Branch

Schlegel's Beaked Blind Snake is egg-laying, producing up to 60 eggs at a time.

The Zambezi Beaked Blind Snake usually has either a striped or blotched appearance.

LOOK OUT FOR

- A medium to large snake with a cylindrical body.
- Has a beaked snout.
- Varies in coloration from plain to blotched or striped.
- The small dark eyes are prominent.

Reproduction: Oviparous, laying between 8 and 60 eggs (20–22 x 10–12 mm), depending on the size of the female. These measure 21 x 11,5 mm and contain partially developed embryos. The eggs hatch within 5–6 weeks.

Subspecies: There are 3 subspecies in southern Africa.

Schlegel's Beaked Blind Snake (*Rhinotyphlops schlegelii schlegelii*), the nominate form, discussed above, has 36–44 scale rows and occurs in the south-eastern parts of Mozambique and the north-eastern parts of KwaZulu-Natal.

The **Zambezi Beaked Blind Snake** (*Rhinotyphlops schlegelii mucruso*) occurs in northern Mozambique, Zimbabwe, eastern Botswana and elsewhere further north. It has 30–36 scale rows around the body and is either striped or blotched.

Peters' Beaked Blind Snake (*Rhinotyphlops schlegelii petersii*) is found in Namibia, northern Botswana and elsewhere further north. It is blotched and has 34–40 scale rows around the body.

Danger to man: None.

Peters' Beaked Blind Snake has blotches on the upper body.

Slender Blind Snake

Typhlops obtusus

OTHER NAMES
Stompkopblindeslang (A)

Length: Adults average 30–35 cm with a maximum length of 37,2 cm.

Scale count: There are 24–26 scale rows around the body with 460–507 dorsal scales.

Colour: Above, shiny dark brown and pale brown below.

Preferred habitat: Humic soil in moist savanna in eastern Zimbabwe, Mozambique and elsewhere further north.

Habits: This snake inhabits forests where it may be found in loose humic soil or under rocks in humic soil. Often found in compost heaps.

Similar species: May be confused with other blind snakes and a variety of harmless snakes as well as the Southern Stiletto Snake (*Atractaspis bibronii*).

Enemies: Other snakes.

Food and feeding: Unknown.

Reproduction: Unknown.

Danger to man: None.

LOOK OUT FOR

- A slender snake with a rounded snout.
- Plain dark brown above with a paler belly.
- Found in eastern Zimbabwe, Mozambique and elsewhere further north.

average 35 cm   maximum 37,2 cm

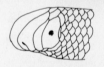

Humic soil in moist savanna is the preferred habitat of this rare species, whose distribution only just extends into southern Africa.

Ian Michler / SIL

HARMLESS

Fornasini's Blind Snake
Typhlops fornasinii

OTHER NAMES
Fornasini se blindeslang (A)

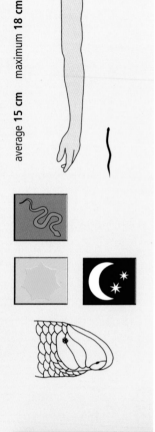

average 15 cm   maximum 18 cm

Length: Adults average 15 cm with a maximum length of just over 18 cm.

Scale count: There are 22–27 scale rows around the body with 232–277 dorsal scales.

Colour: Above, uniform grey to dark brown or blackish brown with irregular yellow blotches, especially on the throat and anal region. These blotches may be visible on the rest of the belly, but are not pronounced.

Preferred habitat: Coastal forest and moist savanna.

Habits: An endemic species that inhabits coastal bush and moist savanna. It is found in alluvial sand where it burrows below leaf litter. This snake is common within its range.

Similar species: May be confused with other blind snakes and a variety of harmless snakes as well as the Southern Stiletto Snake (*Atractaspis bibronii*).

Enemies: Other snakes.

Food and feeding: Unknown.

Reproduction: Unknown.

Danger to man: None.

A common blind snake, often found under leaf litter.

LOOK OUT FOR

- A very small snake with a cylindrical body and rounded snout.
- Has irregular yellow blotches on the throat and beneath the tail.

Bill Branch

Bibron's Blind Snake
Typhlops bibronii

HARMLESS

OTHER NAMES
Bibron se blindeslang (A)

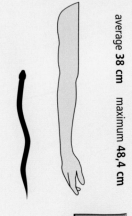

average 38 cm maximum 48,4 cm

Length: Adults average 30–38 cm with a maximum length of 48,4 cm.

Scale count: 30–34 scale rows around the body with 363–453 dorsal scales.

Colour: Above, uniform shiny dark brown to olive brown with a yellowish brown to light brown or pink to fleshy pink belly. The young are usually paler than the adults.

Preferred habitat: Coastal forest, moist savanna and grassland.

Habits: A burrowing snake that, because of its fossorial existence, is seldom seen on the surface, except perhaps after heavy rains.

Similar species: May be confused with other blind snakes and a variety of harmless snakes as well as the Southern Stiletto Snake (*Atractaspis bibronii*).

Enemies: Other snakes.

Food and feeding: Invertebrates, including ant and termite larvae.

Reproduction: Oviparous, laying 2–14 thin-walled eggs (42–43 x 9,5–10 mm). These hatch within 5–6 days and the young measure 10–12,9 cm.

Danger to man: None.

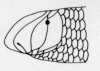

Warren Schmidt

This snake is seldom seen on the soil surface, except after heavy rains.

Bibron's Blind Snake (left) is easily confused with the venomous Southern Stiletto Snake.

Richard Boycott

HARMLESS

Long-tailed Worm Snake

Leptotyphlops longicaudus

average 20 cm   maximum 25,5 cm

OTHER NAMES
Long-tailed Thread Snake (E)
Langsterterdslangetjie (A)
Langstertdraadslangetjie (A)

Length: Adults average 15–20 cm but may reach, or exceed, 25,5 cm.
Scale count: There are 14 scale rows around the body and 10 around the tail with 266–325 dorsal scales and 34–58 subcaudals.
Colour: Above, uniform lilac to grey with a flesh pink tinge. The belly is uniform flesh pink.
Preferred habitat: Moist savanna.
Habits: Because of its fossorial existence, this snake is seldom seen. It may be found under loose stones or beneath rotting logs. If exposed, it will disappear down the nearest hole or attempt to burrow into loose soil or under loose leaves. It will also wriggle furiously. Specimens have been found in the roots of bushes during land-cleaning operations.
Similar species: Worm snakes are very distinct, with highly polished scales encircling their cylindrical bodies, but different species of worm snakes are difficult to tell apart.
Enemies: Other snakes, birds, carnivorous mammals and scorpions.
Food and feeding: Invertebrates, especially termites.
Reproduction: Oviparous, laying 2, 3 or more eggs (18–22 x 4 mm).
Danger to man: None.

Bill Branch

LOOK OUT FOR

- Small slender snake with a rounded head.
- May wriggle furiously if captured.
- Has a cylindrical body.
- Scales are highly polished.

This snake feeds on invertebrates, especially termites.

Cape Worm Snake

Leptotyphlops nigricans

OTHER NAMES
Black Thread Snake (E)
Kaapse erdslangetjie (A)
Swartdraadslangetjie (A)

Length: Adults average 15–17 cm with a maximum length of close to 20 cm.

Scale count: There are 14 scale rows around the body and 10 rows around the tail with 202–260 dorsal scales and 21–33 subcaudals.

Colour: Uniform dark brown to black above and below, sometimes with pale-edged scales.

Preferred habitat: Fynbos, dry savanna, moist savanna and grassland.

Habits: Like the Long-tailed Worm Snake (*Leptotyphlops longicaudus*), this snake is fossorial. Individuals are seldom seen unless uncovered while sheltering under loose stones or beneath rotting logs. It is endemic to southern Africa. In winter, large numbers of these snakes have been known to congregate in a suitable hiding place.

Similar species: Worm snakes are very distinct, with highly polished scales encircling their cylindrical bodies, but different species of worm snakes are difficult to tell apart.

Enemies: Other snakes, birds, small carnivorous mammals and scorpions.

Food and feeding: Invertebrates.

Reproduction: Oviparous.

Danger to man: None.

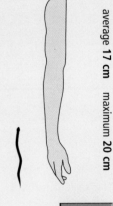

average 17 cm   maximum 20 cm

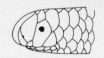

LOOK OUT FOR

- A very small slender snake.
- Uniform dark brown to black in colour.
- Has a cylindrical body.
- Scales are highly polished.

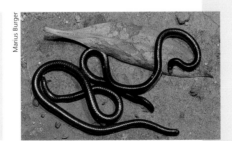

Marius Burger

Cape Worm Snakes average 15–17 cm in length.

Because of its fossorial existence, this snake is seldom seen.

Bill Branch

Slender Worm Snake
Leptotyphlops gracilior

HARMLESS

OTHER NAMES
Slender Thread Snake (E)
Skraal erdslangetjie (A)
Skraal draadslangetjie (A)

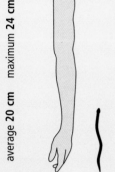

average 20 cm   maximum 24 cm

Length: Adults average 15–20 cm with a maximum length of 24 cm.
Scale count: There are 14 scale rows around the body and 10 around the tail, as well as 305–362 dorsal scales and 24–41 subcaudals.
Colour: Uniform brown to black above and below.
Preferred habitat: Fynbos and karoo scrub.
Habits: An endemic species that inhabits succulent karoo vegetation. Like the other worm snakes, it is fossorial and seldom seen. Large numbers are ploughed up while sheltered in termite mounds.
Similar species: Worm snakes are very distinct, with highly polished scales encircling their cylindrical bodies, but different species of worm snakes are difficult to tell apart.
Enemies: Other snakes, birds, small carnivorous mammals and scorpions.
Food and feeding: Invertebrates.
Reproduction: Probably oviparous.
Danger to man: None.

Note the highly polished scales.

John Visser

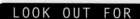

LOOK OUT FOR

- A very slender snake.
- Uniform dark brown to black in colour.
- Has a cylindrical body.
- Scales are highly polished.

Many of these snakes are ploughed up during farming operations.

John Visser

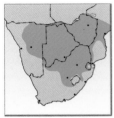

Leptotyphlops s. scutifrons

Peters' Worm Snake

Leptotyphlops scutifrons

OTHER NAMES
Peters' Thread Snake (E)
Peters se erdslangetjie (A)

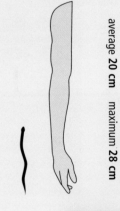

average 20 cm   maximum 28 cm

Length: Adults average 18–20 cm, with a maximum length of nearly 28 cm.

Scale count: There are 14 scale rows around the body and 10 around the tail with 192–309 dorsal scales and 19–30 subcaudals.

Colour: Above, reddish brown to black, with the belly black or paler. The scales may be pale-edged.

Preferred habitat: Varied, including coastal forest, moist and dry savanna, grassland and karoo scrub.

Habits: A fossorial form that may be seen on the surface after heavy rain. Otherwise it may be found beneath stones, rotting logs or in termite mounds. Specimens have been found in semidry cow dung near Harrismith in the Free State. This snake may pretend to be dead if handled in a rough manner.

Similar species: Worm snakes are very distinct, with highly polished scales encircling their cylindrical bodies, but different species of worm snakes are difficult to tell apart.

Enemies: Small carnivorous mammals, birds, snakes and scorpions.

Food and feeding: Invertebrates, especially termites.

Reproduction: Oviparous, laying 2–7 elongate eggs (35 x 14 mm) in midsummer. The eggs may be joined like a string of sausages.

Subspecies: There are 2 subspecies that occur within our range. The typical race of **Peters' Worm Snake** (*Leptotyphlops scutifrons scutifrons*), discussed above, has 225–309 ventrals and 19–30 subcaudals.

Leonard Hoffmann / SIL

Peters' Worm Snake is fossorial, but may emerge after heavy rains.

Eggs of Peters' Worm Snake.

LOOK OUT FOR

- A slender snake.
- Uniform red-brown to black in colour.
- Has a cylindrical body.
- Scales are highly polished.
- The tail ends in a spine.
- Found in a variety of habitats from forests to karoo scrub.

The Eastern Cape Worm Snake (*Leptotyphlops scutifrons conjunctus*) has 192–258 ventrals and 18–28 subcaudals. It lays small eggs (9,2–11,8 x 2,5–3,4 mm) and grows to a maximum length of 19,1 cm. It may have white patches on the underside of the body and the tail.

Danger to man: None.

The Eastern Cape Worm Snake may have white patches on the underside of the body.

Incognito Worm Snake
Leptotyphlops incognitus

OTHER NAMES
Incognito Thread Snake (E)
Incognito-erdslangetjie (A)
Incognitodraadslangetjie (A)

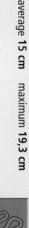

Length: A small snake, the largest specimen measuring 19,3 cm.

Scale count: There are 14 scale rows around the body, 10 around the tail, 223–292 ventrals and 23–35 subcaudals.

Colour: Brown to black above, with a black belly.

Preferred habitat: Varied – from lowland forest to moist savanna and grassland.

Habits: A fossorial form that may be seen on the ground surface after heavy rain. Otherwise it may be found beneath stones or rotting logs, or in termite mounds.

Similar species: Worm snakes are very distinct, with highly polished scales encircling their cylindrical bodies, but different species of worm snakes are difficult to tell apart.

Enemies: Small carnivorous mammals, birds, snakes and scorpions.

Food and feeding: Invertebrates, especially termites.

Reproduction: Oviparous.

Danger to man: None.

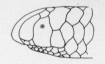

LOOK OUT FOR

- A small, slender snake.
- Uniform black in colour.
- Has a cylindrical body.
- Scales are highly polished.

Bill Branch

The eggs are attached, resembling sausages.

Bill Branch

This snake may be found under stones or logs, or in termite mounds.

HARMLESS

Tello's Worm Snake
Leptotyphlops telloi

average **14 cm**   maximum **18 cm**

OTHER NAMES
Tello's Thread Snake (E)
Tello se erdslangetjie (A)
Tello se draadslangetjie (A)

Length: Adults average 14 cm with a maximum length of close to 18 cm.

Scale count: There are 14 scale rows around the body, 12 around the tail, 241–263 dorsal scales and 24–26 subcaudals.

Colour: Uniform black above and below, with white patches on the head.

Preferred habitat: Restricted to the Lebombo Mountains in Swaziland and Mozambique.

Habits: A fossorial endemic species with a limited distribution. This snake is rare and is seldom encountered.

Similar species: Worm snakes are very distinct, with highly polished scales encircling their cylindrical bodies, but different species of worm snakes are difficult to tell apart.

Enemies: Other snakes, birds, small carnivorous mammals and scorpions.

Food and feeding: Invertebrates.

Reproduction: Probably oviparous.

Danger to man: None.

Tello's Worm Snake is preyed upon by snakes, birds, carnivorous mammals and scorpions.

The remote Lebombo Mountains of Swaziland and Mozambique are the preferred habitat of this rare snake.

Jonathan Leeming

LOOK OUT FOR

- A small slender snake.
- Uniform black in colour with white patches on the head.
- Has a cylindrical body.
- Scales are highly polished.

Ariadne Van Zandbergen / SIL

Distant's Worm Snake
Leptotyphlops distanti

HARMLESS

OTHER NAMES
Distant's Thread Snake (E)
Distant se erdslangetjie (A)
Distant se draadslangetjie (A)

Length: Adults average 15 cm with a maximum length of close to 24 cm.

Scale count: There are 14 scale rows around the body, 12 around the tail, 230–307 dorsal scales and 19–30 subcaudals.

Colour: Grey-black to black above and below, and the scales are often pale-edged.

Preferred habitat: Coastal forest, grassland and moist savanna.

Habits: An endemic species that inhabits a variety of habitats including coastal bush, moist savanna and grassland. It is fossorial and is usually only seen on the surface after heavy rain, when it is flushed from its shelter. Otherwise it may be found under loose stones, beneath rotting logs, in grass tussocks and also in termite mounds.

Similar species: Worm snakes are very distinct, with highly polished scales encircling their cylindrical bodies, but different species of worm snakes are difficult to tell apart.

Enemies: Other snakes, birds, small carnivorous mammals and scorpions.

Food and feeding: Invertebrates.

Reproduction: Probably oviparous.

Danger to man: None.

average 15 cm   maximum 24 cm

LOOK OUT FOR

- A small slender snake.
- Uniform grey-black in colour.
- Has a cylindrical body.
- Scales are highly polished.

Like many of the other worm snakes, Distant's Worm Snake is often flushed to the surface during heavy rain.

Bill Branch

HARMLESS

maximum 12,6 cm

average 9 cm

Southern Forest Worm Snake

Leptotyphlops sylvicolus

OTHER NAMES
Southern Forest Thread Snake (E)
Suidelike wouderdslangetjie (A)
Suidelike wouddraadslangetjie (A)

Length: A very small species with a maximum length of 12,6 cm.
Scale count: 14 scale rows around the body and 10 around the tail.
There are 171–194 dorsal scales and 18–22 subcaudals.
Colour: Black above and paler below, sometimes with white speckles near the vent.
Preferred habitat: Coastal forest.
Habits: A forest inhabitant that was described quite recently.
Similar species: Worm snakes are unique, with highly polished scales encircling their cylindrical bodies, but different species of worm snakes are difficult to tell apart.
Enemies: Other snakes.
Food and feeding: Unknown.
Reproduction: Unknown.
Danger to man: None.

LOOK OUT FOR

- A very small snake.
- Uniform black in colour.
- Has a cylindrical body.
- Scales are highly polished.

Wulf Haacke

This recently discovered snake inhabits coastal forests.

Coastal forest is the preferred habitat of the Southern Forest Worm Snake.

Peter Pickford / SIL

Namaqua Worm Snake

Leptotyphlops occidentalis

OTHER NAMES
Western Thread Snake (E)
Namakwa-erdslangetjie (A)
Westelike draadslangetjie(A)

Length: Adults average 17–20 cm with a maximum length of 32,2 cm.
Scale count: There are 14 scale rows around the body and 12 around the tail, as well as 276–355 dorsal scales and 16–26 subcaudals.
Colour: Above, light brown to grey-brown or purplish brown with a paler belly. The scales on the back have pale edges, giving a chequered appearance.
Preferred habitat: The Namib Desert and karoo scrub.
Habits: This snake, which is endemic to southern Africa, inhabits arid regions in the west. It is fossorial and will seek shelter under rocks and logs. Individuals may be forced to the surface after heavy rains.
Similar species: Worm snakes are very distinct, with highly polished scales encircling their cylindrical bodies. Different species of worm snakes are difficult to tell apart.
Enemies: Other snakes and scorpions.
Food and feeding: Termites.
Reproduction: Probably oviparous.
Danger to man: None.

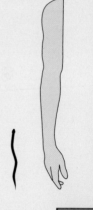

average 20 cm   maximum 32,2 cm

LOOK OUT FOR

- A very slender, small snake.
- The scales on the back have pale edges, giving it a chequered effect.
- Has a cylindrical body.
- Scales are highly polished.

Bill Branch

Individuals may be found under rocks or logs.

An endemic snake that inhabits the drier regions in the west of its range.

Andrew Turner & S Davies

Damara Worm Snake

Leptotyphlops labialis

HARMLESS

OTHER NAMES
Damara Thread Snake (E)
Damara-erdslangetjie (A)
Damaradraadslangetjie (A)

average 17 cm   maximum 30 cm

Length: Adults average 17 cm with a maximum length of nearly 30 cm.
Scale count: There are 14 scale rows around the body and 12 around the tail, as well as 278–338 ventral scales and 18–24 subcaudals.
Colour: Above, greyish brown to brown with pale-edged scales. The belly is paler.
Preferred habitat: The Namib Desert and karoo scrub from northern Namibia further northwards.
Habits: Very little is known about this snake.
Similar species: Worm snakes are very distinct, with highly polished scales encircling their cylindrical bodies, but different species of worm snakes are difficult to tell apart.
Enemies: Other snakes.
Food and feeding: Unknown.
Reproduction: Unknown.
Danger to man: None.

LOOK OUT FOR

■ A slender snake.
■ Has a cylindrical body.
■ Scales are highly polished.

Wulf Haacke

Very little is known about this inhabitant of northern Namibia.

This secretive and poorly known species inhabits the Namib Desert and karoo scrub.

Pungwe Worm Snake
Leptotyphlops pungwensis

HARMLESS

OTHER NAMES
Pungwe Thread Snake (E)
Pungwe-erdslangetjie (A)
Pungwedraadslangetjie (A)

Length: Known from a single juvenile specimen that measured approximately 9 cm.
Scale count: There are 14 scale rows around the body and 10 around the tail, with 252 dorsal scales and 21 subcaudals.
Colour: Brown above and below with darker marks on the head and scattered white patches below as well as under the tail.
Preferred habitat: Coastal forest.
Habits: This endemic snake is known from a single specimen that was found in the Pungwe Flats in Mozambique. It was formally described in 1997.
Similar species: Worm snakes are very distinct, with highly polished scales encircling their cylindrical bodies, but different species of worm snakes are difficult to tell apart.
Enemies: Other snakes.
Food and feeding: Unknown.
Reproduction: Unknown.
Danger to man: None.

This recent discovery is known only from the Pungwe Flats in Mozambique.

average and maximum unknown

LOOK OUT FOR

- A slender snake.
- Has a cylindrical body.
- Scales are highly polished.
- Has dark markings on the head and white speckling on the belly.

Ian Michler / SIL

Jacobsen's Worm Snake

Leptotyphlops jacobseni

average 16 cm   maximum 21 cm

OTHER NAMES
Jacobsen's Thread Snake (E)
Jacobsen se erdslangetjie (A)
Jacobson se draadslangetjie (A)

Length: Adults average 16 cm with a maximum length of nearly 21 cm.
Scale count: There are 14 scale rows around the body and 10 around the tail, as well as 244–289 ventral scales and 18–27 subcaudals.
Colour: Above and below, brown to black with pale markings on the chin.
Preferred habitat: Grassland and moist savanna at an altitude of between 1 300 and 1 700 m.
Habits: Very little is known about this snake. Individuals have been found under stones and in deserted termite mounds.
Similar species: Worm snakes are very distinct, with highly polished scales encircling their cylindrical bodies, but different species of worm snakes are difficult to tell apart.
Enemies: Other snakes, mammalian predators and scorpions.
Food and feeding: Unknown.
Reproduction: Unknown.
Danger to man: None.

LOOK OUT FOR

- A slender snake.
- Has a cylindrical body.
- Scales are highly polished.

Wulf Haacke

This relatively unknown snake was described fairly recently.

GLOSSARY

Agama: Short, stubby lizards of the family Agamidae, with a triangular head and short tail. Agamas are active during the day.

Amphisbaenid: Worm lizard of the suborder Amphisbaenia (family Amphisbaenidae). Amphisbaenids are adapted to a burrowing lifestyle and are closely related to lizards.

Anal: Region of the anus. Refers in squamates (scaled creatures) to the scale in front of the cloacal opening; in snakes, the terminal scale in the ventral series, and is usually larger than the ventral scales. The paired anals in snakes are often referred to as a divided anal.

Anaphylaxis: Increased sensitivity to the action of a normally nontoxic protein, especially on second exposure. Serum sickness in humans is an instance of relatively mild anaphylaxis.

Anterior: Situated at or near the front.

Antivenom: Serum produced from the antibodies of animals injected with venom. Combats the effect of snakebite by blocking access of toxic enzymes to target cells in the body of the victim.

Aquatic: Living in water.

Arboreal: Living predominantly in trees.

Caudal: Pertaining to the tail.

Class: The taxonomic category ranking below 'phylum' and above 'order'.

Cloaca: The common chamber in many vertebrates into which the urinary, digestive and reproductive ducts discharge their contents. Opens to the exterior through the anus.

Clutch: All eggs laid by a female at one time.

Crepuscular: Being active mainly at dawn or dusk.

Cryptic: Hidden or camouflaged.

Cytotoxin: Toxin that adversely affects tissue and cell formation. Predominant in adder venoms.

Diurnal: Being active mainly during the day.

Dorsal: Refers to the upper surface of the body. In snakes, all the body scales except the enlarged ventral and subcaudal scales.

Dorsolateral: The upper surface of the body, bordering the backbone but above the flanks (see 'Lateral').

Elapid: Snake of the family Elapidae. Elapids, e.g. cobras, Rinkhals, mambas, and coral snakes, have rigidly fixed front fangs.

Endemic: Found only in a specific area. A species may thus be classified if more than 90% of the distribution records come from within a specific area.

Envenomation: The delivery of venom by the bites of snakes or the bites, stings or effluvia (gaseous waste) of insects and other arthropods.

Family: The taxonomic category ranking below 'order' and above 'genus'.

Fang: Large specialized tooth adapted for the injection of venom into prey.

Fossorial: Adapted to burrowing and living below ground.

Genus: The taxonomic category ranking below 'family' and above 'species'.

Gravid: Pregnant.

Haemotoxic: A substance that compromises red blood cells or other components of the circulatory system, adversely affecting the blood or the functioning of the circulatory system.

Hatchling: In this context, a newborn reptile produced by an egg-laying species.

Hemipenis: One of the paired copulatory structures present in male squamate reptiles.

Herpetology: The study of reptiles and amphibians.

Incubation: Keeping eggs warm and humid to ensure continuous development.

Interstitial skin: The skin lying between the scales.

Intramuscular: Into a muscle.

Intravenous: Into a vein.

Invertebrate: Any animal without a backbone.

Jacobson's organ: A pair of organs situated in the roof of the mouth, into which the tips of the forked tongue are pressed in order to taste and smell scent particles picked up by the tongue from its immediate environment.

Keel: A prominent ridge, occurring longitudinally on the dorsal scales of some snakes.

Labial: Of the lips. Usually refers to the scales bordering the lips.

Lacertids: Lizards of the family Lacertidae.

Lateral: Pertaining to the sides or flanks of the body.

Lymph: A colourless alkaline fluid carried around the body by the lymphatic system.

Mimic: A species that takes on the appearance of a distasteful, inedible, venomous or aggressive species as a form of self-defence.

Montane: Inhabiting mountains.

Necrosis: The death of cells (bone or soft tissue) in the body, usually within a localized area. Gangrene is necrosis with infection.

Neurotoxic: Toxin adversely affecting neuromuscular function. Predominant in venoms of cobras and mambas.

Nocturnal: Being mainly active at night.

Order: The taxonomical category ranking below 'class' and above 'family'.

Oviparous: Egg-laying. See also 'Viviparous'.

Parthenogenetic: The ability of females to develop fertile eggs without mating.

Posterior: The rear or back part.

Postocular: A scale bordering the posterior edge of the eye.

Prefrontal: One of the scales on the head of a reptile.

Preocular: A scale bordering the anterior edge of the eye.

Ptosis: Drooping of the eyelids.

Recurved: Used here to describe a tooth that bends backwards.

Rhombic: A more or less diamond-shaped pattern.

Riverine: Pertaining to rivers.

Rostral: Pertaining to the scale at the front of the nose (rostrum) of a reptile.

Scale: A thin, flattened, plate-like structure that forms part of the surface covering of various vertebrates, especially fish and reptiles.

Sidewind: Sideways movement of a section of the body, followed by the next section. Often seen in desert snakes on unstable dune sand, where usual forms of locomotion are not effective.

Sloughing: The casting or shedding of the outer layer of skin.

Squamate: Scaled creatures.

Subcaudal scales: In snakes the ventral scales, either paired or single, found between the vent and the tip of the tail.

Subcutaneous: Under the skin.

Subspecies: A population of a species that is distinguishable from other populations of that species.

Substratum: The nonliving material on which a plant or animal lives.

Sympatric: Living in the same region.

Taxonomy: The science of classification – hierarchical arrangement of animals and plants in groups based on their natural relationships.

Terrestrial: Living on the ground.

Ventral: Pertaining to the underside of the body.

Vestigial: Being smaller than (or a remnant of) an evolutionary ancestor.

Viviparous: Giving birth to live offspring from eggs that hatch within the uterus or as the egg is laid or shortly after laying. The egg has a transparent membrane and lacks the leathery white outer layer seen in oviparous snakes.

Opposite: The Olive House Snake.

BIBLIOGRAPHY

Akani, GC & Luiselli, L. 2000. 'Aspects of the natural history of *Natriciteres* (Serpentes: Colubridae) in Nigeria, with special reference to *N. variegata* and *N. fuliginoides*'. *Herpetological Natural History* 7 (2): 163–168.

Alexander, GJ. 1990. 'The reptiles and amphibians of Durban, South Africa'. *Durban Museum Novitates* 15: 1–41.

Alexander, GJ & Marshall, CL. 1998. 'Diet activity patterns in a captive colony of rinkhals, *Hemachatus haemachatus*'. *African Journal of Herpetology* 47: 27–30.

Alexander, GJ, Mitchell, D & Hanrahan, SA. 1999. 'Wide thermal tolerance in the African elapid, *Hemachatus haemachatus*'. *Journal of Herpetology* 33: 165–167.

Alexander, GJ & Brooks, R. 1999. 'Circannual rhythms of appetite and ecdysis in the elapid snake, *Hemachatus haemachatus*, appear to be endogenous'. *Copeia* 1999: 146–152.

Auerbach, RD. 1978. *The amphibians and reptiles of Botswana*. Mokwepa Consultants (privately printed), Gaborone.

Barker, D & Barker, T. 1996. 'The maintenance and reproduction of the Dwarf Python of Angola and Namibia'. *Vivarium* 7 (1): 30–34.

Bauer, AM, Lamb, T, Branch, WR & Babb, RD. 2001. 'New Records of two rare snakes from northern Namibia, with comments on the trans-Kunene distribution of Mopaneveld Squamates (Squamata: Serpentes: Colubridae)'. *Herpetozoa* 14 (1–2): 75–79.

Bayliss, PS. 2001. 'Life history note: *Lamprophis fuliginosus* (Brown House Snake). Predation'. *Herpetological Review*. 32 (1): 48–49.

Boycott, RC. 1995. 'Notes on the distribution and ecology of *Amblyodipsas concolor* (A Smith, 1849) in Swaziland (Serpentes: Colubridae)'. *African Journal of Ecology* 33 (4): 417–419.

Boycott, RC. 1996. 'Life history notes, Serpentes: Colubridae. *Lamprophis fuscus* Yellow-bellied House Snake. Size, lepidosis and distribution'. *African Herp News* (25): 40–41 (October).

Branch, WR. n.d. *First aid treatment of snakebite*. Cedar Press, Port Elizabeth.

– 1985. 'The pressure/immobilisation first aid treatment of snakebite'. *Journal of the Herpetological Association of Africa* 31: 10–13.

– (ed) 1988. *South African Red Data Book – reptiles and amphibians*. South African National Scientific Programmes Report No. 151.

– 1989. 'A new adder (*Bitis*) from the Cedarberg, and the status of *Bitis inornata* (A. Smith, 1849): Preliminary observations'. *Journal of the Herpetologial Association of Africa*. 36 (Proceedings of the 1987 HAA Stellenbosch Conference): 64–67.

– 1992. 'Life history notes. Serpentes: Colubridae. *Psammophis crucifer*. Cross-marked Grass Snake. Size'. *Journal of the Herpetological Association of Africa* 41: 44 (December).

– 1992. 'Life History Notes. Serpentes: Colubridae. *Psammophis notostictus* Karoo Sand Snake. Size'. *Journal of the Herpetological Association of Africa* 41: 44 (December).

– 1995. 'Geographical distribution, Reptilia, Serpentes: Colubridae. *Philothamnus semivariegatus semivariegatus*'. *African Herp News* 24: 29–30 (December).

– 1997. 'A new adder (*Bitis*: Viperidae) from the Western Cape Province, South Africa'. *South African Journal of Zoology*. 32 (2): 37–42.

– 1997. 'Life history notes. Serpentes: Typhlopidae. *Typhlops bibronii*. Size'. *African Herp News* 26: 28 (July).

– 1998. *Bill Branch's field guide to snakes and other reptiles of southern Africa*. 3rd ed. Struik Publishers, Cape Town.

– 1999. 'Dwarf Adders of the *Bitis cornuta-inornata* complex (Serpentes: Viperidae) in southern Africa'. *Kaupia. Darmstadter Beitrage zur Naturgeschichte* 8: 39–63.

– 2002. 'The conservation status of South Africa's threatened reptiles'. In GH Verdoorn and J le Roux (eds), *The state of South Africa's species*. Published conference proceedings. Endangered Wildlife Trust, Johannesburg.

Branch, WR & Griffin, M. 1996. 'Pythons in Namibia: Distribution, conservation and captive breeding programs'. *Advanced Herpetoculture* 1: 93–102.

Branch, WR & Haagner, GV. 1996. 'Life history notes – Serpentes: Leptotyphlopidae. *Leptotyphlops conjunctus incognitus* Incognito Worm Snake. Reproduction'. *African Herp News* 25: 40 (October).

– 1999. 'Geographic distribution: Serpentes: Sauria: Colubridae/Scincidae. *Psammophis brevirostris* and *Acontias* sp. The value of road kills'. *African Herp News* 30: 37–38 (December).

Branch, WR, Haagner, GV & Shine, R. 1996. 'Is there an ontogenetic shift in mamba diet? Taxonomic confusion and dietary records for black and green mambas (*Dendroaspis*: Elapidae)'. *Herpetological Natural History* 3 (2): 171–178.

Broadley, DG. 1990. *FitzSimon's snakes of southern Africa*. Jonathan Ball & Ad Donker, Parklands.

– 1996. 'A review of the tribe Atherini (Serpentes: Viperidae), with the description of two new genera'. *African Journal of Herpetology* 45 (2): 40–48.

– 1996. 'A revision of the genus *Lycophidion* Fitzinger (Serpentes: Colubridae) in Africa south of the Equator'. *Syntarsus* 3: 1–33.

– 1998. 'A review of the African *Elapsoidea semiannulata* complex (Serpentes: Elapidae)'. *African Journal of Herpetology*, 47 (1): 13–23.

– 1999. 'Geographic distribution: Serpentes: Colubridae. *Prosymna lineata'. African Herp News*, 30: 36–37.

– 1999. 'The South African Python, *Python natalensis*, (A Smith 1840), is a valid species'. *African Herp News*, 28: 31–32 (January).

– 2001. 'A review of the genus *Thelotornis* (A Smith) in eastern Africa with the description of a new species from Usamabara Mountains. (Serpentes: Colubridae: Dispholidini)'. *African Journal of Herpetology*, 50 (2): 53–70.

– 2002. 'A review of the species of *Psammophis* (Boie) found south of latitude 12 ° S (Serpentes: Psammophiinae)'. *African Journal of Herpetology*, 51 (2): 83–119.

Broadley, DG & Broadley, S. 1999. 'A review of the African worm snakes from south of latitude 12° S (Serpentes: Leptotyphlopidae)'. *Syntarsus* 5: 1–36 (August).

Broadley, DG & Schätti, B. 1997. 'A new species of *Coluber* from northern Namibia (Reptilia: Serpentes)'. *Madoqua* 19 (2): 171–174.

Broadley, DG & Wallach, V. 1997. 'A review of the worm snakes of Mozambique (Serpentes: Leptotyphlopidae) with the description of a new species'. *Arnoldia* 10 (11): 111–119.

– 1997. 'A review of the genus *Leptotyphlops* (Serpentes: Leptotyphlopidae) in KwaZulu-Natal, South Africa, with the description of a new forest-dwelling species'. *Durban Museum Novitates* 22: 37–42.

Christensen, PA. 1969. 'The treatment of snakebite'. *South African Medical Journal* 43: 1253–1258.

Cunningham, PL. 2002. 'Natural history notes, Reptilia, Serpentes, Colubridae. *Lamprophis fuliginosus* Brown House-snake. Foraging'. *African Herp News* 34: 28–29.

– 2002. 'Natural history notes, Reptilia, Serpentes, Elapidae. *Naja nigricollis nigricincta* Western Barred Spitting Cobra or Zebra Snake. Diet'. *African Herp News* 35: 12–13.

De Villiers, AH. 1995. 'Life history notes. Serpentes: Colubridae, *Psammophylax rhombeatus rhombeatus* Spotted Skaapsteker. Reproduction'. *African Herp News* 24: 26–28 (December).

Douglas, R. 2001. 'If you are going to get bitten by a snake – get it right!' *Culna* 56: 18–19.

Ernst, CH, Walsh, T & Lammerzahl, AF. 1999. 'Reproduction of the Rufous-beaked Snake, *Rhamphiophis oxyrhynchus* (Colubridae, Lamprophinae) [sic]'. *British Herpetological Society Bulletin*. 66: 19–25 (= *R. rostratus*).

Flemming, AF. 1994. 'Reproductive cycles of the snakes *Psammophis crucifer, P. leightoni trinasalis* and *P. notostictus* (Serpentes: Colubridae) in the Orange Free State, South Africa'. *Journal of the Herpetological Association of Africa* 43: 19–27 (June).

Foley, SC. 1998. 'Notes on the captive maintenance and reproduction of Oates' Twig Snake (*Thelotornis capensis oatesii*)'. *Herpetological Review* 29 (3): 160–161.

Greiff, I. 1999. 'Natural history notes: Serpentes; *Philothamnus natalensis occidentalis* Western Green Snake. Size and reproduction'. *African Herp News* 28: 36–37.

Griffin, M. 2000. 'The species diversity, distribution and conservation of Namibian reptiles: a review'. *Journal of Namibia Wissenschaftliche Gesellschaft* 48: 116–141.

Griffin, M & Hauch, J. 1999. 'Natural history notes: Serpentes: Colubridae: *Prosymna frontalis* Southwestern Shovel-snout. Reproduction'. *African Herp News* 30: 30–31.

Haagner, GV. 1997. 'Life history notes. Serpentes: Colubridae, *Mehelya capensis capensis* Cape File Snake. Size'. *African Herp News* 26: 29 (July).

Hebbard, S & Cunningham, PL. 2002. 'Natural history notes, Reptilia, Serpentes, Boidae. *Python anchietae* Angola or Anchieta's Dwarf Python. Reproduction'. In *African Herp News* 35: 8–9. (October).

Hughes, B. 1997. '*Dasypeltis scabra* and *Lamprophis fuliginosus* – two pan-African snakes in the Horn of Africa. A tribute to Dan Broadley'. *African Journal of Herpetology* 46 (2): 68–77.

Jacobsen, NHG. 1989. 'The distribution and conservation status of reptiles and amphibians in the Transvaal'. Project TN 6/4/1/30. 1621 pp. Unpublished MSc.

Le Roux, J (ed.). 2002. *The biodiversity of South Africa 2002. Indicators, trends and human impacts*. Struik Publishers, Cape Town.

Marais, J. 1985. *Snake versus man – A guide to dangerous and common harmless snakes of southern Africa*. Southern Books, Johannesburg.

– 1992. *A complete guide to the snakes of southern Africa*. Southern Books, Johannesburg

– 1999. *Snakes and snakebite in southern Africa*. Struik Publishers, Cape Town.

Mattison, C. 2002. *The encyclopaedia of snakes*. Cassell Paperbacks, London.

Pantanowitz, L, Scott, L, Southern, J & Schrire, L. 1998. 'Development of antivenoms in South Africa'. *South African Journal of Science* 94: 464–469.

Pietersen, D & Pietersen, E. 2001. 'Life history notes. Serpentes: Leptotyphlopidae, *Leptotyphlops longicaudus* Long-tailed Thread Snake'. *African Herp News* 33: 16 (July).

Reitz, CJ. 1978. *Poisonous South African snakes and snakebite*. Department of Health, Pretoria. Perskor, Pretoria.

Schrire, L, Muller, GJ & Pantanowitz, L. 1996. *The diagnosis and treatment of envenomation in South Africa*. SAIMR, Johannesburg.

Shine, R, Branch, WR, Harlow, PS & Webb, JK. 1996. 'Sexual dimorphism, reproductive biology and food habits of two species of African file snakes (*Mehelya*: Colubridae)'. *Journal of Zoology* (London) 240: 327–340.

– 1998. 'Reproductive biology and food habits of horned adders, *Bitis caudalis* (Viperidae) from southern Africa'. *Copeia* 2: 391–401.

Shine, R, Haagner, GV, Branch, WR, Harlow, PS & Webb, JK. 1996. 'Natural history of the African Shield-nose Snake *Aspidelaps scutatus* (Serpentes: Elapidae)'. *Journal of Herpetology* 30 (3): 361–366.

Shine, R, Harlow, PS, Branch, WR & Webb, JK. 1995. 'Life on the lowest branch: Sexual dimorphism, diet and reproductive biology of an African Twig Snake, *Thelotornis capensis* (Serpentes: Colubridae)'. *Copeia* 1996 (2): 290–299.

Simelane, TS, & Herley, GIH. 1997. 'Recognition of reptiles by Xhosa and Zulu communities in South Africa, with notes on traditional beliefs and uses'. *African Journal of Herpetology*. 46 (1): 49–53.

Spawls, S, & Branch, WR. 1995. *Dangerous snakes of Africa*. Southern Books, Johannesburg.

Spawls, S, Howell, K, Drewes, R, & Ashe, J. 2002. *A field guide to the reptiles of East Africa*. Academic Press, London.

Tilbury, CR. 1993. 'A clinical approach to snakebite and rationale for the use of antivenom'. *South African Journal of Critical Care* 9 (1): 2–4.

– 1996. 'A comparative analysis of the epidemiology and economics of human bites and snakebite at the Jwaneng Hospital'. *Hospital Supplement*: 20–24 (April).

Visser, J & Chapman, DS. 1978. *Snakes and snakebite*. Purnell, Cape Town.

Webb, JK, Branch, WR & Shine, R. 2001. 'Dietary habits and reproductive biology of typhlopid snakes from southern Africa'. *Journal of Herpetology* 35 (4): 558–567.

A Western Natal Green Snake eating a tropical house gecko.

INDEX

Numbers in bold refer to photographs.

A

Adder
  Albany 78, **78**, **79**
  Berg 38, 39, 68, **68**, **69**
    antivenom 44
  Burrowing 143
  Common Night 90
  Desert Mountain 72, **72**, **73**
  Gaboon 37, 66, **66**, **67**
    antivenom 40, 45
  Horned 22, 82, **82**, **83**
  Many-horned 38, 70, **70**, **71**
  Namaqua Dwarf 84, **84**, **85**
  Night **28**, 38
    antivenom 44
  Péringuey's 86, **86**, **87**
  Plain Mountain 74, **74**
  Puff **8**, 11, 23, 37, 63, **63**, **64**, **65**, **75**
    antivenom 40
  Red 76, **76**, **77**
  Rhombic Night 90, **90**
  Snouted Night 92, **92**, **93**
  Southern 80, **80**
adder
  Albanie- 78
  Berg- 68
  Gaboen- 66
  Gewone Nag- 90
  Horing- 82
  Moeras- 88
  Namakwadwerg- 84
  Namibduin- 86
  Ongemerkte berg- 74
  Péringuey se 86
  Pof- 63
  Rooi- 76
  Suidelike 80
  Veelhoring- 70
  Wipneusnag- 92
  Woestynberg- 72
Amblyodipsas concolor 195
Amblyodipsas microphthalma 199
Amblyodipsas microphthalma nigra 200
Amblyodipsas polylepis 197
Amblyodipsas ventrimaculata 201
amphisbaenids (worm lizards) 18
Amplorhinus multimaculatus 179
anatomy 18
antivenom 40
  administering 44–45
  development 40
  polyvalent 44
  snakebite kits 41
  useful contacts 47
Aparallactus capensis 190
Aparallactus guentheri 193

Aparallactus lunulatus 192
Aparallactus nigriceps 194
Aspidelaps lubricus 116
  antivenom 44
  venom 38
Aspidelaps lubricus cowlesi 117
Aspidelaps lubricus infuscatus 117, **117**
Aspidelaps scutatus 118
  antivenom 44
  venom 38
Aspidelaps scutatus fulafula 119
Aspidelaps scutatus intermedius 119, **119**
Atractaspis bibronii 38, 143
  antivenom 44
Atractaspis congica 147
Atractaspis duerdeni 145
Auroraslang 218

B

Bangweulu-moerasslang 233
Bark Snake
  Eastern 175, **175**, **176**
  Viperine 177, **177**
basslang
  Oostelike 175
  Westelike 177
Beaked Snake
  Dwarf 151, **151**
  Rufous 150, **150**
binomial system of nomenclature, 27
Bird Snake 138
Bitis albanica 78
Bitis arietans 11, 37, 63
  antivenom 40
Bitis armata 80
Bitis atropos 38, 39, 68
  antivenom 44
Bitis caudalis 22, 38, 82
Bitis cornuta 38, 70
Bitis gabonica 37, 66
  antivenom 40, 45
Bitis inornata 74
Bitis peringueyi 86
Bitis rubida 76
Bitis schneideri 84
Bitis xeropaga 72
Black White-lipped snake 200, **200**
Blind Snake
  Bibron's 287, **287**
  Boyle's Beaked 280
  Delalande's Beaked 281, **281**
  Fornasini's 286, **286**
  Peters' Beaked 284, **284**
  Schinz's Beaked 282, **282**
  Schlegel's Beaked 283, **283**

  Slender 285
  Zambezi Beaked 284, **284**
blindeslang
  Bibron se 287
  Boyle se haakneus- 280
  Delalande se haakneus- 281
  Fornasini se 286
  Schinz se haakneus- 282
  Schlegel se haakneus- 283
  Stompkop- 285
Blompotslang 279
body temperature control 22
Boomslang 19, 21, 39, 135, **135**, **136**, **137**
  antivenom 40, 44, 45
bosslang
  Gespikkelde 244
  Suidelike 242
Burrowing Asp
  Beaked 145
  Bibron's 143
  Duerden's 145
  Eastern Congo 147
  Southern 143
Bush Snake
  Spotted 244, **244**, **245**, **248**
  Variegated 244

C

captive snakes 50
  breeding 57
  diseases 58
  eggs and hatchlings 58, **58**
  enclosures 52–54
  feeding 54–55, **55**, 56, **56**
  guidelines 51
  handling 52, **53**
  heating 53
  obtaining specimens 51–52
  recordkeeping 59
  transporting 52
caterpillar-like movement 23
Causus defilippii 92
Causus rhombeatus 38, 90
  antivenom 44
Centipede-eater
  Black 193, **193**
  Black-headed 190, **190**, **191**
  Cape 190
  Mozambique 194
  Reticulated 192, **192**
children
  antivenom administration 45
Chilorhinophis gerardi 202
classification systems 26–27
Cobra
  Anchieta's 104, **104**, **105**
  Black-necked Spitting 11, 37,

39, 110, **112**
antivenom 40
Black Spitting **2**, 11, 37, 39,
47, **111**, 112
antivenom 40
Cape 38, 100, **100**, **101**
antivenom 40
Egyptian 102
Forest 38, 106, **106**, **107**
antivenom 40
King 11
Mozambique Spitting 11, 37,
38, 39, 108, **108**, **109**
antivenom 40
Snouted 38, **94**, 102, **102**, **103**
antivenom 40
Zebra 11, 38–39, **110**, 112
Coluber zebrinus 277
Common Tiger Snake 181, **181**
concertina-type progression 23
Coral Snake 116
Angolan 117, **117**
Cape **116**, 117, **117**
antivenom 44
venom 38
Western 117, **117**
Cream-spotted Mountain Snake
208, **208**, **209**
Crotaphopeltis barotseensis 189
Crotaphopeltis hotamboeia 187
cytotoxic venom 37–38

D

Dasypeltis inornata 273
Dasypeltis medici 275
Dasypeltis scabra 270
Dasypeltis spp. 54
Dendroaspis angusticeps **5**, 38, 98
antivenom 40
Dendroaspis jamesoni
antivenom 40
Dendroaspis polylepis 12, 23, 36,
38, 95
antivenom 40, 44
Dipsadoboa aulica 185
Dipsina multimaculata 151
Dispadoboa flavida 186
Dispholidus typus 19, 21, 39, 135
antivenom 40, 44
draadslangetjie
Damara- 298
Distant se 295
Incognito- 293
Jacobsen se 300
Langstert- 288
Pungwe- 299
Skraal- 290
Suidelike woud- 296
Swart- 289
Tello se 294
Westelike 297
Dromophis lineatus 152
Duberria lutrix 253
Duberria lutrix rhodesiana **254**
Duberria variegata 255

Dwarsgestreepte slang 186
Dwerghaakneusslang 151

E

Eastern Bird Snake 141
Eastern Vine Snake 141
Echis spp.
antivenom 40
Egg-eater
Common 270, **270**, **271**, **272**,
276
East African **1**, 275, **275**, **276**
Rhombic 270
Southern Brown 273, **273**, **274**
'egg-tooth' 16, **16–17**
eggs 21
eiervreter
Gewone 270
Oos-Afrika- 275
Suidelike bruin 273
Elapsoidea boulengeri 123
Elapsoidea guentheri 120
Elapsoidea semiannulata 122
Elapsoidea spp.
antivenom 44
Elapsoidea sundevalli 125
Elapsoidea sundevalli decosteri
127
Elapsoidea sundevalli fitzsimonsi
126
Elapsoidea sundevalli longicauda
126
Elapsoidea sundevalli media 126
envenomation 37
erdslangetjie
Damara- 298
Distant se 295
Incognito- 293
Jacobsen se 300
Kaapse 289
Langstert- 288
Namakwa- 297
Peters se 291
Pungwe 299
Skraal 290
Suidelike woud- 296
Tello se 294
evolutionary history 18

F

facts and fallacies 10–11
File Snake
Angola 267
Black 268, **268**, **269**
Cape 265
Southern 265, **265**, **266**
first-aid measures 42–43, **43**
venom in eyes 44
Flowerpot Snake 279, **279**

G

garden environment 12
Garter Snake
Angolan 122, **122**
Boulenger's 123

De Coster's **126**, 127
Günther's 120, **120**
Highveld 126, **126**, **127**, **131**
Kalahari 126
Long-tailed 126, **127**
Sundevall's 125, **125**
Zambezi *121*, 123, **123**, **124**
Gebande slang 186
Geelslang 100
Gerard se swart-en-geel-grond
slangetjie 202
Gerard's Black & Yellow
Burrowing Snake 202, **202**
Gestreepte moerasslang 152
Global Positioning System (GPS) 31
graafneusslang
Angola- 236
Gespikkelde 238
Jan se 234
Suidwestelike 237
Sundevall se 239
Tweestreep- 235
Visser se 241
Grass Snake
Grey-bellied 174, **174**
Leopard 156
Montane 167
Olive 153
Short-snouted 155
Green Snake
Angola 247, **247**
Eastern 251
Eastern Natal 27, 251, **251**, **252**
Natal 251
Ornate 246, **246**
South-eastern 249
Western 247
Western Natal 252, **252**
systematic classification 28
groenslang
Angola- 247
Natal 251
Rooistreep- 246
Suidoostelike 249
Gryspensgrasslang 174
guide to book 14–15

H

Haakneusslang 150
Dwerg-151
habitats 13 *map*
haemotoxic venom 39
Halfgevlekte slang 242
Harlequin Snake
Spotted 128, **128**, **129**
Striped 130, **130**
hatchlings **16–17**, 58
hearing 19
Hemachatus haemachatus 11, 21,
38–39, 113
antivenom 40
Hemirhagerrhis nototaenia 175
Hemirhagerrhis viperinus 177
Herald Snake **20**, 187, **187**, **188**
hibernation 22

Homoroselaps dorsalis 130
Homoroselaps lacteus 128
honderdpootvreter
    Gebande 192
    Mosambiekse 194
    Swart- 193
    Swartkop- 190
Horingsman 70, 82
House Snake
    Aurora 218, **218**
    Black 217
    Brown 215, **215, 216**
    Fisk's 220, **220**
    Olive 217, **217**
    Spotted 219
    Yellow-bellied 221, **221**
house snakes 21, 52
huisslang
    Bruin- 215
    Fisk se 220
    Geelpens- 221
    Olyf- 217

I
identification 28
Imamba 95, 98
Imamba eluhlaza 98
Imamba emnyama 95
Imbululu 63
Inambezulu 244
Inhlangwana 265
Inhlwathi 211
Inkamela 116
Inkwakhwa 215
Intlangu 265
Intlwathi 211
Inyushu emdaka 223
Iphimpi 113
Irhamba 63
Irhamba lamatye 68
Ivusamanzi eliluhlaza 251
Ivuzamanzi elimdubu 225
Ivuzamanzi limnyama 223
Izilenzi 225

K
kapel
    Koper- 100
    Bosveld- 102
killing 12–13
kobra
    Anchieta se 104
    Bos- 106
    Kaapse 100
    Mosambiekse spoeg- 108
    Swartkeelspoeg- 110
    Wipneus- 102
Koraalslang 116
kousbandjie
    Gestreepte 130
    Gevlekte 128
kousbandslang
    Angola- 122
    Günther se 120
    Sundevall se 125

Zambezi- 123
Kunene Racer 277, **277**
Kuneneslang 277

L
Lamprophis aurora 218
Lamprophis capensis 215
Lamprophis fiskii 220
Lamprophis fuscus 221
Lamprophis guttatus 219
Lamprophis inornatus 217
Lamprophis swazicus 222
Leptotyphlops distanti 295
Leptotyphlops gracilior 290
Leptotyphlops incognitus 293
Leptotyphlops jacobseni 300
Leptotyphlops labialis 298
Leptotyphlops longicaudus 288
Leptotyphlops nigricans 289
Leptotyphlops occidentalis 297
Leptotyphlops pungwensis 299
Leptotyphlops scutifrons 291
Leptotyphlops scutifrons
    conjunctus 292
Leptotyphlops sylvicolus 296
Leptotyphlops telloi 294
Limnophis bangweolicus 233
Linnaeus, Carolus (Carl von Linné)
    27
Lined Olympic Snake 152, **152**
local tissue necrosis 37, **45**
locomotion 22, **22**, 23, **23**
luislang
    Anchieta se dwerg- 213
    Angoladwerg- 213
    Suider-Afrikaanse 211
Lycodonomorphus laevissimus 223
Lycodonomorphus leleupi 228
Lycodonomorphus obscuriventris
    227
Lycodonomorphus rufulus 225
Lycophidion capense 256
Lycophidion hellmichi 261
Lycophidion multimaculatum 259
Lycophidion namibianum 260
Lycophidion nanum 264
Lycophidion pygmaeum 263
Lycophidion semiannule 262
Lycophidion variegatum 258

M
Macrelaps microlepidotus 38, 148
Mamba
    Black 12, 23, 36, 38, 95, **95,**
      96, 97
      antivenom 40, 44
    Green **5**, 38, 98, **98, 99**
      antivenom 40
    Jameson's
      antivenom 40
mamba
    Groen- 98
    Swart- 95
Many-spotted Snake 179, **179, 180**
Marmerslang 185

Marsh Snake
    Olive 231, **231**
      Southern Forest 232, **232**
Mehelya capensis 265
Mehelya nyassae 268
Mehelya vernayi 267
Meizodon semiornatus 242
M'fezi 108
mites 51–52
Mole Snake 21, 229, **229, 230**
Molslang 229
Montaspis gilvomaculata 208
Mopanieslang 175
Mopane Snake 175
movement 22–23

N
Nagslang 217
Naja anchietae 104
Naja annulifera 38, 102
    antivenom 40
Naja melanoleuca 38, 106
    antivenom 40
Naja mossambica 11, 37, 39, 108
    antivenom 40
Naja nigricollis 11, 37, 39, 110
    antivenom 40
Naja nigricollis nigricincta, 11,
    38–39, 112
Naja nigricollis woodi 11, 37, 39,
    47, 112
Naja nivea 38, 100
    antivenom 40
Natal Black Snake 38, 148, **148**
Natalse swartslang 148
Natriciteres olivacea 231
Natriciteres sylvatica 232
nest fallacy 11
neurotoxic venom 38–39
Nyoka yasebusuku 90

O
Ophiophagus hannah 11
organs of Jacobson 19

P
Pelagic Sea Snake 132
Pelamis platurus 39, 132
    antivenom 44
persglansslang
    Gewone 197
    Kalahari 201
    Natalse 195
    Oostelike 199
Philothamnus angolensis 247
Philothamnus natalensis 251
Philothamnus natalensis
    occidentalis 27, 252
      systematic classification 28
Philothamnus ornatus 246
Philothamnus semivariegatus 244
Philothamus hoplogaster 249
precautions for outdoor activities
    46
preserving specimens 31–32, **33**

labelling 32–33
prey-licking fallacy 11
Proatheris superciliaris 88
Prosymna angolensis 236
Prosymna bivittata 235
Prosymna frontalis 237
Prosymna janii 234
Prosymna stuhlmannii 238
Prosymna sundevalli 239
Prosymna sundevalli lineata 240
Prosymna visseri 241
Psammophis angolensis 169
Psammophis brevirostris 155
Psammophis crucifer 167
Psammophis jallae 162
Psammophis leightoni 159
Psammophis leopardinus 156
Psammophis mossambicus 153
Psammophis namibensis 161
Psammophis notostictus 158
Psammophis orientalis 165
Psammophis subtaeniatus 163
Psammophis trigrammus 157
Psammophis trinasalis 160
Psammophylax rhombeatus 21, 170
Psammophylax tritaeniatus 172
Psammophylax variabilis 174
Pseudaspis cana 21, 229
purpergrondslang
    Gewone 197
    Kalahari 201
    Natalse 195
    Oostelike 199
Purple-glossed Snake
    Common 197, **197**, **198**
    Eastern 199, **199**
    Kalahari 201, **201**
    Natal 195, **195**, **196**
Python
    Anchieta's Dwarf **3**, 213, **213**, **214**
    Angola Dwarf 213
    Burmese 7
    Rock 211
    Southern African 21, 211, **211**, **212**
Python anchietae 213
Python natalensis 21, 211
Pythonodipsas carinata 178
pythons, anchoring fallacy 11

Q
Quill-snouted Snake
    Bicoloured 205, **205**, **206**
    Elongate 207, **207**
    Sabi 203
    Save 203, **203**
    Striped 206, **206**
    Transvaal 204, **204**
    Waterberg 206

R
Ramphotyphlops braminus 279
recordkeeping 31, 59
Red-lipped Snake 187

Reed Snake 179
reproduction 21, 57, **57**
Rhamphiophis rostratus 150
Rhinotyphlops boylei 280
Rhinotyphlops lalandei 281
Rhinotyphlops schinzi 282
Rhinotyphlops schlegelii 283
Rhinotyphlops schlegelii mucruso 284
Rhinotyphlops schlegelii petersii 284
Rietslang 179
Rinkhals 11, 21, 38–39, 113, **113**, **114**, **115**
    antivenom 40
Rock Snake
    Spotted 219, **219**
    Swazi 222, **222**
Rooilipslang 187
Roomgevlekte bergslang 208
rotsslang
    Gevlekte 219
    Swazi- 222

S
Sand Snake
    Cape 159
    Cross-marked 167
    Dwarf 169
    Eastern Stripe-bellied 165, **165**
    Jalla's 162, **162**
    Kalahari 160, **160**
    Karoo 158
    Namib 161, **161**
    Pygmy 169
    Western Stripe-bellied 163, **163**, **164**
    Western 157
sandslang
    Dwerg- 169
    Jalla se 162
    Kalahari- 160
    Namib- 161
    Oostelike gestreepte 165
    Westelike gestreepte 163
scale counts **29–30**
    body 29
    head 28–29
    subcaudal 30–31
    ventral (Dowling system) 30
scorpion stings 39
Semiornate Snake 242, **242**, **243**
serpentine movement 23
shedding of skin **18**, 20
    in captivity 56
Shield-nose Snake
    Common 118, **118**, **119**
        antivenom 44
        venom 38
    Eastern 119
    Intermediate 119, **119**
Shovel-snout
    Angola 236
    East African **210**, 238, **238**
    Jan's 234, **234**

Lined 240, **240**
Mozambique 234
South-western 237, **237**
Sundevall's 239, **239**, 240
Two-striped 235, **235**
Visser's 241, **241**
Side-stabbing Snake
    Beaked 145
    Bibron's 143
    Duerden's 145
    Eastern Congo 147
    Southern 143
sidewinding movement 23
skaapsteker
    Gestreepte 172
    Gevlekte 170
    Rhombic 21, 170
    Spotted 170, **170**, **171**
    Striped 172, **172**, **173**
skeleton **18**
skerpneusslang
    Save- 203
    Transvaalse 204
    Tweekleur- 205
    Westelike 207
Skildneusslang 118
skin sloughing/shedding 20, 56
skull structure 18
slakvreter
    Gevlekte 255
    Gewone 253
sloughing of skin **18**, 20
    in captivity 56
Slug-eater
    Common 253, **253**, **254**
    Spotted 255
    Variegated 255, **255**
    Zimbabwean 254
smell, sense of 19–20
snake classification, 26
snakebite 36, **41**
    antivenom kits 41
    envenomation 37
    haemotoxic venom 39
    local tissue necrosis 37, **45**
    neurotoxic venom 38
    prevention 46
    treatment guidelines 41
        first-aid measures 42–43, **43**
        medical measures 44
    useful contacts 47
specimens. see preserving specimens
spitsneusslang
    Save- 203
    Transvaalse 204
    Tweekleur- 205
    Westelike 207
spitting cobras 11
spitting snakes
    venom in the eyes 39
    first-aid, 46
Stiletto Snake 38
    Beaked 145, **145**

Bibron's 143, **143**
Duerden's 145, **145**
Eastern Congo 147, **147**
Southern 143, **143**
Swamp Snake
Bangweulu 233, **233**
Eastern Striped 233
Swart-en-geel-seeslang 132
sweepslang
Dwerg 169
Kaapse 159
Karoo- 158
Kortsnoet- 155
Kruismerk- 167
Luiperd- 156
Olyf- 153
Westelike 157
sypikslang
Haakneus- 145
Oos-Kongolese 147
Suidelike 143

T
Tabakrolletjie 253
taxonomy
definitions 27
Telescopus beetzii 183
Telescopus semiannulatus 181
Telescopus semiannulatus polystictus 182
Thelotornis capensis 138
Thelotornis capensis oatesii 140
Thelotornis mossambicanus 141
Thelotornis spp. 19, 39
antivenom 44, 45
Thread Snake
Black 289
Damara 298, **298**
Distant's 295
Incognito 293
Jacobsen's 300
Long-tailed 288
Peters' 291
Pungwe 299
Slender 290
Southern Forest 296
Tello's 294
Western 297
tierslang
Beetz se 183
Gewone 181
tongue, forked 11, **11**, 19, **20**
Tiger Snake
Beetz's 183, **183**, **184**
Common (Eastern) 181, **181**, **182**
Damara 182, **182**
Namib 183
treatment guidelines (snakebites)
antivenom administration 44–45
first-aid measures 42–43, **43**
medical measures 44, **45**
Tree Snake
Cross-barred 186, **186**

Marbled 185, **185**
Twig Snake 19, 138
Typhlops bibronii 287
Typhlops fornasinii 286
Typhlops obtusus 285

U
Ukhokhothi 138
Umhlwazi 163
Umhlwazi 249
Umzingandlu 215
Unomofuthwana 90
Unompondwana 70
Uphempthwane 113
useful contacts 47
user's guide to book 14–15

V
venom
antivenom (see antivenom)
cytotoxic 37–38
in eyes 39
first-aid 46
haemotoxic 39
neurotoxic 38–39
Vine Snake 19, 39, 138, **138**
antivenom 44, 45
Eastern 141, **141**
Oates' 140, **141**
Southern 140, **140**
Viper
Eyebrow 88
Floodplain 88, **88**, **89**
Lowland Swamp 88
Mole 143
Saw-scaled Viper
antivenom 40
vision 19
vleislang
Olyfkleurige 231
Suidelike Woud- 232
voëlslang
Oostelike- 141
Savanne- 138
vylslang
Angola- 267
Suidelike 265
Swart- 268

W
Water Snake
Barotse 189
Common Brown **9**, 225, **225**, `226`
Dusky-bellied 223, **223**, **224**
Floodplain 227, **227**
Green 249, **249**, **250**
Mulanje 228, **228**
waterslang
Barotse- 189
Bruin- 225
Groen- 249
Mulanje- 228
Swart- 223
Vloedvlakte- 227

Westelike gekielde slang 178
Western Keeled Snake 178, **178**
Whip Snake
Cape 159, **159**
Crossed 167, **167**
Dwarf 169, **169**
Karoo 158, **158**
Leopard 156, **156**
Olive 153, **153**, **155**, **166**
Short-snouted 155, **155**
Western 157, **157**
Wolf Snake
Cape 256
Common 256, **256**, **257**
Dwarf 264
Eastern 262, **262**
Hellmich's 261, **261**
Namibian 260, **260**
Pygmy 263, **263**
Spotted 259, **259**
Variegated 258, **258**
wolfslang
Bont 258
Dwerg- 264
Gespikkelde 259
Gewone 256
Hellmich se 261
Kaapse 256
Namib- 260
Oostelike 262
Pigmee- 263
worm lizards 18
Worm Snake
Cape 289, **289**
Damara 298, **298**
Distant's 295, **295**
Eastern Cape 292, **292**
Incognito 293, **293**
Jacobsen's 300, **300**
Long-tailed 288, **288**
Namaqua 297, **297**
Peters' 291, **291**, **292**
Pungwe 299
Slender 290, **290**
Southern Forest 296, **296**
Tello's 294
worm snake eggs **21**

X
Xenocalamus bicolor 205
Xenocalamus bicolor lineatus 206
Xenocalamus bicolor australis 206
Xenocalamus mechowii 207
Xenocalamus sabiensis 203
Xenocalamus transvaalensis 204

Y
Yellow-bellied Sea Snake 39, 132, **133**, **133**
antivenom 44

Z
zoological classification
definitions 27